= D+D

Ee/Co

Ever After

WILLIAM WHARTON

Ever After

A FATHER'S TRUE STORY

Newmarket Press

Copyright © William Wharton 1995
Published in Great Britain by Granta Books
under the title Wrongful Deaths

This book is published in the United States of America.

10   9   8   7   6   5   4   3   2   1

Library of Congress Cataloging-in-Publication Data

Wharton, William.
    [Wrongful deaths]
    Ever after: a father's true story / William Wharton.
    p.   cm.
    Originally published : Wrongful deaths. London: Granta Books. 1994.
    ISBN 1-55704-223-3
    1. Wharton, William—Trials, litigation, etc. 2. Oregon—Trials, litigation,
etc. 3. Wrongful deaths—Oregon. 4. Traffic accidents—Oregon.
5. Grass seed industry—Oregon. 6. Burning of land—Oregon. I.Title.
    KF228.W425W47   1995
    346.7303'23 — DC20
    [347.306323]
                                                                94-45326
                                                                CIP

*To Kate, Bill, Dayiel, and Mia. And to Margaret
who brought a beacon of light to the darkness*

W.W.

CONTENTS

Foreword   IX

PART ONE: Kate   1

PART TWO: Will   65

PART THREE: Settlement   119

Epilogue   238

FOREWORD

AS A RESULT of the experiences described in this work, I have come to the conclusion that everything coming through the mind of man or woman is fiction. So-called truth is a convenience and a comfort for which we all search. This search seems natural and necessary to humans.

In science, observations are established as truth by replication. A concept or observation is considered true when numerous repetitions of the same concepts, observations and conclusions have been completed and verified.

However, for a long time, scientific man was convinced the sun went around the earth. This phenomenon fulfilled all the requirements for truth in its day.

History considers an event to have been true when it has a significant volume of primary, secondary and tertiary evidence, enough to warrant a statement of validity. However, it is, in the long run, merely a consensus truth. That is, most people think it is true. And, typically, they only consider it true for a limited time.

Religion takes its truth from revelation to individual humans, sometimes called prophets: superior or alien beings with special powers, who are generally not of this world. From these revelations, various versions of dogma evolve among humans which purport to be truth. Many people live their lives by these "truths," will kill or be killed for them.

I've gathered as much evidence, primary, secondary and tertiary, as I could. I pray the event herein described will not be replicated. I do not expect, or ask, belief from you, the reader, in the unique revelation with which I was blessed. It is reported only as part of the total experience, the holy horror of it all.

I am writing this work of biography-autobiography-fiction, concerning the event which changed our lives, in the form of a documentary novel. In the interest of the aesthetics involved in novel-writing, I have needed to employ certain novelistic devices.

There are conversations I did not hear, for example, between my daughter and her husband, which I create. They are, however, related to the unfolding events as I know them. I tell part of this tale from the point of view of my daughter, Kate, in her voice, as teenager and adult. It was necessary to use the novelist's techniques of personal projection to do this. I hope it does not invalidate for the reader the sequence of events I wish to tell. It is not meant to.

I am a novelist. This along with painting is my mode of communication. I hope the reader will be able to enter into the events related and the emotions experienced with at least the "feeling of truth" for truth.

To protect the privacy of those concerned with this tale I have changed all names except for some first names of my immediate family. To those, I've given my writer's surname.

I don't intend that this be a book of complaints except as it is necessary to explain certain events as I experienced them. I am the first to admit that bias enters all communication, even when an effort to represent truth is being made.

> William Wharton
> 15 April 1993, Port Marly

PART ONE

CHAPTER 1

OUR NEIGHBORHOOD in Paris was what the French call a *quartier populaire*, a nice way of saying "slum." Actually it was an area where furniture was made, and most of the people were artisans—carpenters, upholsterers, window-makers, printers, that kind of thing. There were also artists—more and more of them the longer we lived there. But I was too young to appreciate a good thing; I wanted to live in the sixteenth *arrondissement*, or some other posh place like that.

That's where Danny, my boyfriend from the American School, fits in. His father had been an ambassador and now worked for some top-secret international organization. Once an ambassador, always an ambassador; so his calling-card had his whole title written out. I was very impressed.

Danny wasn't a very good student, but he was good-looking and really did live in the sixteenth *arrondissement*. He was the only student on campus to own an automobile. He was older than the other kids and had a French driving license. In France you need to be eighteen to drive.

We went together all during our last two years of school. I remember Christmas of our senior year especially.

We spent it down at the mill, an old, stone water-mill in the Morvan, a part of Burgundy, where our family goes for Christmas. It's always cold and there's nothing to do.

I was afraid I was pregnant, even though I wore a diaphragm—Mom and Dad insisted on it when I turned thirteen. On top of everything, Robert, my little brother, who was only about three or four, kept singing the Christmas song

3

"Mary had a baby." Each time he did, Danny and I either moaned or giggled, depending on our mood. If we got to giggling, we couldn't stop. I know it drove Mom crazy.

Later, Danny asked me to marry him, although I wasn't pregnant. It was just before I graduated. When I told Dad and Mom, Dad looked at me a long time before he said anything.

"Well, Kate, I think he'll make a great first husband."

I thought that was awfully cynical, but he turned out to be right. Danny did make a good first husband.

Right after high school, Danny and I went to California and studied at a junior college. We lived in a tiny apartment. Neither of us had paid enough attention in school to enter a real university. Also, as my parents were still California residents, I didn't need to pay tuition. We lived together two years and then, when Danny transferred to UCLA, got married.

The wedding was in California, arranged by my Aunt Emmaline, Mom's sister, but the real wedding was at the mill.

I'm not religious, but wanted a wedding in the little village church on top of the hill that looked down over the mill. Danny wasn't even baptized. Dad took my baptismal certificate and used it to make one for Danny, hand-lettered in Dad's usual crooked, artistic way, and then photocopied it. It looked better than mine. We then sent our certificates off to the bishop and I guess they wound up in the Vatican. I don't know.

Dad describes the wedding in a book he wrote called *Tidings*. An old war buddy of his played the music from *Fiddler On The Roof*. We passed out translations to the people in the church, most of whom were French and couldn't understand a word. All of us cried when he played "Where Is That Little Girl I Carried?" The recessional was "Sunrise, Sunset." It made for terrific marriage music.

The mill was fixed up, and there was lots of food and music. The men in the village shot shotguns in the air, and a couple of them built a fire in the garage under the grange where we were dancing. This was to add a little more excitement. Excitement we didn't need.

Dad had his beard long, with his hair pulled back in a little pigtail tied with a ribbon. He didn't have all that much hair so it looked a little strange. Mom was beautiful and graceful in her "butterfly dress" made for her by a rich Arab lady, mother to one of the kids in her kindergarten. The woman designed dresses for Christian Dior. What a crazy mixture our lives were.

It was a great wedding. The people in the village kept showing up with string beans. It was late string-bean season. We accepted them all, even though we had to bury some of them down by the old water-wheel.

Danny and I spent our wedding night up at the hotel in Montigny next to the church.

We went back to California and I was miserable. I worked cleaning houses, then as a secretary for a refrigeration company. Finally I got a real job, working for Korean Airlines. Through all this, I talked to Mom and Dad. They wanted me to continue in school. They're great believers in education. But I needed to earn enough to help Danny through school. His parents, with all their money, weren't contributing much, if anything at all.

Mom came and found a terrific apartment for us near the miracle mile in Los Angeles. It wasn't too far from where I worked, or from UCLA. It was also near the LA County Museum, where I spent any time I could get. I loved art. I liked things old-fashioned and traditional.

Then I got pregnant. The apartment was a great place for a couple, but with a baby we'd need more space, and, with Dad's help, we found a nice little house in Venice, near the beach.

Mom came to help with the birth of Wills. We wanted a natural childbirth and I did all the lessons and exercises, but in the end, they had to do a Caesarean.

❊ ❊ ❊

Dad also wrote about me in his book called *Dad*. He called me Marty and described finding the little house in Venice where Danny and I lived while I was pregnant. We lived there about four years.

Mom or Dad would visit sometimes, and we'd bicycle along the path right on the beach. It was idyllic.

It was during this time I began falling out of love with Danny. It wasn't anything he was doing; it was more what he wasn't. I kept asking myself what was wrong with me. I had so many friends who were having *real* trouble with their husbands: drinking, womanizing, drugs, and all. Danny worked hard every day and, except for smoking, didn't do much of anything wrong. He found a good job as a salesman for a steel company, and he was wonderful with Wills. It would make me jealous sometimes watching them play together. I think, in a way, Danny never grew up. Maybe neither of us did.

The big trouble was Danny bored me. We couldn't maintain a decent conversation. I came from a family where there was conversation all the time, maybe even a bit too much, at least for me. Sometimes I couldn't keep up with my own family. They'd go on about things so fast.

But with Danny, life was only long evenings when he'd read the papers, watch TV, or go over his bills and orders from work, then go to sleep. He seemed to love playing with that little calculator of his, making up for the fact he couldn't pass Algebra II, I think.

I got so desperate, I remember calling Dad long distance. I asked him, Just what was love anyway? I wanted to know if I loved Danny. He told me to hang up and he'd call me back later. In about half an hour he called.

"Kate, I've thought about it. I'm no expert, ask your mother. But as far as I can see, love is a combination of admiration, respect, and passion. If you have one of those going, that's about par for the course. If you have two, you aren't quite world class but you're close. If you have all three, then you don't need to die; you're already in heaven."

At the time, it didn't seem to help. But I continued thinking about what Dad said for the whole of the next month. That's when I decided I definitely had a zero. I don't really know what Danny thought, but don't believe it was any different for him. He just wouldn't admit it.

I wanted to move out of Venice. Wills was starting to grow up and we were in the middle of a big drug scene. The clinic where people would stand outside in the morning to get their "meth" was only a block from our house.

Dad came up with the idea we might enjoy living in Idylwild. This is a place in the Los Angeles mountains above Palm Springs, more than a mile high. It's well located for Danny's "territory."

We all drove up there, and I loved it right away. We lucked out and found just the kind of house I always wanted. Dad had made money writing *Birdy* and lent us some so we could buy the place.

Danny and I were getting along better. Wills loved it up there. There were rocks to climb, the smell of pines, snow in the winter, and beautiful, clear, star-filled nights. Blue jays and raccoons, pine cones and acorns were everywhere. Wills adored his little nursery school and I sometimes worked there. Danny didn't have any more driving to do than he did in Venice. His territory was huge. Idylwild was in the middle of it. The only trouble was the long drive up through the hills. But he was terrific about it.

Then, Danny was offered a chance to work for Honeywell Bull. Dad had helped Danny write his application and résumé, and we were happy because it was much more money, with better prospects, than selling steel. The trouble was we had to move to Phoenix, Arizona, where Danny was put into a training program.

It meant selling the house of my dreams. In a certain way, that was when the dream really ended. We sold the Idylwild house for a profit, paid back Dad, and bought a place in Phoenix. It was a new house, sitting in a bare space surrounded by other houses just like it, without even a lawn. I couldn't get accustomed to living in an oasis surrounded by desert. I'd never lived like that. I couldn't believe it was me living in this house, with Danny off to work most of the time.

I did everything I could to make it a real home but I hated to look out the windows. Everything was so barren. I'd been spoiled by Idylwild, and even by Venice, but especially by living with my parents in Europe most of my childhood. At least there was always something interesting to see. Here there was nothing. It was so hot. Practically no one walked in the streets.

Wills started school, and I announced to Danny I wanted a divorce. There were no other men in my life but I knew there would be soon and I just wanted out. Danny was broken up about the whole thing and we were up night after night, talking it all over. God, it was hell. Looking back, I can see I must have seemed a real bitch to him. Maybe I was.

Dad and Mom couldn't understand at all. Dad sat down with me for a quiet talk the way he did when things seemed to be getting out of hand. Most of the time he kept out of my private life, wanting me to work things out for myself, but once in a while he couldn't hold himself back. It was the same when I started smoking. Then, again, when I first started having sex. It was the same with drugs. He'd explain his ideas and it was hard to argue with him.

On the smoking thing, he talked very quietly to me in my bedroom, first asking if I smoked. There was no lying about it. I smelled of cigarettes all the time, I was getting up to a pack a day, and the teachers had told Mom I was spending time between classes in the smoking area. He was quiet.

"Listen, Kate. I know it's your life, but in a certain way your life is ours, too. We've spent a hell of a lot of time and effort getting you this far along, clearing up diaper rashes, pumping your stomach out when you drank Chlorodane, getting you through fevers when the doctor thought you had polio, keeping you from being run over, nursing you through chicken-pox, measles, mumps; the whole thing. We fed you vitamins, made sure you had all the shots to keep you from getting the worst diseases. You know you never had any other milk to drink except your mother's milk or goat's milk until you were four years old. I pulled milk from the teats of our goats every morning and evening.

"It really makes us unhappy seeing you do this to yourself. Do you know why you smoke?"

God, he could be so hard and mean in his quiet, tension-filled voice. I promised I'd stop but I didn't. He knew I wouldn't but he'd done what he felt he had to do. That's the way Dad is.

Then, with sex, he told me to be careful for health reasons, make sure the guy wears a condom. But he had to go on.

"More than anything else, Kate, sex is one of the greatest joys on earth, like Christmas. But it can be the same as having Christmas every day in the year if one becomes promiscuous. There won't be any thrill left." He tried to talk to me about the difference between romance and sex, that when sex came in the door, too often romance went out the window, cornball things like that.

I didn't know what the word promiscuous meant. When I told some of my friends what he'd said, they thought it was cute, and awfully funny.

With the drug thing, they were having a big crackdown at school: even the president of the Board of Trustees' and the Headmaster's kids got busted. Sometimes I think there was more pot than cigarettes in the smoking area. This was the early seventies and we were all trying to catch up to the sixties. Dad cornered me in my room again. He pulled out a small bottle with about three ounces in it.

"Look, Kate, do you know what this is?"

He didn't wait for me to answer.

"It's Mexican golden, some of the best pot you'll find. A friend of mine sold it to me. He was going back to America and was afraid of customs.

"This bottle will always be on the top shelf in my closet in the bedroom. Any time you want to smoke, take some, but only smoke it in the apartment here, and with none of your friends around.

"The French are very tough on this stuff. If you get caught, since I'm not with a big company, we'll all have to leave France in forty-eight hours. I really don't want to do that. We like it here. You have to think about our lives, too."

He considered pot, and all other drugs, a cheap shot at what can be earned the hard, real way by personal creative activity. He was convinced it stopped people, chemically, from making the tremendous effort to get a personal "high" based on their own capacities.

"You see, Kate, when I was an art student at UCLA, I read Huxley's *Doors of Perception* and was deeply impressed. I volunteered to participate in some experiments on LSD 25. That's what they called acid back then. They wanted artists, and paid us thirty-five dollars a day to be guinea-pigs. I did it twice. They injected the stuff into my arm. After about five minutes, I became aware of the clothes on my body. It was really erotic. I could hear the clinking of neon lights, and was fascinated by the shadow of a typewriter being used by a secretary across the room.

"They took me to the LA County Museum where they asked me to describe the paintings. The colors seemed phosphorescent and in different layers. On the way back to the university in the car, driven by the experimenters, I was suddenly on the edge of a bad trip and curled up on the seat.

"The cars out the window seemed to be getting bigger and smaller. It was only normal perspective changes but my mind wasn't up to that kind of rational realization.

"I went back one more time when they wanted me to try

painting after the injection. I thought I was painting the most beautiful painting in the world and was so happy I cried.

"But after they'd cooled me off in a dim room for a few hours, I came out to look at the painting I'd done and it was just paints smeared together into a uniform brown, the kind of thing an untalented kindergartener might do.

"I think I learned something, Kate. What happens with those drugs is the thinking part of the brain is repressed so feelings are very strong. The ability to discriminate, to make decisions, to understand the nature of the physical world is distorted.

"Now, that's fine if you have an ordinary brain and don't have any plans for it. But you have a fine brain, Kate, and I'd hate to see you screw up the wiring, short-circuit yourself.

"You know, after that experience, it was almost two months before I could work up the enthusiasm necessary to do any valid painting. Remember the word 'enthusiasm' comes from the Greek for 'with the gods.' It takes real discipline and involvement to paint well and I'd almost lost that.

"I wouldn't touch any of that stuff again for love or money. It's only a way of saying you don't have any confidence in your own identity. In a certain way, I think people who become dependent on drugs are like alcoholics. They have so little self-respect, they want to escape from themselves. It's a form of psychic suicide."

He stared at me with those marbled blue eyes of his sunken under his chimpanzee brows. But he convinced me, and I stayed away from it all. I might be one of the only ones of my generation who got through the test-by-fire without getting burned.

That's the way Dad is. He'll be so laid back most of the time, sometimes you think he just doesn't care. But he respected us. He wanted us to make our own world but he didn't want us to get hurt.

When I told him I wanted to divorce Danny, I knew I was probably in for a bad time. He came to visit, and I spent about half an hour trying to explain. He sat on a little stool with his legs spread apart, his elbows on his knees and his chin in his hands. He watched every movement in my face or else he just looked down between his legs. He didn't say a word until I was finished.

"Do you think Danny loves you?"

"Yes, I think so, but . . . "

He held out his hand lightly.

"Does he love Wills?"

"You see him, Dad. You know he does."

"Do you have reasonable sexual relations? I don't mean whammers every time, but good married sex?"

I didn't think he'd ask that. Mom would never ask anything in this area. I took a deep breath.

"I guess, compared to most other women I've talked with, we have as good sex as most."

"Do you have orgasm?"

He looked me straight in the eyes.

"Not always. But I can get it off myself when I want. I don't need Danny for that."

I never thought I'd be able to talk about this with either of them.

"He doesn't beat you, or drink secretly, or take drugs or anything, does he? Does he have other women?"

"No to the first questions. The last one, I don't think so, so far. I think I'd know."

"So it just comes down to your being bored with him. Do you think you'd be bored with some other man?"

"I don't know. Dad, I've been all wrapped up with Danny since I was sixteen. I don't know how I'd feel around another man."

"Maybe you ought to find out, before you do anything drastic, Kate. Remember you're going to hurt both Danny and Wills, probably yourself as well, if you do go through with this divorce. These are some pretty nice people. Make sure."

12

"But, Dad, you aren't really asking me to go out and have affairs are you? I don't think I'd like that."

"Well, then why not make the most of what you have? It isn't the worst situation in the world."

"You aren't asking me to live my life out with a boring man?"

"Lots of other people do. Men live with boring women and women with boring men. Sometimes boring women live with boring men, that's the way it is.

"You know, Kate, you can't say you didn't really know Danny when you married him. You two had been like married for two years before you actually went through the formalities. It was a free choice. You must have had some idea."

I grew quiet. I knew I had to stick it out some more. I didn't want to. I wanted to take Wills and just split. Dad then asked me if I'd spoken to Camille, my younger sister.

"She's had a lot more experience than you, Kate, even though she's five years younger. There's something of the street-fighter in her. Ask her opinion about what her life's like. She's free as a bird. I'm not sure she can really fly but there's plenty of sky around her. Ask her what she thinks."

I hadn't talked with Camille about anything. She's so aggressively positive about things and, like Mom, always sounds as if she's living in some high-school play. But it was an idea.

Wills came in and grabbed Dad by the hand and pulled him out into the yard to be pushed by him on the swing. I've pushed that swing so often I've developed monster shoulder-muscles. I spread out on the couch and cried for the first time in weeks.

Well, I did divorce Danny. It was messy, and the lawyers were the only ones getting anything out of it until Danny and I sat down and worked something out ourselves. I didn't want alimony, only what Danny could afford for child-support. We'd split whatever we could make on the house, but it wouldn't be much.

Danny lost his job at Honeywell Bull, as did a whole lot of other people, and he returned to selling steel, but with another company. He moved back to Venice, a small apartment.

I figured the only way I could support myself and Wills was to finish my degree and earn a teaching credential.

It was an uphill battle at my age with a child, but I enrolled at ASU, Arizona State University, and wangled a couple of jobs on campus. One was in the geology department, where I thought briefly of becoming a geologist, both because it paid well and because so many of the geologists were men. There wasn't much female competition, either. The other was in the German department, where I was in charge of putting out their bimonthly periodical. I learned plenty about writing and publishing—although I almost got fired when they discovered my written German wasn't as good as my spoken.

I enrolled Wills in a nursery school on campus and paid his bill by putting in a few hours a day there. I was very busy, but also surprised at how well I could do in my classes now I was motivated.

Dad and Mom came through with some money once in a while to help cover the bad spots, but in general, I was on my own. I was growing more and more confident, both as a student and as a woman. I began going out and liked being able to pick the men I wanted instead of being locked in with one.

I did the first half of my practice teaching at Arizona State and applied to do my second half at the American School in Paris, where Mom taught. I wanted to get back to Europe. I never really fit into the American scene.

So, at almost thirty, I came home, lived with Mom and Dad on their houseboat, and learned how to teach. I felt closer to the family than I ever had before. The boat, like the mill, had never been one of my favorite places, but now I loved it. Mom and Dad had a knack for finding places that were unique.

Dad took Wills to the French school every morning and picked him up in the evening. It was tough for Wills, but I think he had a good time with Dad. He began to learn some

French, and the river-banks were a terrific place for a seven-year-old boy to play. He made friends with a few French kids, despite the language barriers.

He loved going to the top of the Eiffel Tower. He varied between calling it the "Awful Tower" and the "Eyeful Tower" but said he liked it more than Disneyland. He also enjoyed climbing up on the lead roof of Notre Dame with Dad, the two of them looking as if they'd just conquered Everest. Neither Mom nor I could look at them; we both have a terrible fear of heights, as does my brother, Matt. There are four children in my family. I'm the eldest.

I received good reports on my teaching and a high recommendation from the head of the school. I had done my practice teaching in first grade and decided to remain at this level—kindergarten or first grade. It was the same grade levels as Mom taught. It turned out that when my younger sister Camille did her practice teaching later, at La Jolla in California, she would come to the same decision. It runs in the family. I never thought Camille and I would wind up kindergarten teachers.

CHAPTER 2

WHEN I'VE finished my practice teaching, I sit down to write out a curriculum vitae that will sound good. Although I did graduate *cum laude* from Arizona State, I hadn't quite finished my credential. It's hard finding a job in an overseas school without at least two years' US experience. But I decide to try anyway.

I mail out sixty letters, then buy a Eurail pass and start on my journey. It's May. Mom is still teaching, Wills is in school. Dad says he'll take care of Wills when Mom isn't home. I hate to depend on them so much, but there's no other way.

I travel at night from one city to another. I sleep on the train to save hotel bills. I do quite a bit of criss-crossing Europe, looking for the night train-rides that are about eight or ten hours long. When I get off a train in the city where I'm going to be interviewed, I head to a phone, confirm the rendezvous, then look for a reasonable restroom where I can put myself in order. I take more "bird-baths" in sinks of train stations than I ever thought I'd take in my whole life.

Most of the interviews are discouraging. People are usually interested in the fact I can speak French, German, and English, and have a good academic background, but they hold the lack of experience against me. I try to beef my résumé up with my nursery-school teaching in Idylwild and Phoenix, but it doesn't help much.

After two weeks on the road, with one or two interviews every day, I still have nothing definite. The next stop is near Munich. In fact, I have one interview at an international school right at the head of the Starnberger See near the city of Starnberg. We lived nearby, in Seeshaupt, when I was a child and Dad was on sabbatical from his teaching. It's only a half-hour trip on the train from Starnberg to Seeshaupt.

The last time I saw Dad, he said he'd just started writing a new book, part of which takes place in Seeshaupt. He said it's built around the stories he told us in the morning about Franky Furbo, a wonderful magic fox. In fact, I was the one who suggested he could make a great adult book from those stories. I'd love to have read it, but I guess I never will. Or maybe there is a way. I just don't know about those things yet. It's a strange situation we're in.

The man who interviews me in Starnberg, Stan, is one of the smilingest men I've ever met. We get along right away. But it's the same thing: he doesn't think he can hire someone without experience. The fact I speak such good German impresses him. I'm impressed too because he, an American, can speak incredibly good German himself. It turns out his first wife, who has died, was German.

He asks me to wait a few minutes in the office and he'll be right back. I think maybe he's going to the bathroom. I've already given up. After around twenty rejections, one loses confidence. I'm hoping to catch a train down to Seeshaupt before dark.

He comes back smiling. But then he's always smiling. He rubs his hands together.

"You're lucky, Kate. I talked the director into it. I exaggerated your nursery-school experience a bit, even more than you did, so don't make a liar of me. But you're the kind of teacher I'm always looking for, optimistic, smiling, full of enthusiasm and energy. Maybe after you've had two years' experience, you won't be that way, but you're hired to teach first grade. You'll get the same salary as the other first-grade teacher I hired last year. I'm sure you'll love her."

I could have fallen over right there in his office; I have a hard time to keep from crying. It's all been so difficult the last few years and now it looks so beautiful. I know I must have thanked him but I don't remember. He comes around his desk.

"Come on, Kate, let me show you the school. We're really proud of it. The German government built this place for us and about half our students are German. Their parents don't like the strict, old-fashioned ways of German schools. We have the best mix of Germans, Americans, and all other nationalities, but we teach an American curriculum. It's an exciting place."

We walk over to the campus, which is in the country, with modern buildings and old cow-barns and a small castle. My room is bright and neither too big nor too small. Stan says they try to keep the classes to under twenty students. God, it's like a dream. I can't believe it. I'm still a little teary.

"Do you have a place to stay, Kate?"

"I have friends near here, in Seeshaupt. I think I can stay there. Then I'll start hunting for a place in Starnberg and be ready to teach in September. Is there any chance I can come out during the summer to get my classroom ready?"

"Anything you want. Boy, this is great for me. Usually I need to hunt up a place for new teachers because they don't speak German. But you're all set. Are you sure you don't want anything?"

I find I'm smiling, and then I laugh.

"How about a contract? I'd actually like to sign a contract so I know this is all true. I can't wait to tell my parents. My little boy, Wills, is just going to love it here. Do faculty children get to go to this school free?"

"Absolutely, completely free to faculty kids. Who do you think I am, Scrooge?"

"More like Santa Claus, Stan."

The temptation to put my arms around him and give him a big kiss is enormous, but I resist. I don't want to do anything to screw up this chance.

I phone Dad and Mom. They're as excited as I am. I find a little furnished apartment near the lake, and work like crazy getting it into shape. I make curtains, wax all the furniture. It's a little nest on the second floor with a beautiful view of the lake. I have a large room with a corner kitchen and a curved nook eating area. Almost everything's made of wood. I've decided to keep everything simple. I buy two dishes, two cups, two spoons, two knives and two forks. It'll be just Wills and me, no social life, at least for a while. I can't wait till Wills comes.

In the evenings I study my books from Arizona State and plan lessons. I want everything to be just right when I start. I'm very nervous.

I have a little stove but no refrigerator. I'll buy some kind of used refrigerator as soon as I get my first check; for now, I'm almost flat broke. I have enough to pay Wills's air fare and we can get by on food till my first check, but that's it.

Wills arrives at the airport in Munich the same day school lets out at MIS. MIS stands for Munich International School, my school. We both cry, hugging each other outside customs.

We take the S-Bahn home and Wills loves everything—the lake, the town, our apartment. But he falls asleep on the floor in about ten minutes. I carry him to his bed and undress him. I imagine he hasn't slept much the night before with all the excitement. I'd had a hard time getting to sleep myself. I whisper in his ear that I need to go to school for a while but I'll be back when he wakes up.

I'm supposed to go to an end-of-the-school-year party. Stan asked me to come, even though it's the day Wills arrives.

There are six new teachers for the next semester. Stan introduces me and I stand up. People clap. I meet most of the other teachers. One is a huge, bearded guy who doesn't have much hair. I can't get over how much he looks like Dad and my brother Matt. He's flirting with the new librarian. When introduced, he says he comes from Oregon, although he's just been teaching in Southeast Asia. I don't see a wife around. The married teachers seem to have their spouses with them.

❄ ❄ ❄

I work like mad getting my classroom in order. Wills comes with me every day and plays: on the soccer field, kicking a ball, or at the gym, trying to shoot baskets. They have a great playground here, too. Sometimes he'll come in and give me a hand, pushing desks around.

A couple times the big, bearded guy from Oregon comes in. He's going to be teaching computing and is getting his room fixed up, too. He speaks very slowly, but the more we talk, the more I like him. He doesn't waste time with anything that isn't worth talking about. Chatter is about ninety percent of all conversations anyway, but when he says something it's usually interesting. He can't believe I can really speak German and I'm not German. I try explaining, but I'm not sure I come across.

I find a refrigerator being sold by an elderly German couple, at a price I can pay. They're willing to hold on to it till I get my check, but I need to find someone to move it.

The next time Bert, that's the name of the bearded Oregonian, stops in my classroom, I ask if he could help me move a refrigerator. I promise him a home-cooked meal, American-style, in return. He stares at me a minute, then lifts an eyebrow and says, "Spare-ribs?"

I have no idea where I can find spare-ribs in Germany, although I do know how to cook them. That's one advantage of those years cooking at home instead of washing dishes. So we make the deal. He wrestles that machine out of the cellar of these old people, across town, and up my stairs, single-handedly, as if it were a portable radio or something. He's bushed when he's finished and flops down on my couch.

"You don't perhaps have some of this great German beer around, do you, Kate?"

By luck, I have one bottle. I don't drink beer myself. It isn't cold because we haven't plugged in the refrigerator yet, but he doesn't seem to mind. He has a bottle-opener on the knife with his keys, and drinks it out of the bottle before I can find a glass. Just then, Wills comes running in. Bert lolls back and smiles.

"Hi there, buster, what's your name?"

Wills, his mouth open, is taking in this hunk of a man. Bert has to be six-three and 200 pounds.

"Wills, sir."

"Well, Wilzer, I've seen you shooting baskets down there in the gym. You like basketball?

"Yeah, but I can't get the ball up high enough to go through the basket. It's too high."

"Sure you can. Next time I see you down there, I'll show you how. You'll be dropping in baskets like Magic Johnson."

I've prepared most of the dinner. I've borrowed some dishes and cutlery—so much for my bachelor life. I've let the spare-ribs simmer for three hours, basting them with my ersatz barbecue sauce. I've set the little table. Wills is as excited about having spare-ribs as Bert is. I haven't done any real cooking in quite a while.

Both Wills and Bert eat with such gusto that my hokey barbecue sauce is spread all over the kitchen. No cook can ever complain when people dig in like that, and I don't.

For me, Bert looks part grizzly bear, yet, strangely enough, it's attractive. He's physical, is deeply into sports; likes beer, chasing women, horsing around with the boys. He's exactly the kind of man I've spent most of my life trying to avoid. I also recognize in him some of the things in my dad which drove me up a wall. I wonder what Mom would think of him: dismiss him probably as one of the unwashed peasants. But I admit his very simplicity gets to me. I know I'll need to watch myself.

For Wills, Bert is just some other kid to play with. Bert actually listens to him ramble on, and shows him about ten different silly things you can do with a knife, fork, and spoon, including drumming. They start drumming on the table, the glasses, the dishes, anything they can touch, while Bert sings or hums, "When the Saints Come Marching In." That's how a lot of the sauce is spread all over the place.

In self-defense, I move over to the kitchen and begin taking things off the table. But all the time my eyes are glued on Bert and he knows it. He's acting up. He knows when I look at his massive forearms or the hair squeezing up over his T-shirt. That's right, he's wearing a T-shirt at the table, a dirty, sweaty T-shirt. After all, he's just moved a refrigerator. I'm giggling, thinking to myself: what would it be like, making love to a grizzly bear?

I have the answer that night. After Wills is in bed, we begin chatting. He tells me about his home town in Oregon, a place called Falls City. His best friends are still his high-school buddies, especially the ones he played basketball with. He's thirty-two, a year older than I am and has never been married, says he has no intention of getting married, at least not for a long time yet.

He makes simple moves, the kind adolescent boys make, and I don't resist. It's been months since I've had a chance to be with a man.

He doesn't so much make love, as cuddle, and hold, wrap himself around me, all in slow motion, like one of those underwater love scenes. His hands are strong and gentle. He never hurries, doesn't seem nervous at all. It's as if making love is the most natural thing in the world, and all men and women who aren't making love just then, at that moment, are really missing something. It's a bit like making love with a real animal, maybe not a grizzly bear or a gorilla, but a powerful male. I don't think I've felt so safe and comfortable with any man in my life.

He giggles a lot. He hardly talks when we're loving, but makes all kinds of quiet purring, growling, contented noises. We fall asleep after about two hours of fore-, center-, and after-play.

In the morning, he's up before I am, sitting in the little alcove-kitchen with Wills, playing cards; actually he's performing card tricks while they both eat cornflakes raw—I mean dry. He's made some coffee. Soon as he realizes I'm awake, he calls out to me.

"Cuppa Java?"

I nod. I'm still in bed. I wonder what Wills is thinking. I've always tried to keep the men in my life away from Wills because he still loves Danny so, and I don't want to make him feel things are as bad between us as they really are.

Bert ambles over to the kitchen stove and pours me a cup. He's wearing a pair of boxer shorts. He doesn't even have shoes on. He has wide feet that won't sink in any mud, and a tattoo on his left ankle. He smiles down at me.

"Hope you don't mind my staying over. Little Wilzer was up and moving about before either of us, so I just slithered out of bed and joined him. I don't think he's noticed much."

This he says in what passes as a whisper for him. As I get to know Bert, I learn his idea of a whisper can be heard at fifty meters. But Wills is concentrating on the cards, trying to build a card house to match the one Bert's made on the table.

I sit up and drink the coffee. It's been a long time since anyone's brought me coffee in bed. My hair is a mess. I'm sure my make-up is smeared all over my face, but I know Bert doesn't mind too much. He leans over and gives me a quick, light kiss. I'm astounded again at how such a big, seemingly clumsy man can be so gentle. He straightens up.

"Well, I'd better get back to my place. My landlady watches me like a hawk. We don't want to start any rumors before we even begin teaching. Old Lister, our beloved headmaster, would blow his crispy, blond top."

That's how it starts. I expect him to move over to the next available woman but it doesn't happen that way at all. We begin to go out a little even before school officially starts, just to the local *Gasthauses*, usually with Wills. I have a hard time keeping from calling him Wilzer myself. That gives some idea of the quiet power of Bert's personality.

Bert invites me to his place. I go, after Wills is asleep; the lady downstairs said she'd listen for him. I meet him at the Dampher Steg, my favorite place, a little gazebo near the docks for the local cruising boat. It's a wonderful spot to wait for someone, with the swans and ducks and the sun setting over the lake.

But, as the weeks go by, I rarely have to wait because Bert is usually there before me. He always has something special, a piece of German chocolate, or some wild flowers he's picked, or a particularly beautiful stone he's found by the side of the lake and shined up for me. He's always whittling something, such as two links in a chain, or a heart with our names on it. It's like a high-school romance, but so much more powerful because we're older, old enough not to expect too much and to take it as it comes.

He's there, waiting for me, and we go to his place. He puts his finger to his lips and makes a big deal about sneaking up the back staircase. The landlady was adamant that he was to bring no women to his room. The Germans can be awfully uptight, especially the older ones. Bert says he almost didn't take the place because of this "no women" business but couldn't find anything better in his price range.

It's a real nest, like a bear's cave or fox's warren, one big room with a bed nestled under an eave. In fact, everything is tucked under an eave one way or another. But it's cozy. He makes me a cup of coffee and pours a bit of brandy in it. Usually, I don't drink alcohol, but this is special. He's so proud of himself I just can't say no, so I sip slowly and try getting it down without choking. Mom and I both have this problem of choking on anything spicy or strong.

Bert and I naturally grab onto each other and then drop into that bed where a person can scarcely sit up. I'm beginning to feel I could be falling in love with this creature of a man. This doesn't fit my plans at all. I want some time, at least two years, to prove myself as a teacher and establish my independence.

We aren't even halfway through the first semester when Bert gives up his place and moves in with me. I don't fight it. He makes me feel valued, not just precious, but intrinsically valued, in a way that no one, not even my own parents, who I know love me dearly, ever could.

We have become the "romance" of the school. Bert's very overt in his affections, taking my hand when we walk, or throwing one of his monster arms over my shoulders. We have a little coffee-clatch of elementary-school teachers who meet at lunch every day and he joins us. At first, a few object, but they quickly accept him. I keep catching him gazing at me.

And the change in Wills is remarkable. He's always hated school. Now he drives there with Bert and me. Bert chatters along about his math, asking him what parts are hard, and showing him the magic, secret ways he has to lick different kinds of arithmetic, as if they're fighting off some multi-armed dragon. Bert, who isn't, himself, much of a reader, can also light a fire under Wills, just by reading to him. He'll go along, then at critical parts ask questions about what's happened or what Wills thinks is going to happen. He'll sometimes act as if he's stuck and ask Wills to sound out a word. What a fine first-grade teacher he'd make.

He also gets Wills interested in both calculators and his computer. He sucks him in with games, then has him checking his homework, sometimes with the calculator, sometimes with the computer.

Homework actually begins to be fun-time at home. After dinner, Bert opens a beer and Wills spreads his work over the kitchen table. Bert leaves Wills alone till he's stuck, then comes charging in. It's like Tom Sawyer whitewashing the fence. Wills will end up begging to do the next part and Bert will keep pushing him off till Wills starts to be mad, then takes over and finishes with joy.

Bert likes to smoke cigars, the most vile cigars I've ever smelled. When he moved in, I told him he couldn't smoke those things in the house. Then I told him he couldn't smoke in the car either, even when I'm not with him. When he can't stand it any longer, he'll go outside and take a walk to have his "stogie." Invariably, Wills wants to join him. So now I've made a new rule: "no stogie walk" until Wills is in bed. I don't know why Bert puts up with all this.

With each new rule, and there are many, Bert just tilts his head, looks at me to see how serious I am, then shrugs his massive shoulders. I hate bringing up any of these rules. I see how he suffers. I also don't want to lose him. How often does a woman get a chance at a man like this one?

Bert plays in a basketball league of local Germans and Americans. This is the kind of thing he really likes. Wills loves to watch him. Bert plays like a bull in a china shop, none of the usual slinking around of basketball players. He'll just dribble, watching for someone to whom he can pass, and if nothing comes up, he'll find the smallest hole and charge right through it. He has several impressive shots besides a right- and left-hand lay up—especially a stop-and-jump shot with one hand.

I learn the names of these things from watching and having them explained to me after each game. Before, I didn't know a thing about basketball. Sports, especially team sports, were not exactly favored in our family.

Afterward, Bert likes "goin' out with the boys." They go to one of the local *Stüben* and have a few beers, smoke cigars, and participate in some good old-fashioned male camaraderie crap.

He'll come home a bit silly, usually bearing some goofy thing he's picked up, as a love gift, like a beer coaster on which he's written "Bert loves Kate." Then he'll climb in bed and fall right to sleep. I can't bring myself to ask him to stop.

At Christmas, I talk Bert into coming to the mill and having Christmas with the family. I know he'll like it: the stuff about the mill that I hated will be just his thing. I tell him that we'll chop down and steal our Christmas tree as we do every year. Dad will write about it later, in a book called *Tidings*. I'm Maggie in that book.

Bert fits right in with the family. The morning after we arrive, he's padding around the main room in a sweatsuit and bare feet. Nobody, not even Dad, walks around at the mill in bare feet. The floor is freezing. Bert's feet just don't seem to feel the cold. Bert's enthusiastic about everything—the pond, the hills, the dark mystical quality of the Morvan, the whole family.

He says it's the closest thing to Oregon he's found in Europe, and, in some ways, it might even be better. He connives with the tree-napping, helps mount a ten-footer in the corner next to the fireplace, puts on the highest balls and wraps the lights and garlands around it. He works right in with the family, as if he's always been there.

Late one evening, after Christmas, when everyone has gone to bed, I have a few moments alone with Dad.

"What do you think of Bert, Dad?"

"Well, to be honest, I'm not sure he isn't a member of the family who's been hiding out on us. I can look at Robert, Matt, and Bert and see them as brothers. I think he's terrific. What do you think of him?"

"You remember what you said when I was considering divorcing Danny and I asked you, long distance, what love was?"

"I'll never forget it. I was very upset. I didn't want you to divorce. Now it seems to have worked out, but I still feel sorry for Danny."

"Don't worry about Danny. He's living a yuppie life in Venice, California. But that isn't what I want to talk about.

"You said love was admiration, respect, and passion. I thought you weren't being helpful, but you were. Do you remember what you said about having all three?"

"Yup."

"Well, now I know I don't have to die to go to heaven."

But I did.

CHAPTER 3

B Y N O W , Bert's moved into my place with most of his
junk, and we need more privacy. We need a bedroom
to ourselves.

One of the teachers tells us about an apartment up on the
hill overlooking town. We go see it. Although it isn't perfect,
it's the right price and gives us just about what we want. It's
second floor again with an outside metal spiral staircase. We
can also enter through the front door, up a real marble
staircase on the inside, but then we need to pass through Frau
Zeidelman's part; she's the owner of the place. We decide to
use the outside staircase, unless we're desperate—ice, or
snow, or something like that.

The apartment's basically a corridor, with rooms on each
side. The rooms on one side open onto a terrace looking out
over the town to the lake. It's a beautiful view. On that side we
decide to put the living-room, our bedroom and Wills'
bedroom. On the other side is the toilet-room with one of
those crazy German toilets where the shit sits on a platform so
you can inspect it while it smells up the entire room before
you flush.

But it's clean, everything is ungodly clean, and well-built in
the German style, with double windows that swing open in all
kinds of weird ways with levers and locks. The doors are so
big and heavy, fitted so tightly, you could cut your fingers off
without trying.

Because we're the school romance, everybody on the
faculty pitches in with furniture, even some of the parents, so

28

that in no time, we have the place nicely furnished. I haven't felt so part of a place since we lived in Idylwild.

Bert hates to sleep in a bed. There's more than a little hippy in him. He wants a mattress on the floor. He usually gives in to me but not on this one.

I've got to admit it's comfortable, and it helps my back, but getting up and out of this "floor bed" in the morning is almost more than I can manage. Unless he gives me a push or a pull, I have to spin around on my knees and crawl out backwards. Also, it's hard to make. I honestly don't think Bert ever made a bed in his life. I need to show him how to make hospital-type corners that won't come out, and then how to fold the top sheet over the covers. He thinks it's all very amusing.

Because he stretches out in the evenings on the bed to read—says he can't read or think in a chair—it's usually a mess again before I climb in anyway. His idea of a great evening is slipping into his gray sweatsuit, then flopping on the bed with a copy of *Stars and Stripes* or the *Herald Tribune* and nibbling on some of those big, fat German pretzels while slugging down a beer or two.

Lots of times, Wills snuggles in beside him, and I have the house to myself. I'll sit in the living-room and read something and pretend I'm Mom. Later, after Wills has fallen asleep, I'll take him down the hall to the toilet, then to his own bedroom.

After I've tucked him in, most times I go back to our bed. Bert half wakes and softly explores all over me, mumbling and singing in his half-sleep. If I want to, I only need to show some interest and we're off. If I'm tired or just not interested, it doesn't take much, and his consciousness, or whatever it is, will slowly recede, and he'll roll on his back and snore quietly.

When summer comes, Bert's crazy about going to Greece. Danny and I've made a deal: I can take Wills with me to Europe, provided he stays with Danny through the summer. Actually, by the terms of the divorce, Danny could have stopped me from taking Wills out of the country at all.

Danny has a new job, a good one, selling stainless steel, and has married a very nice woman. I feel reasonably comfortable about Wills going off to California. The only thing that worries me is he'll probably find himself all wrapped up in TV and TV dinners while he's there. But as Bert says, "He's Danny's child as much as he's yours. You just have to let go."

It's a teary goodbye at the airport. As soon as I put Wills on the plane, I telephone Danny to verify that he'll be there at the airport in Los Angeles to pick him up. Danny can sometimes forget even the most important things. We split the cost of the fare.

So Bert and I take off for Greece, camping. I've always hated camping. We didn't do much of it in our family. Dad said that during World War II he'd had all the camping he'll ever need for the rest of his life. The idea of sleeping out on the ground in what he calls a "fart sack" has no appeal to him.

I'd been camping with other kids in high school. They all lived in big houses with maids, and roughing it was fun for them. But in Paris, we lived in a small apartment, only 300 square feet, all five of us, which was already halfway to camping. Then, when we went to the mill, we had no electricity and needed to haul water from the well; it was freezing cold at Christmas and there was no way to wash your hair. I don't look forward to camping at all. But Bert's so excited by the idea I agree to go.

We drive all over Greece, camping in campgrounds, and it's as bad as I expected. Then Bert sprouts the idea we must climb Mount Olympus.

"Why do a crazy thing like that? It looks awfully high to me. We could get lost and never be found again."

"But, Kate, it's the home of the gods. There are paths and trails all the way up. We could never be lost. If you get tired, I'll carry you."

I give in. Bert's always so easy to live with except when he has one of his fixations, these goofball notions. Then he's like someone possessed.

He carefully makes tight knapsacks for each of us, his about twice as big as mine. He checks my hiking boots and socks. I'd forgotten Bert's a farm boy who knows how to handle himself in rough country. Maybe he wants me to go with him so he can show off.

At first, it isn't so bad, and we sing as we walk along. Then it starts getting steeper. I want to turn back. The top is still far off. Also it's beginning to feel cold, in the middle of July!

"Come on, Kate, we're more than halfway. Think of it. We might meet some of the gods; it's the chance of a lifetime."

"You go ahead, Bert. I'll wait here."

"Give me your hand, Kate. I'll pull with each step."

I give him my hand. We slug along for another half hour. Then I sit down on a rock. I look up to the top. We don't seem to be any closer.

"Honestly, Bert. I can't make it. I'm not the athletic type. You go on and I'll start back."

"Let's just take a little rest, Hon. Then we'll see. Look, the view from here is beautiful. It must be sensational on top."

I'm too tired to argue. I have a headache and I'm beginning to feel faint. What kind of guy am I living with?

After another half hour, I have my breath back. I'm ready to start down. Bert stands up, windmills his arms around in big circles, helps me wrestle my pack up on my back again.

"Kate, try 200 more steps. I know you can do it. If you come this close to the top of Mount Olympus and turn back, you'll never forgive yourself."

So we start trudging on, Bert practically dragging me along behind him. I begin to understand the meaning of the word "enthusiasm," one of Dad's favorites. I don't know how many times I've heard him say it meant "with the gods" in Ancient Greek or something. Bert's definitely with the gods, or, at least, wants to be.

I'd been counting, trying to give my mind something to do, and once we reach 200 I stop. If it weren't so cold, I'd be sweating down into my boots. The top looks closer, but not close enough. Neither of us says anything. Bert drops his pack and helps me off with mine again. We sit on the rocky side of that damned hill. Even Bert is puffing.

"Well, we're getting close, Honey. I'll bet not many women have made it this far. I'm proud of you."

He's being so slick, which isn't like him. Maybe living together is a big mistake. What other goofy ideas does he have? Mount Everest? I feel I might be getting hysterical.

"OK, Bert. I'll try to reach the top of this goddamned mountain but when we come down, we're finished. I don't want to live with a madman."

"Oh, come on, Kate. You don't mean that. If you feel that way, let's just turn on back right now. I didn't realize. I'm sorry."

I look at him and stand. He pushes the pack up on my back and then pulls on his. He starts on his way down the hill. I turn and start up. I'm determined to shame him, make him realize what he's been doing. I'm sure I'm going to die of exhaustion or a heart attack and it will be his fault. He hurries after me.

"You OK, Kate? Come on, let's go back. Your face is white."

I don't answer. I keep my eyes down and take one step at a time. If this is the last thing we ever do together, at least I'm going to do it right. He trudges along behind me. I don't even think to worry about Wills. I'm that mad. Bert tries to take the pack off my back but I shrug him off. He doesn't say anything.

I don't know how I do it, but we reach the top. I check to be sure there's no higher place, then plop down. I'm sure I'm going to faint, but I don't. I look out. It *is* beautiful. Bert's on his knees beside me, looking into my face.

"Please don't be this way, Kate. I just got so excited by the whole idea I didn't think. Come on, give me another chance."

I stare at him. Then I see tears in his eyes. I'd never even thought Bert could cry. He knows. He knows how close he's come to losing me. More than anything else, I know how much he really loves me, not just romance or sex but love with a capital L-O-V-E. I fall over into him.

We sit on top of that cold, uncomfortable hill through most of the afternoon.

"Kate, we'd better start back down before sundown. I'm not sure I can find our way back to the camp in the dark."

I stand up. I look at him.

"Bert, I know you can."

He looks me in the eyes carefully, gives me a hug, and we begin walking.

It's hard to believe how easy it is going down. Although my legs are like rubber and my big toe feels as if it's going to push its way right out the front of that heavy boot, we make it just as the sun sets. Bert has both packs. I know he's incredibly excited about having made it all the way to the top but he doesn't want to say anything until I do. And I'm just too tired.

When we arrive at the tent, I flop on the sleeping-bag. I hurt all over. Bert piles our packs in the corner, then kneels at my feet and unlaces my boots. I'm too tired to stop him. He gets off my boots and socks, then begins massaging my feet. Having my feet massaged is one of the things I like most in this world. How did he know? Immediately my headache starts to fade. I begin to be proud we've actually made it. He covers my feet and crawls up to my head. He looks into my eyes.

"Kate, you did it. You climbed to the top of Mount Olympus. That makes you a goddess. I always knew you were one, but this proves it."

He reaches into his pack and pulls out, of all things, a bottle of champagne, a warm bottle. He's toted it all the way up that mountain and then back again.

"I hoped we could drink this up there, but it wasn't the right time. Will you drink some with me now, before it explodes?"

I smile and reach up for him. He comes down on me and gives me one of his most loving and enfolding bear hugs. Up there on that hill was the closest I came to losing the best man in the world. We drink the warm champagne slowly. Bert undresses and undresses me. We climb into the sleeping-bag. We haven't even finished the bottle when I fall asleep with my head on his shoulder. I imagine he finishes the bottle himself, but I don't remember a thing.

We stay at the camp another day while I recover from my stiffness and my poor feet heal enough so I can walk on them again. It's warm now and I spread out in the sun. I have to admit I keep looking up at that mountain, not believing I've really done it. I can't think of any one thing, except having Wills, that was so hard or so worth doing.

A few days later, we go to a monastery, which for centuries allowed only men inside. We're hauled up a cliff in a wicker basket. I'm scared to death. They house us in neat, clean, small rooms that used to be cells for the monks. We eat at a big long table with the monks and a few other tourists. The food is simple but good. There's no electricity so we go to bed early. Bert starts making his moves. Then I remember.

"Bert, I left my diaphragm down in the car, and it's the wrong time."

He doesn't stop but keeps fondling, stroking, nuzzling me.

"I'll tell you, Honey, much as I love you, I'm not going down in that basket in the dark to get it."

I turn into him.

"I'm not either."

We make love, simply, almost reverently, in a way somehow like the food and the whole place, simple and rewarding. Afterward, as I lie stretched out on my back, I look up at the ceiling and try to read what's written out in gold and red in a ring around the wall. I can't figure out much but there's one word in that crazy complicated printing that looks to me like *Dayiel*.

Three weeks after we're back, I know I'm pregnant. I check with a kit and sure enough it's so. This is the very last thing I want. I know abortion is out for me. It has nothing to do with religion or anything. I just don't like the idea of anybody violating my body and then having nothing for it; it's like a negative number somehow, something you can see, but less than zero: nothing. I tell Bert.

It makes him crazy. He picks me up and swings me in the air. I think he's going to drop me.

"It was in that monastery, wasn't it? Tell me."

"As far as I can figure, it wasn't on Mount Olympus."

"I knew it. I could feel it. I felt a third person with us in the cell that night and the next morning. It was as if you had an angel on your shoulder or some kind of aura all around you. I just knew it."

"I'm glad you didn't tell me. Now what do we do? I'll never finish the two years' teaching experience I need to get a job in an international school. I'm back where I started, depending on a man. Goddamn it, Bert, I worked so hard to free myself."

"Think about it, Kate. We're going to have a baby, somebody new who's the two of us put together. Doesn't that make you excited? God, I'm almost dizzy thinking about it. Come on, let's go down to the *Rathaus* and find out what we should do to get married. Imagine, I'm going to be a father and you're going to be my wife."

"No, I'm not. I did that once. The only ones who profit from marriages are lawyers. Either you love me and will stick around to help or you won't. Priests or mayors or *Burgermeisters* or anybody waving sticks over our heads or throwing smoke in our faces doesn't change anything. I just hope if you want to split, you'll be straight enough to help me until the baby's in school and I can go back to work."

"Damn, Kate. You sound so cold-hearted. I really want to marry you. I want us to be Mr. and Mrs. Woodman. I'm so proud of you and I want everybody to know. Don't you understand?"

"That's just male egotism talking. You have to remember: I've been through all this. I suffered from it. I'd like to think it would be different for us—I know I love you and am more than half-sure that you love me—but nothing lasts. Life is change and if you don't like change you don't like life. I like life."

But I can feel myself getting excited. I love children; that's why I enjoy teaching kindergarten and first grade. I'm like Mom that way. I can feel myself melting. I swore I'd never be trapped like this again, but here it is. I smile and snuggle into Bert's arms.

"Bert, I'm glad you're the father and feel the way you do. I've just had so many bad experiences with men. You're the first man I've ever trusted. I'll be happy to be the mother of our child. In fact, if it's a girl I want to call her Dayiel."

Bert holds me close, but has already started sucking in his little beer-belly so it won't push against me. We stand there in the hall, rocking back and forth, almost as if we're dancing. Bert even starts to hum. He stops.

"Did you say Dayiel? How do you spell it? Where did you find such a name?"

I tell him about reading it on the ceiling where the baby was conceived. He laughs, rears back. There are tears in his eyes again.

"What if it's a boy?"

When Wills comes home at the end of summer, I'm beginning to show a little bit and have tender nipples. We wait till after supper on the first night. I've made some chocolate milk and then bring out cookies, German *Liebkuchen*. These Wills really likes. We're in the kitchen. Bert brings it up.

"How'd you like a little brother or sister, Wilzer?"

Wills looks at him carefully.

"Where do you mean, here, or with Daddy and Sally in California?"

That stops Bert. Neither of us had thought of that. It's easy to forget how Wills lives in two different worlds with two different sets of people, and he's just come from the other world.

36

"I mean here with us, Wilzer, with your mom and me."

"But you aren't my dad. He might get mad if Mom and you have a baby."

"They don't live together any more, Wilzer. They're divorced. I live with your mom now."

"But you aren't married the way Dad and Sally are. How can you have a baby together?"

"Well, we are married in a way. We consider ourselves married. That's why I'm living here with you."

"Do I get to go to the wedding?"

I lean forward and hold Wills tight to me. It's the first time I realize how alone he must feel. It's hard on kids when parents break up. They don't show much at first but afterwards nothing surprises them any more.

That night I call Mom and Dad in Paris. Mom's even more excited than Bert. I can tell Dad is, too. They both have always loved children and, so far, Wills is their only grandchild. I have a hard time getting them off the phone; we don't really have the money to afford long-distance calls to Paris.

Bert is all over me while I'm pregnant, not only to make love, but also to put his face, his ear, even his nose against my stomach as it gets bigger. I feel movement early, just before the fourth month. When Bert feels it, he becomes excited, jumping up and down like one of those Indian dancers you see.

"Bert, you'll wake Frau Zeidelman. Stop acting like an idiot and come back here."

He lowers himself onto the bed and puts both his hands and his face against me.

"There it is again. It's live. It's pushing right against me. Just feel that."

"I feel it, Bert. Now relax."

After that night, he climbs in bed with me every evening after I've read to Wills, and talks to the baby. He not only talks, he sings—crazy songs. I can't imagine how he knows so many. And some have the dirtiest lyrics I've ever heard. He says he learned them as a kid in Oregon. He sings so I begin giggling and then the baby jumps around. It's ridiculous, but I love it.

Then Wills hears us, of course, and wants to join in. He'll have his head on one side of my belly and Bert his head on the other. At first, Bert doesn't sing his dirty songs but then I say it's OK, and Wills laughs so hard he almost falls off the bed. They're just the kind of songs little boys like most.

Now Bert really starts putting pressure on us to get married.

"Look, Kate. My folks come from a small town with only 600 people. They're Catholic, although the only one who's actually religious is my little sister. We don't need to have a church wedding, but they'll feel peculiar if we have our baby without any kind of wedding at all."

Finally I give in. It's also my parents. They tell us we can have the wedding on the houseboat with a big dance afterward. My parents have a two-story houseboat they put together—a wooden boat on top, with a metal hull underneath. The downstairs is fifty feet long and is almost all one room. The boat looks like an ark and is perfect for parties. This could be our personal Halloween party, to chase away all the ghosts. This was before I knew there are no ghosts, not the way people think, anyway.

So that's what we do. Nobody in Bert's family has ever been to Europe, but the whole passel of them say they're coming. We decide, because we have a five-day holiday for All Saints' and All Souls' Day, to celebrate the marriage on November first. That day will also honor my Aunt Emmaline, Mom's sister. It's her birthday.

I have two aunts, Aunt Emmaline, and Dad's sister, Aunt Jean. They were girlfriends in high school. In fact the two of them brought Dad and Mom together when they were all teenagers. Aunt Jean married a PE teacher in a junior high school and has had five kids, all by Caesarean. Aunt Emmaline was an actress. She got married on her fortieth birthday. It was her first and only marriage. It lasted five years even though she was married to one of the nicest men I've ever met.

I adored Aunt Emmaline when I was a little girl. She lived in gorgeous apartments and wore fancy clothes. She was always on TV in some series or another and was in several films. She was glamorous. She bleached her hair, which normally was sandy-colored like mine, so she looked like a real blonde, and wore heavy make-up. She had a great figure.

Aunt Emmaline was the dream aunt for a teenage girl, a fairy godmother. She'd take me out to eat and buy me clothes. She was as different from my mother as anyone could be. Mom is the same size, but with dark hair and dark eyes. She doesn't dye her hair. She has the same beautiful figure but you'd never know it from the way she dresses. Mom has always been quiet. In fact, I can't remember Mom ever once raising her voice.

But before Aunt Emmaline was fifty, she was a drunk. She'd call us on Christmas Eve almost every year and give what Dad called her "goodbye-goodbye" speech. Dad made it a rule that nobody was to answer the phone on Christmas Eve but him. We could always tell from his face who it was. He'd just listen and nod his head. Normally my dad isn't a great listener. Then he'd say, "Is that all, Em?" He'd pause. "Well, I hope you have a happy life and Merry Christmas. Take care of yourself." Then he'd hang up. It was always the same. We never knew what she was saying. When I finally asked, he told me she was threatening to kill herself because nobody loved her.

My last dealings with Aunt Emmaline were sad ones.

My younger sister, Camille, and I were living in California. I was in Venice, and Camille in Culver City. Mom's mother, our grandmother, was living in Santa Monica. Emmaline was living in West Hollywood. Grandma was more than eighty at the time.

Grandma called Camille and said she'd been trying to phone Emmaline for three days and nobody answered. She'd taken a cab over to her place but it was all locked up. She wondered what she should do. She was crying.

Camille phoned me. It was evening and Danny was home so I asked him to watch Wills. I drove over to Camille's and from there we headed to Emmaline's. Neither of us was particularly concerned. It wasn't the first time Emmaline had gotten so far out she didn't answer the phone. But we weren't looking forward to it, either.

From previous visits, we knew how to climb through the bathroom window. We parked the car, walked up the hill to her apartment. We knocked several times and rang the bell, but nothing happened. We went around to the back. We promised each other this was the last time we'd ever do this.

I pushed Camille through the little window and she came around to open the front door for me. It was dark, and we turned on some lights. We called out, then saw that the light was on in her bedroom, coming out from a crack under the door.

When we went in, I almost fainted. Even Camille, who's pretty tough, turned her back and screamed.

Aunt Emmaline was stretched out on the floor beside her bed, practically naked. There was shit and piss on the bed, on her and on the floor. We could see right away she was dead. Camille turned back around and stared.

"We've got to phone somebody, the police or somebody."

But the phone was beside the bed, just in front of where she was spread out. We stood there. Then Camille went around the other side of the bed, reached across and gathered in the phone. She sat down on the floor. I tried to move close to make sure Aunt Emmaline was really dead. She was. She was beginning to stink and it wasn't just the shit and everything. I slunk around and scrunched down on the floor beside Camille. She had the phone on her lap and looked at me.

"I think we ought to call Mom and Dad. They'd know best what to do. What time is it there?"

We figured it had to be about seven in the morning. Camille made two mistakes dialing but finally got it. Her hands were trembling.

She explained the situation as carefully as she could. Dad was on the phone and Mom was on the extra ear-extension they have on French phones. We could hear Mom crying. Dad wanted to know how we were, what we'd done so far.

Camille told him. There was a long quiet pause; we figured he was talking to Mom.

"OK, first look around and see if there's any kind of a note, anything like that."

We put down the phone and started looking. Camille found a bunch of insurance papers all spread out on the desk. It was good having something to do. I kept trying not to look into the open eyes of Aunt Emmaline. We came back and told Dad what we'd found.

"Put them back into the drawer of the desk, sort of spread around. Don't touch anything else. Just make sure there are no notes."

We did that.

"Now call the police and an ambulance. Stay there till they come. Then, as soon as possible, go home and, if you have any, take a sleeping pill. I'm sorry you kids had to do this, but it was bound to happen. Just remember, it's what your aunt wanted."

We did all that and everything went off fine. They put it down that Aunt Emmaline had died of a stroke or something; a friend arranged this with the police so Aunt Emmaline could be buried in holy ground, and so Grandma wouldn't know. It seems this kind of thing is always happening in that part of the world. West Hollywood is sort of the place where failed actresses and actors wind up their careers, one way or another.

I don't know if there's any way I can contact Aunt Emmaline now, I'm not sure I want to, but I chose Aunt Emmaline's day for the wedding: I guess because I'm the closest thing to a child she had. One good thing that came out of the experience was my determination never to drink or fool around with drugs, and I never have.

After the wedding, I return to working at the school, but I begin having trouble with bleeding. I'm sick every morning and feel terrible all day. I'd had an emergency Caesarean with Wills in Los Angeles and the incision was done vertically, both through the stomach wall and the uterus: not exactly what you'd call a "bikini cut." I want this one naturally, but the doctors in Germany say it's probably impossible. However they also say they'll try.

I've found a *Frauenklinik* nearby, right on the Starnberger See. The baby seems to be growing nicely, but the contractions and bleeding continue. The doctor says I must stay in bed or I could very easily lose the baby.

I tell them at school and show them the doctor's certificate that I should stop teaching. Stan is very sympathetic, and comes several times to see how I am. Ruth, his wife, comes regularly to help keep the place up. I'm surprised how the faculty and parents all help. I knew I had some really good friends, Ellen, Pam, Cindy, Dallas, but I never expected they'd dash into the fray so willingly.

Bert does the laundry, keeps the apartment reasonably neat, takes care of Wills, feeds him, dresses him, all the things that have to be done. He comes home directly from school and gives up his basketball team. I feel spoiled. I keep thinking I'm better, that it's passed, but after half an hour on my feet I'm dizzy and need to slide back into bed again.

I'm glad when that seventh month passes. The doctor says, now, no matter what happens, he can probably save the baby, but he's given up on letting me have a natural birth. He says it's too risky, still I beg him to let me try anyway.

By the middle of the ninth month, my contractions begin and we rush to the *Frauenklinik,* and during seven hours of labor, we try for a natural delivery. But the doctor finally says it's too dangerous and performs a Caesarean. I cry.

Dayiel weighs almost eight pounds. She has to be the most beautiful baby ever. She already has strawberry blonde hair and the biggest, deepest blue eyes anyone could imagine.

Bert comes to visit me in the hospital during his lunch-time, eating sandwiches in the car. He holds the baby, fooling with it, his crazy beret perched on his head, while looking up at me and smiling like a demented fool. I know I'm smiling back in the same way. I have never been so happy.

Then, right in the middle of sedate Starnberg, we have a typically Oregonian event. A group of Bert's old cronies from his high school basketball team, five of them, decide, practically overnight, to visit us from the United States. They want to check out Bert's new baby girl—as well as the famous German beer: a private *Oktoberfest* in mid-April.

Bert's at home when the local policeman leads them to the apartment. They don't speak any German; to be honest, their English isn't so hot. The celebrations had started at the first *Gasthaus* they came across.

The next day, Bert brings them into the hospital. They're all wearing heavy-knit sweaters, lumber jackets, jeans, hard-tipped boots with thick-ribbed woolen stockings folded over at the top. The boots have yellow leather thongs lacing them up. They all have different multicolored stocking caps with pom-poms.

And loud! They seem to think they're out in the woods. The nurses are running and buzzing around, yammering at them, like farmers in the Morvan trying to control a herd of cows as they move it down the road. Bert stops them all outside my room. He doesn't have to explain much. I've figured it out. His Oregon animal buddies have somehow found us. I pull my nightgown shut—I've just finished nursing—and prepare myself for the worst.

Bert's all apologies. He's sheepish, but I know that, underneath, he's pleased they've come all this way.

"OK, Bert. Let them in. We'll just take it as it comes."

They're quiet for the first few minutes. Bert gives one of them the baby, and he holds her like a cut log, and then she's

passed from one to the other, each holding her in a slightly
different way, as if she were a water-bucket in a lumberjack
fire brigade. Little Dayiel looks each one in the eyes as if this is
the most natural thing in the world. Bert's beside me, holding
my hand, and as obviously proud as any proud papa could
be. Any moment I'm expecting one of them to try a lay-up
shot with this strange-shaped basketball. I'm glad when she
comes back to Bert and then to me. She smells of cigarettes,
sweat, and, I'll swear, Oregon spruce trees.

Finally they're ready to leave. Bert needs to return to school
and he gives them the key to our apartment. It's the one to the
door at the top of the spiral staircase we use as an entrance.

Just before dinner, Bert comes again on his way home. He
and Wills ate at the pizza place but didn't see the mob. He
hasn't been home yet. I hate to think of what these woodsmen
will have done to our nice little nest—maybe built a fire in the
middle of the living-room floor to keep warm.

At about nine o'clock Bert phones, just after I've given Day
her bedtime feeding. He still hasn't heard or seen anything of
his friends. He'd made arrangements to show them around
town and maybe keep them out of trouble, but they didn't show.

"Lord, I hope they don't mess things up, Kate. They can be
real hellraisers when they get into the spirit of things."

"Don't worry about them, Bert. They're big boys and not
our responsibility. Just go to bed. Make sure Wills drinks some
warm milk to help him sleep."

With that, I hang up. And in a few minutes I'm asleep.

The next thing I know is an awful clattering, shouting, and
hollering. It's almost like a chant but I can't quite make it out.
Day wakes too. I listen. It's "WOODMAN!" Someone is
chanting: "WOODMAN! WOODMAN!"

My God! I know who it is immediately. What can I do? I
ring for the nurse. She comes running in all excited. I explain
in German to let one of them in, only one, and bring him to
my room. She stares at me. I repeat. Just *one*, only one. *Nur
eins*. She scoots out of the room.

44

I don't know how she picked the one she has but he's absolutely stoned. Maybe he was the only one upright. He stands, more or less, at the foot of the bed, holding onto it, rocking back and forth, his head rolling on his shoulders.

"Don't you understand, this is a hospital? You can't just barge in like this. What are you thinking of?"

He looks up at me. It takes about three tries before he can get a word out.

"The key—lost the key."

I almost laugh. It's too much. I reach over to my purse on the table beside my bed.

"Why didn't you go to the apartment? Bert has a key."

Again, a long lapse before he answers.

"Did. Nobody answered. We yelled and nobody came."

I believe it. Bert can sleep through almost any noise. I guess if you live around sawmills, you can ignore most sounds. I give him my key.

"Don't lose it! You know the right way to go in?"

"Yeah, we'll be fine now we have the key."

He's holding it out in front of him like a gold nugget he's found under a rock. He goes out the door to my room that way. What a crowd of idiots Bert grew up with.

When Bert comes in the next day during his lunch period I don't even have to say anything. They've told him. Bert's holding out his hands, both of them, as if he's a cop trying to stop traffic.

"It's OK, Honey. They're all very sorry. They're on the S-Bahn, leaving for Heidelberg, first to Munich and then onward. I know they seem like a bunch of untamed animals, but they're a great bunch of guys. They just can't handle this German beer."

I put out my arms and Bert comes to me. He's such a shaft of strength coming from that tangle of wilderness. I'm so lucky to have him. I'm anxious to be home with him soon as possible.

❉ ❉ ❉

When I come home, there are flowers everywhere. My friends have cooked different meals for the whole week and put them in the refrigerator. All Bert needs to do is heat them up. I spend practically all that first week at home in bed, except for going to the bathroom. I play with Dayiel whenever I have the energy. She's such a wide-awake baby, already looking around at everything. It seems like such a new start on things. I figure I'll have one more baby seven years from now. That way I can have three children and each one will be like an only child. The older ones will be old enough to help me, too. I have it all planned out. Ha! What one doesn't know.

CHAPTER 4

AYIEL IS a doll but she's a devil, too. At four months, she's already biting my nipples when I nurse her, and she doesn't even have teeth. Bert thinks it's funny, and I think Dayiel does it because he laughs.

She's on her hands and knees almost as soon as she can roll over onto her stomach. She rocks back and forth, laughing out loud as if she's just robbed a bank. It isn't long before she develops her own way of crawling—not on her knees but on her hands and her feet—and is scooting around the apartment, like a dog or cat. Nothing is safe. I do everything to baby-proof that apartment, but nothing is Dayiel-proof.

She never sleeps through the night. She's up three or four times. Then after being nursed, she wants to play. Even at six months, she's sleeping less than eight hours a day. She seems to love life so much she hates to close her eyes. It's as if she knows.

Bert and I become zombies. We take turns getting up and fetching her. Then we let her stay in bed between us. I think she'll be safe that way, but she figures how to crawl out from the bottom. Bert wakes up with a start the first night she does it.

"Kate, where's Day?"

I'm still groggy.

"I don't know, maybe one of us put her in her crib when we were half-asleep."

"I didn't."

He leaps out of bed in one jump the way he can, like a jack-in-the-box. He leans back into our room.

"She's not there!"

I sit up, scared now.

"Maybe she's in Wills's room. Maybe he took her in bed with him because she was crying."

I crawl out of bed and stand up. I have a terrible headache. Bert's running up and down the hall. Now I'm worried. Where, in a locked apartment, can a baby go? Could she have hurt herself?

Then I hear Bert laughing. The baby is laughing, too. They're in the bathroom.

Day is sitting in the bottom of the shower, playing with the toys I put in there when I give her a bath. I know she likes to take a bath, it's one of her favorite things, but in the middle of the night, without water, in the dark? She's pointing up to the faucets, wanting us to turn on the water. She's filthy from crawling around and soaked through. Bert leans over and starts undressing her. Day keeps pointing up at the faucets.

"OK, Day. This one time. But no more baths at three o'clock in the morning. Understand?"

She smiles and slaps her hands on the bottom of the shower the way she does when there's water.

"Bert, do you mind if I go back to bed? I'm pooped and I have a terrible headache."

"Go ahead, that's OK, Babe, I can handle this. You go to bed, try to get some sleep. I'll see if I can put her down after her bath. Boy, am I ever going to be a mean math teacher tomorrow."

He turns on the water and I can hear it running as I pad back and crawl into bed. I don't even hear Bert come in; maybe he doesn't, because he's gone off to school when Day screams from her crib and wakes me up.

Mom and Dad come to visit several times. Dad is wonderful with Dayiel. I never expected that. He follows her around the house, wherever she wants to go, letting her do what she wants as long as it isn't dangerous. He says it's like having a puppy, and that spending so much time on the living-room floor, crawling with her, he's acquiring an entirely new view of the world. He also gives her airplane rides, pushing her up over his head or lifting her up on his legs or his feet or letting her sit on his stomach and bounce. I remember him doing all those things with me and Matt and Camille. I'd forgotten.

Having a baby brings back so many things from your own life that you might never have remembered. If I hadn't seen Dad with Dayiel, I wouldn't have remembered these acrobatics he did with us. It's funny how one forgets. Probably forgetting is the closest thing to death most living people ever know. It isn't sleep.

Mom reads to Dayiel. It seems to calm her. Mom tells me about a study that says a little child, from infancy on, should have three books read to it a day. The same study says that any normal child who has had 3,000 books read to it before going to school will do much better all the way through to university. My God! Three thousand books.

As Day gets older and the weather improves, Mom takes her into our garden or down by the *See* to feed the ducks and swans. Day's great, as long as you don't try to make her do something she doesn't want to do, or not let her do something she wants. Then she can be so stubborn I could almost kill her. But Bert and I also love her, despite, or maybe because of, all the devilment she gets into and the constant watching she takes.

Everything is going along fine, but then I find out I'm pregnant again. Day's only thirteen months old, and, naturally, still in diapers. Even Bert, who now knows enough about how hard it is to rear a child, is concerned.

I go to the *Frauenklinik* and no one is too happy about my having another baby so soon after a Caesarean. But we decide to have it anyway, then Bert will have a vasectomy; or, if it's possible in the middle of a Caesarean, I'll have my tubes tied. We'll never be able to afford rearing more than three kids.

This time I'm sick from the beginning and I have very low blood pressure. I can hardly eat, and what I eat, I usually throw up. Bert's worried. He says I ought to consider having an abortion; it isn't too late.

I sleep on the idea, but in the morning I know I want this baby. This way all our kids will be in school by the time I'm forty. We can carry on teaching together, maybe even here, at the International School, with the children at the same school with us. It isn't the way I'd planned it but now it seems like a good idea, if only I can survive another Caesarean.

Mia is born on December seventeenth. I beg the doctors to let me go home for Christmas Eve, and they agree, but I have to go right back in. On Christmas Day the doctor comes to see me. He says he hated to cut me open again and ruin all that neat embroidery he'd done before but that he's done just as well this time. He's thinking about taking up crocheting.

It's Day's first proper Christmas and she loves it. Mom and Dad fly from Paris and are there the day I come home with the baby. He has his video camera, calls me "mamma Mia," and takes some beautiful pictures of Dayiel kissing Mia while she's nursing and then of Dayiel trying to nurse herself on the other nipple. Mom distracts her with one of the Christmas gifts; it's another book. Day's already pointing, not just at the pictures, but at the words. She'll be reading before she's five.

It's the best Christmas I remember and we've had some great Christmases in our family. I feel I've made it as an adult. I have a wonderful husband and three children. Dad always said you know you've grown up when you'd rather have Christmas at your own home with your own kids, than go off to your parents' house. That's a bit sad, but I think he's right. I feel grown up. I never have before.

Just before Mia is born, Bert's dad dies. He's had a bad heart for a long time. And although he was in good enough shape to come to the wedding, he looked pale. He just drops dead. He's sixty-four, only a few years older than my dad.

Bert dashes off for the funeral, helps his mom settle things, and then gets back the week before Mia is born. But he is a wreck.

I was surprised by Bert's crying before. Now, he can't mention his dad without breaking down. He continues working at school because he feels he needs to be doing something. But it's hard for him and it's hard for me because I can't help him. Even if I were well, I probably couldn't do much. It's hard to understand why we humans don't seem able to learn about death, the quiet simplicity of it all.

We agree that Bert should quit the International School, and that we should move to Oregon for a year or two so he can be near his mom. Claire's all alone now in a big house where she's reared four kids, and doesn't know what to do. Bert felt terrible leaving her.

Oregon will be a good temporary solution. Besides, Danny wants Wills for one full school year, and if we're in Oregon, I'll be able to call him every evening. Danny's wife Sally has delivered a boy they named Jonathan, and they've bought a nice duplex in Redondo Beach. I can't really say so, but I'm not thrilled.

In the meanwhile, having two babies at the same time is quite a job. I think poor Bert spends half his free time down in that basement filling and emptying washing-machines and hanging clothes, mostly diapers.

Although I recuperate more quickly than I expected, all the muscles in my stomach seem to have turned to mush. It's a month before I can do one sit-up. I look at my jogging shoes and think I'll never jog again. It's very depressing.

But Mia is a love. She's so different from Day. It seems she is smiling and trying to talk from the first moment I see her. I can look in her eyes and she'll look right back at me and it's magic somehow. I feel I've known her a long time, that she's very wise and loves me deeply. I know this is considered kooky talk by most people but they just don't know. I know now I was right.

We need to put the apartment back in perfect condition or we'll lose our deposit; three kids can really wreck a place. We scrub everything, then paint. To us it looks perfect but we know to a German eye it's a pigsty. But Frau Zeidelman gives us back our money anyway.

The goodbye parties seem to go on forever. It's worse than three Christmases and New Years thrown together. But it's wonderful. The washing-machine we give to Camille and her husband Sam. The VW "hulk" we pass on to Matt. We give away most of the furniture the same way it had been given to us. On the last night we have just the crib for Mia, our mattress on the floor with Day between us, and Wills on a pillow. Friends are going to pick those up the next day.

In the dark, Bert turns toward me.

"You know, Kate, I thought I'd never learn to like old Krautland, but if it weren't for my mother being alone, and Wills going to live with Danny, and the fact we don't have any furniture, I'd go right back to Stan and tell him I'm going to stay after all. These people here at the school are even nicer than Oregonians and that's saying something."

Traveling with kids is never fun, and this trip starts out wrong. First, we need to wait six hours in Munich before the plane is allowed to take off. On the trip to Paris, strong winds make the plane dip and roll. The flight from Paris to New York is even worse. And then I get sick. I haven't been sick on a plane since I was twelve years old, but I go into the tiny plastic restroom and vomit till I think I'm going to die. One of the attendants hears me, or maybe Bert sends her back, but she knocks and I manage to pull back the lever to let her in.

She's nice and considerate, and puts me in one of the seats reserved for the crew, tips it back and gives me a pill. She asks if I'm pregnant. I point up the aisle toward Bert, Mia, Day, and Wills.

"They're mine."

I'm sure the stewardess thinks I'm either some kind of Arkansas hick or a fanatic Catholic. But she, like everyone else, is so kind. Different attendants help Bert and Wills with the babies during the whole trip.

When we finally land at JFK, we're six hours late.

Mom is waiting at the airport, and has been for almost six hours. She's come up from the beachhouse they have in New Jersey, where they've spent the last seven summers. It's a really old-fashioned house in an old-fashioned town called Ocean Grove. I loved it when I visited them there about five years ago. But it would've cost 700 additional dollars to make the stopover this time, and we couldn't afford it.

I get off the plane dead white, Mia in my arms, Bert's balancing Dayiel and our hand luggage. Wills is toting another bag. It's a deep, low point. And there's Mom, smiling as ever, as if she'd just met us on the street by accident. I cry. I don't feel much like a grown-up. I feel like a little girl who's gotten lost and just found her Mommy.

When it all settles down, Bert is looking at our tickets.

"Well, Babe, we've missed our connecting flight. Could I leave Dayiel with you while I go see what's happening?"

I can only nod. Mia is nursing. I'll bet the milk she's getting is sour. But it keeps her quiet. When Mia drops off to sleep, Mom takes her. She watches Wills watching Day, and I drop off, dead to the world.

When I wake, Bert's back and he's all smiles.

"They were going to put us up in a Hilton Hotel or something until tomorrow, but I told them we have a place to stay if they could just hold us over until the flight next week.

"There was a whole bunch of palaver, but in the end we agreed, so if it's OK with Rosemary, we're on our way to Ocean Grove, in a car, yet. Think of that."

We arrive in Ocean Grove after midnight. Dad's asleep. He jumps out of bed the way he does, stark naked. He says he'd held the place at the banquet they were supposed to be attending, until the lady took the food away. Then he came home, worried, checked at the airport, found the flight from Munich was delayed, then decided to grab some sleep and worry more in the morning. The idea of catastrophes happening in our family just never seems to come up. Somehow we've all lived in a kind of never-never land where nothing ever happens to us, only to other people.

For twenty years, while Dad was supporting the family as a painter, we lived without life assurance, car insurance: we had no liability insurance of any kind, no social security, nothing but Dad's little disability pension from when he was wounded in World War II. My parents were crazy, lucky, or dumb. Maybe it was crazy-dumb-luck, because we hardly ever even got sick. I don't think that any of us four kids saw a doctor more than six or seven times in twenty years, and then it was mostly to get shots.

Mom is a bit of a witch, a good witch. She has fixed up the whole upper floor of that big house in New Jersey just for us, with a crib for Dayiel, a bassinet for Mia, and separate beds (and rooms) for Wills and us. We aren't even supposed to be coming. Could she have bewitched that plane? When I was a teenager, I used to think she had some special power, the way she'd always know things. Now I see it has nothing to do with witches. She just has strong intuitions that she believes in and then acts on them. She'll never believe what's happened to us—that's not the kind of witch she is. She's a practical one.

We sleep like dead people. It's ten o'clock before I hear Bert rolling out of bed to get Mia. She's slept through the night for the first time. Or maybe she did wake but we didn't know it. He tucks her in beside me and she begins to nurse furiously. Bert climbs out of bed, and goes downstairs. Wills is still asleep.

I know that Dad and Mom, even after being up late the night before, will have already played tennis, swum, gone for a bike ride, or maybe a little jog.

Dad's something of a fading jock, but Mom was always the most unathletic person I've known. Now, she's out there, hitting a tennis ball two-handed, and hitting it hard. She runs her two miles every morning, slowly, but she does it. I wonder if, after the kids have grown some, I'll ever get back in shape. I'm the same as Mom, no athlete, but I like feeling good.

We have a wonderful week. Dayiel's in and out of the water, playing in the sand with her granddad, making castles, ball ramps, and running around on a beach that seems to have no limits.

Bert is a regular water-bug and Wills even more so. They're in and out of the ocean with Dad about twenty times a day. Wills has more friends than he can play with and disappears for long stretches. Both Bert and Dad are a lot more confident about the kids than I am and don't seem to be watching them. Bert comes up to a shower that's attached to the boardwalk, washing off Mia. After he's changed her, I go over.

"Aren't you watching Wills? He's out there in those high waves, riding on one of those boogie boards, and he could sink, or even float out of sight. You're as bad as Dad. You never expect anything dangerous to happen."

Bert squints up at me into the sunlight.

"Look, Kate. You see those guys sitting up on those white stands, wearing the red jackets? Those are lifeguards. They're watching everybody, especially little kids, and they know this water like the back of their hands. I was talking to one, in fact the captain of the lifeguards, and do you know that, in the almost hundred years since they started having lifeguards here, nobody has ever drowned on this beach? This is probably the safest place in the world. So relax and enjoy."

I turn away. This is so like him. But he's right. From then on I try to relax and enjoy. It's like coming home.

Mom and I share the cooking, and the boys take care of the little ones. Even Uncle Robert, my tall little brother, does his share. He likes Day, although generally he hates little kids.

After watching her, he then has to explain to us, in his slow, methodical way, why she's exceptional.

Mom drives us to the plane. Everything is on schedule. If Mom is involved I have the feeling that everything will be fine.

We arrive in Oregon, and Bert's brother Steve picks us up. I have no idea what to expect. The road from the airport is so full of weird vehicles, RVs, cars pulling trailers, vans, caravans, all driving fast, really fast, and cutting in and out all the time, that I finally say something to Bert's brother.

"Steve, don't they have any speed limits here? You're doing seventy and almost everybody is passing you. I thought France or Germany was bad, but this makes their driving look almost sane."

"Everybody in Oregon is going somewhere in a hurry it seems, Kate. I don't understand it myself. But if you go under seventy you'll be run right over. You know, Oregon is one of the few states that went back to the sixty-five mile speed limit. This means they drive seventy-five without the cops doing anything. Maybe it's the frontier spirit."

He looks over at Bert and laughs. We're in a big American car with plenty of space for our luggage and us. The three kids are in back with me—without seat belts, so I have to hold onto Day and Mia, one in each arm, and I tell Wills to hold onto the armrest. In California and in Germany, I always drove using special seats with straps for the kids, which in turn were held down by seat belts. It's the law in both those places, but I'd do it anyway. A little kid doesn't have a chance, even if you only need to stop fast. Bert looks back at me from the front seat.

"See, Kate. We're in the wild west here. That fifty-five mile-an-hour speed limit saved more lives than any law that's been passed in the United States, but in Oregon they'd rather be dead than safe. They don't like anybody else telling them what to do."

I hold tight onto the kids till we come off the highway. It's early evening and the countryside is beautiful, except there seems to be a terrible smog, worse than in Los Angeles.

"What's all the smoke, Bert? Do they have big industry up here?"

"That smoke's from field burning, Kate. One of the biggest crops in Oregon is grass seed. The farmers burn hundreds of thousands of acres of stubble from the fields after they harvest the grass seed. It's been going on for almost forty years. Everybody tries to fight it but the seed growers are making hundreds of millions of dollars a year growing the stuff. It's hard to stop them.

"All kinds of organizations have tried, but nobody seems to get anywhere. The people in Oregon are paying for it. Their eyes sting, and there are darkened skies, constant smoke, and cancer-giving pollutants. All just so a few farmers can get rich. It isn't really farming either, it's agri-industry, a pall over Oregon.

"I used to be head of a group at the university that fought them; in fact I was arrested once for picketing the governor's mansion. Sometimes, it makes me ashamed to be an Oregonian."

I wonder how the smoke is going to affect Wills and me. We're both terribly allergic. But then, next week, Wills will be flying down to Los Angeles. In all the fuss, I almost forget I won't be seeing him much during the next year. He has been my best friend and closest companion. I'm going to miss him. But as Bert says, he's Danny's child, too. In many ways, in the way he is inside, he's more Danny's child than mine.

I know something about Bert's family. His father was a butcher who had his own shop in Falls City, a small town with only 600 people. His father expanded the shop to sell other goods so people wouldn't need to go all the way to the next town to buy the little things they've forgotten.

He made a reasonable living. Bert and the other kids in his family all worked in the store. I also know that his dad bought some land just outside town and built a house there on seventeen acres. He tried to grow holly bushes to sell at Christmas, but it didn't work out.

When we drive into the Woodman place I'm enchanted. I have no idea that the house would be so personal, so handmade. It's a bit run-down, mostly needing some nails, a hammer, and a coat of paint, but it's beautiful and fits right into the countryside. It's surrounded by horse fences, and there are two ponies. Wills goes wild.

Claire—that's what she insists I call her—seems happy to see me and especially the two little girls. She's only had one other grandchild, by her youngest son. The little girls take to her immediately. She has a very grandmotherly, soft, loving way about her. But there's also a deep sadness. She was married to that same man, Bert's dad, forty years, and has lived most of those years in this house, raising her kids. Now he's gone and the kids are making their own lives.

Both our little ones are happy in her lap and fall asleep. She's fixed up Bert's old room for us to sleep in. She carries Mia, while Bert takes Dayiel. We don't even undress them, just pull the covers up and turn out the lights. Claire tells me how both the crib and bassinet are the same ones Bert and all her other three kids used.

The house has a good feeling about it, like the feeling we had in Germany, living in Seeshaupt, where we would eat at hundred-year-old tables that had been in the same family the whole time, generation after generation. I like to think of time as something that glues one part of a family to the next as each takes its turn. Now I know it isn't quite like that. It's actually much more complicated.

Bert is hot to fix up the house and get it painted. He has long talks with Claire as to whether she should sell it and move into a small apartment in the next town or stay out here. She hates to leave, but is lonesome. Also, it's a big house for a woman in her sixties to care for. I know Bert and the other kids hope she'll stay on, but I think that's mostly for selfish reasons. They want to think the old homestead is still in the family. They also want to think of it as a place they can come visit.

None of them, except Bert, is more than twenty miles away. And for the next year or two at least, Bert and I won't be that far away either, probably down in Eugene. We're still undecided. It all depends on how much I like Oregon; also, on how much Bert likes it. He's been away a long time.

Whatever his decision, Bert is determined to paint the house and he's going to organize everybody to help, including his old basketball buddies. I dread seeing those clowns with paint-brushes. I can just imagine the result.

Bert buys four twenty-five gallon cans of white paint. Then he keeps adding different colors. He wants a color that will fit in with the surroundings and at the same time stand out as something different. He asks me to decide. I settle on a color that's like the cedar chips all over the ground, a mix of raw sienna, burnt sienna, burnt umber, and red oxide. We keep mixing and painting strips on the house until it dries just right.

Somehow I've become the expert. After going with me to a few museums in Munich and Paris, Bert is convinced I'm a real art connoisseur. He's apparently spread the word around. In our family, all of us were dragged from one museum to the other since we could walk. Either Mom or Dad would talk about the paintings and sculpture we saw so we all had the equivalent of a university art course by the time we were twelve years old.

Bert sets brushes and ladders out for everyone, with pans and rollers, and a whole vat of turpentine. It's a mob scene with everybody swinging a brush or pushing a roller and getting covered with paint. And while it's not as big a mess as I expected, it isn't neat either. I must say those basketball players really work when they want to, if they don't get too drunk. We have barbecues to feed the painters in the evenings, and picnics galore for lunch.

In three weekends, that entire hundred gallons of paint is used up. And at least as much beer has been swilled. We've put on three coats, and it looks great. I was afraid it might be too pinkish, but when it dries, it's just right. I choose three colors for the trim: a white where it won't weather too badly, a burnt sienna for around the window frames, and a mix of burnt and raw sienna for the frames themselves. This takes another week.

Afterward, we all stand around congratulating ourselves and prepare a big party. Doug, Bert's best buddy, brings out an additional keg of beer and almost everybody gets staggering drunk. Thank goodness we've put the paint away in the shed and locked it. They might have started painting the trees. This painting orgy is about the biggest thing to happen in Falls City for years.

Claire just can't believe we've finished the whole job so quickly. She thought it would take months. I begin to understand something of what Bert was missing about Oregon. It's a kind of camaraderie which includes women.

CHAPTER 5

OUR NEXT PROJECT is to register at the University in Eugene, check out the married student accommodation, and start looking for a house to buy. We think it might be the best investment we can make with our $40,000—my savings, Bert's, and what we've put away while we've been together. This includes the $5,000 Mom and Dad gave us when each of the little ones were born, and, on top, $5,000 on each of their birthdays, tax free.

We'd like to buy a house near the University to fix up. We'd work on it during the two years of our stay, then either rent it to students for income, or sell it. Bert hasn't had much experience building but thinks he can manage. It's the kind of thing I've always wanted to do. Dad is the biggest fixer-upper of old houses I know. He claims to have made more money fixing up old houses and selling them than he has in twenty years' painting.

Doug, Bert's best friend, lends us his VW van to make the trip to Eugene. I borrow a pair of good kiddy seats and fasten them to the seat belts in back. We decide if I need to nurse Mia on the way, we'll pull over to the side of the road and sit there till she's satisfied. We're in no hurry. This is the way we did it in Germany. I have the feeling Mia is about ready to stop nursing. I've started giving her a bottle at night and she seems to like it.

At the last minute, as we're about to pull out of the driveway, Wills decides he'd rather stay with Claire, to play with Doug's son and the ponies. I feel safe leaving him.

61

We're going to stay with Don and Roni, good friends of Bert's who live in Eugene. They have already been searching out a house for us. It's wonderful being brought into this complex of interlocking friends that makes up Bert's life. I never realized how popular he is; how much he means, in some symbolic way, to the people around Falls City. I see what Claire has lost having him so far away.

We go through the first stages of registering at Oregon State, trying to claim residence through Bert's mother, hoping they won't check too closely. We both want to finish our master's degrees; it would be Bert's second. His first was in mathematics; this one would be in computer science.

We look at about ten different houses. I can't believe it. There are places less than ten blocks from the university that can be bought for around $40,000–$40,000 wouldn't buy a garage in Los Angeles or Phoenix, or Germany, or France.

We find one we both like that's listed at $48,000 but the realtor says it can be negotiated. We offer $38,000 for starters. We're willing to go as high as $42,000 but don't want to go into debt, and we'll need money to pay for the renovation.

It's a nice two-story house with four bedrooms. We feel we could easily convert it into six bedrooms without much work. The roof, electricity, beams, foundations, all seem good to us. Don, who's built his own house, comes out to inspect, and says it looks solid to him too. We make our official bid at the realtor's around eleven in the morning, and phone Claire to tell her we'll be home for dinner. We pack up, say goodbye to Don and Roni, then start off. It's about a two-hour drive along Interstate 5, I-5, straight north. It's not too far for Bert to go see his mom whenever he wants to.

Both kids drop off to sleep in the back. I try not watching the traffic. For about fifteen or so miles, all the traffic has been redirected to our side, the northbound lane, because of work that's being done on the southbound lanes. This jams up cars and trucks so closely together we can hardly breathe. I wonder if I'm going to make it in America. The cars are tailgating each other, going at about seventy miles an hour. Bert tries to slow down but an eighteen-wheeler behind us keeps flashing his lights for us to hurry up. God, it's scary.

Then, finally, just before Salem, the two sets of lanes, north and south, are open again. Cars and trucks zoom past us, trying to make up time. The sky is white with smoke. I concentrate on looking at what I can see of the scenery, trying not to watch the traffic, as vehicles keep cutting each other off, slipping in and out of our lane with their boat-trailers, their regular trailers, their trailers packed with furniture piled on and precariously tied down. There are huge pickups with wheels almost as high as the roof of the van. Up ahead I see what looks like a yellow stain across the road.

"What's that, Bert?"

"That's what I was telling you about, Kate. They're burning the stubble from grass seed and smoke is blowing across the road. Watch out, this can be dangerous."

We try to slow down but another big eighteen-wheeler is right behind us, practically touching our back bumper. Bert tries to move over into another lane but can't. There's another eighteen-wheeler beside us, and on the other side it's soft shoulder. Bert rolls up his window to keep out the smoke. He turns on his lights.

First, it all gets yellow, then amber, then it's almost completely dark. I look back at the kids but see only that huge truck, that eighteen-wheeler, tailgating us, still there; he's just turned his lights on. He's too close; he'll never be able to stop. I turn back to the front, but can't see a thing. It's now total darkness. Bert's pumping the brake, trying to signal the truck behind us to back off, when he bumps the car in front of us, ever so slightly, and then somehow manages to bring the van to a stop. Then, there's a terrible crunch, an unbelievable noise, the incredible shock of the jolt from behind. I look back for the babies and hear them cry.

There's nothing we can do.

PART TWO

M Y SON Robert and I push our bikes along the narrow alley between the house and the fence of the house next door. We're dripping wet from a three-mile run we've just made in Asbury Park. The race is every Thursday evening at seven on the boardwalk and conducted by the local YMCA. We've ridden the mile or so from there back home. The air is soft and soothing.

Rosemary's already home, having driven back. We've invited good friends who run with us to dine at our house. She's come home early to set the table and put things out. Albie and Linda are stopping to buy the pizza. Bobbie, another friend, is with them. Robert and I have enjoyed riding slowly through the darkening evening and look forward to showers and good pizza with family and friends.

As I push my bike past the dining-room window, I catch the movement of Rosemary coming back through the kitchen. I park my bike near the trash cans. Robert parks his along the fence leaning over the marigolds we've planted. He rushes in past Rosemary to get his shower started so I can have mine after him. I figure I'll help Rosemary.

She pauses in the little covered back porch, on the platform outside the kitchen door. I'm just stepping over the small sill into the porch when she comes quickly down the steps to me. It's enough out of the ordinary that I take notice. I see she's crying.

She comes into my arms. I hold her tight. She's sobbing so hard I can feel it through her whole body and mine. I think:

what in heaven's name can be wrong? My wife is not an easy crier. I'm just beginning to think about all our loved ones, the few older aunts and uncles. Then she looks up, takes my head in both her hands, stares into my eyes. I can scarcely make her out in the dark.

"Will, darling, a terrible thing has happened."

She stops to take a deep, stuttering breath.

"They're all dead. Kate, Bert, Mia, Dayiel. They're all dead. I just finished talking to Claire Woodman. They were killed in a terrible crash and fire on the highway in Oregon. They're dead, all of them, except Wills. He stayed at home with the Woodmans."

She leans her head into my sweaty shoulder and cries harder. I hold onto her, as much to keep myself up as anything. I'm surprised at my reaction. I don't believe it. Somebody's made a mistake. I can't accept it. All the usual reactions people have to things they don't want to believe. But I'm not crying. I've just started shaking my head against Rosemary's.

"When did it happen? How? Are you sure?"

She talks into my shoulder. "It happened yesterday at about four o'clock, Oregon time. There was a fire that blew across the road. Seven people were killed. Thirty cars piled up. Claire was crying so hard it was hard to understand her. I still don't understand."

"It happened yesterday? What took so long? What kind of people won't even tell you right away when something like this happens? Are you sure?"

"I wish I weren't. They're dead. They're gone forever. We'll never see them again. I don't know how I can live."

I hold her tighter. I'm beginning to shiver. I feel cold all the way inside myself. How could this happen? These are the kinds of things that happen to other people. We've always been so lucky. Bert's such a careful driver, and Kate even more so. She won't go around the block in a car with the babies unless they're strapped into baby seats, like astronauts with wide straps crossed over and around them.

I turn Rosemary and lead her back up the steps into the kitchen. She's slumped against me. I'm still not crying. It hasn't registered yet. I hear the Jeep pulling in, parking out front.

Our friends are standing on our front porch. I open the door. They're wearing jackets against the chill after the run. Albie's holding the grease-stained, cardboard pizza box. He's smiling; the women are behind him. They know right away something has happened; something is wrong.

"I'm sorry, we've just had some terrible news."

For the first time, I feel I might break down crying. Somehow, telling it to someone else will make it more real, irrevocable.

"Kate, Bert, Mia, and Dayiel have been killed in a multiple automobile accident in Oregon. Rosemary just phoned and talked to Bert's mom. It happened yesterday afternoon."

Albie puts the pizza down on the table by the window.

"And they're only telling you now?"

It's the same reaction I had. Rosemary begins talking behind me. I know her. She doesn't want anyone thinking badly of somebody else when they aren't guilty of anything wrong.

"They didn't know themselves until just about an hour ago. It's only afternoon there. The accident was so horrible they couldn't identify the bodies for a long time. The Woodmans were expecting them home for dinner last night."

She stops to get her breath, to hold back her sobs. She goes on through her tears.

"They didn't come. The family thought the car had broken down or that maybe they'd decided to stay over with friends. They're the same as we are, thinking this kind of thing doesn't happen to family. The accident is in all the Oregon news, television, everything, all over the country, but they didn't think this kind of thing could happen to their family."

She stops, leans forward with her face in her hands. Linda goes over, gets down on her knees, holds onto Rosemary. I realize I'd better get off my feet or I'm going to fall down. I slump onto the floor with my head against the side of the couch, the way I watch baseball on television. Bobbie pulls some pillows off the couch and tucks them under my head. Both Linda and Bobbie are crying now. Both have children of their own.

Albie pulls my legs out straight, goes into the dining-room, and brings out a chair. He lifts my legs up onto the chair; Bobbie puts another pillow under my legs. I realize from their reactions that I must be going into shock. I know I feel terrible. I can't stop shaking my head. It's totally involuntary.

Linda takes the pizza into the kitchen. She comes back with wet towels for both Rosemary and me. I'm beginning to feel as if things are passing me by. I want to go over, comfort Rosemary, but I'm numb. Albie's on his knees beside me now.

"Do you want me to get the first-aid people? I can call and they'll be here in five minutes."

I shake my head no. It interrupts my regular rhythm of head shaking.

"No. I think we should just be alone for a while. I still have to tell Robert. He doesn't know yet. We'll be all right. You people go home to your families and enjoy them."

Rosemary sits up in her chair, ready to play hostess.

"Yes, please go home. We'll have too many things to do. Nobody can do anything for us right now. If we need any help, we'll call. Honest."

Bobbie leans toward Rosemary.

"I know I won't sleep tonight, so any time, just call and I'll be right over. Dave can help, too. You know lifeguards are trained in first aid. You don't need to take this all alone."

Linda and Albie are standing. It's uncomfortable knowing they want to help, but all of us knowing there's nothing they can do. Rosemary's right: we need to work it out ourselves.

They leave. I try to have them take the pizza but none of us feels much like eating. I see them off the porch and into the Jeep. I look around at the quiet street in the night. Ocean Grove is famous for its peace. I wonder if it will ever be the same for me, for us. I turn back into the house. I go over and kneel before Rosemary, take her hands in mine. Her crying has subsided some. She looks me in the eyes.

"During the twenty minutes or so when I knew and before you came back, oh, how I envied you those twenty minutes of not knowing. I have the strange feeling that if we don't know, it won't be. I staggered over from the phone and sat at the foot of the steps. I was wishing with everything I am that I could scream or pray."

I hear Robert coming down the stairs. I stop him at the bottom of the stairs.

"Robert, I have something to tell you."

Robert is usually quite diffident. But he catches something in my voice, my face. Still, he's carrying through what is for him the normal sequence.

"I left enough water for you to shower and there's still a dry towel."

"Robert, I have some bad news, something terrible has happened."

He stands there, hanging his hands loosely at his sides. I wish I didn't have to say it, ruin his calm. We could allow him one more night's peaceful sleep. But it has to be done.

"Robert, I know this is hard to believe, but Kate, Bert, Mia, and Dayiel were killed in a massive automobile crash in Oregon. Mom just talked to Mrs. Woodman. That's how we found out."

His face blanches. He stands there, blank, for a few seconds. He peers into the living-room.

"How's Mom taking it?"

"It's hard but she's OK."

"Is there anything I can do?"

"Not now. Do you want some of the pizza? It's right there on the table."

"No, I couldn't eat. Is it all right if I take a walk down by the ocean? I don't think I can handle this. I'm even afraid to go in and talk with Mom."

"Sure, I understand, and so will she. Be back before ten o'clock because I don't know when we'll be leaving for

Oregon and the funeral. In fact, I don't know when the funeral will be, but we'll probably be leaving tomorrow."

"OK. I'll be right back."

I can tell he's on the edge of breaking down. I don't think I've heard him cry since he was under ten. Walking along the beach or boardwalk in the dark, crying, is more his style. He goes out the back door. I go into the living-room again. The running costume I'm wearing is looking more and more ridiculous.

It's just then I remember that Sunday we're supposed to be part of a big family reunion outside Philadelphia at my Aunt Alice's. I'll need to call them right away. I also want to call my sister in California.

I slip off my Bill Roger's warm-up jacket. It's beginning to dry on me. I also slip off my soaking wet running shirt. I'm doing these things automatically. I keep looking up at Rosemary. She's staring out the window, tears running down her face. I need to shower and put on some dry clothes but I don't want to leave her alone. I don't want to be alone myself.

"Will, you go on up and take a shower. I'm fine. When you come down, we can make arrangements for a flight and a limousine to pick us up for Newark. But, first, I want to sit here a few minutes to pull myself together, pull our lives together if that's possible. You go up and shower."

She smiles. I smile. We're being silly. We should hold onto each other and cry our hearts out. Neither one of us expresses emotions easily. We've been lucky enough that it hasn't been necessary very often.

I let the shower run over me for ten minutes. Here I can cry. I wonder if Rosemary can cry downstairs. I dress in a pair of light slacks and a T-shirt, not exactly a mourning costume, but mourning costumes aren't our thing either. I go down the steps slowly, preparing myself. Rosemary has moved from the chair by the window to the chair at her desk. She has the *Yellow Pages* in her lap and is talking on the phone. She hangs up.

"Well, we have a flight out of Newark for Portland, leaving at ten-oh-five tomorrow morning. There was nothing this evening. We stop over in Chicago, arrive in Portland at about noon. I'll call Claire Woodman now and tell her what time we come in. I think she told me the funeral is supposed to be Tuesday, but I'm not sure. I wasn't paying much atten—" This is where she breaks down. I go over and hold her head against my chest. She puts her arms around my waist.

"Imagine—all those beautiful young people and we're going to their funeral. It isn't fair. They never had a chance at life."

I hold her more tightly and try to hold tightly onto myself. I wonder how she got herself together enough to call the airlines. She constantly amazes me. I know this is all a horror and a shock for me, but for her it must be impossible. Her life has been the kids. I have my painting and writing, other kinds of children in a way. But she's just lost her much loved first-born Kathleen, along with Bert and those two beautiful babies.

She gently pushes me away.

"Let me get this over with, then I can collapse."

She calls Claire Woodman and tells her what time we hope to arrive. Bert's brother, Steve, will pick us up at the airport and drive us down. Rosemary hangs up.

"I don't know how the both of us got through that. Claire was constantly stopping to cry. Bert was her first baby, too. I didn't think of that."

She pulls out her address book and dials again. This time it's the limousine service, and she arranges for pick-up at seven o'clock in the morning. She hangs up.

"I can't do any more. Would you call and tell Aunt Alice we can't come tomorrow? Then call Jean. She'd want to know."

"Don't you think we ought to call the kids first?"

"I figure it's about three o'clock in the morning. We don't want to wake them, do we?"

"I think they'd never forgive us if we didn't tell them right away."

She stares out that window again.

73

"You're probably right. I guess we should call Camille. Please tell them not to come for the funeral. There's nothing they can do and they don't have much money."

I know the number by heart. It rings about ten times, then I hear Camille, sleepy-voiced, our only daughter now. I almost can't speak because the sobs are building up.

"Camille, this is Dad."

I stop there, take two deep breaths with my hand over the phone.

"What's the matter?"

"Something terrible has happened, Camille."

"What is it? Could you speak louder?"

I might as well get right into it. I don't have any choice. I'm sobbing as I say it.

"Kate, Bert, Dayiel, and Mia were killed in a horrendous automobile crash in Oregon."

"What! Who told you that? How did you find out?"

I can't go on. Rosemary takes the phone. She's crying but not sobbing.

"I called to find out about Kate's gynecologist appointment, how it went. I got Wills, but Claire took the phone from him and she told me. It's hard to believe but it must be true. We can't believe it, it's so impossible."

I take the phone from Rosemary. Camille is crying, practically screaming. She's trying to tell Sam, her husband, what's happened. I say her name, try to get her attention.

"Camille!"

There's a long silence, then she says between sobs, "I'm here."

"Don't bother coming to the funeral. It's too far and Mom and I are sure we can handle it."

"Whatever you say."

That's not like Camille. She's generally against what anybody has to say. It's her way.

"Listen, Camille. Would you tell Matt? We have no way to reach him. Maybe it's best to wait till morning."

"It's morning now."

"You know what I mean, real morning."

"No, Matt would never forgive us. He'll want to know right away. Sam's already dressed and getting the car out so we can drive over. We'll want to be together, anyway."

She sounds more herself. Rosemary takes the phone from me.

"We really mean it, Camille. Don't come. We'll handle it and there's nothing you can do."

"I hear you, Mom, I hear you. We'll work it out. When are they having the funeral?"

Rosemary takes the phone from her ear, tears rolling down her face. She hands the phone to me.

"She wants to know when the funeral's going to be. I just know she'll come and probably Matt, too. But it's such a long way and all for nothing, a terrible waste of money they can't afford. Talk to her, she doesn't seem to understand."

Camille's crying uncontrollably now. She's the most emotional of the family. I wait.

"Listen, Camille. The funeral's Tuesday, but please don't come. Think about it. You know Kate wouldn't like it. Funerals don't help. More important is for you and Sam to go over to Matt's to help him and Juliette. You're the ones we're worried about; you're all we have left."

There's a long silence. Not quite silence. She must be muffling the phone because I can hear her sobbing.

"Dad, we'll decide what we have to do. We're grown up now. I'll talk to Matt and we'll decide together. We probably can't get all the way from here to there in that short a time anyway. The main thing is you and Mom take care of yourselves. Could you have some of your friends come over to help?"

"We want to be alone, Camille. We've made arrangements for getting there and will arrive in Portland at noon tomorrow. Steve, Bert's brother, is picking us up."

Talking about the practical aspects of this impossibility seems to help me. I'm not crying.

"Dad, I'm going to hang up. Sam's out in the car. We'll call and let you know what we're going to do. My God, this is just awful. I can't even think of those two little girls dead. I don't think I can live with this."

Then the line goes dead. She's hung up. I put the phone back in the cradle the wrong way, then turn it around. I look at Rosemary. She's sitting at the bottom of the steps to the bedroom with her elbows on her knees and her head in her hands. She's crying so hard she can hardly breathe.

"Camille's going to go tell Matt and Juliette. I'm not sure I convinced her not to come."

Rosemary doesn't respond. I stand there, confused, feeling that I'm going to faint. I've never fainted in my life, but I think I now know what the feeling must be like.

"I'm going to call Aunt Alice first. They have to know. Is there anything special you want me to say?"

She's slow responding.

"Just tell them what happened and we're sorry we can't come. After all this reunion they were holding was for us. You know as well as I do what to say. I just can't do it right now."

She's still sobbing, wiping her eyes, her nose, the corners of her mouth with a Kleenex.

I look in her address book to find the number. My hands are shaking so much I misdial twice. I look at my watch. It's almost ten o'clock. They're probably asleep, but there won't be time to call in the morning. Aunt Alice answers.

"Oh, hello, Willy. How are you?"

"Did I wake you up, Aunt Alice?"

"No, we were just watching a ball game."

"I think it might be a good idea for you to sit down, Aunt Alice."

"Why, do you think I'm so old I can't stand up late at night?"

"No, just sit down."

I take a deep breath. As each person learns it, it all becomes more real, a part of everyday life, one of the ordinary things that happens.

"Aunt Alice, we can't come Sunday. I'm sorry."

She doesn't respond. She's waiting. I try to put my thoughts, my emotions together.

"A horrible thing has happened."

I pause, still no response. It's her way. I never realized it until just that moment.

"There's been an awful accident out in Oregon. Kate, Bert, and the two babies were killed. We've just found out. We're flying out tomorrow for the funeral."

I'm glad to get it all out.

"That's terrible, Willy. Oh, my. Are you sure?"

"We're pretty sure, Aunt Alice. I'm sorry. You all have the reunion just as if we were there. We don't want to disappoint anybody. All right?"

"All right, Willy. Thanks for calling."

That one's out of the way, at least. One more, and then it's finished. I dial my sister's number in California. It'll be just about dinner time there. Leo answers on the third ring.

"Leo, this is Will. Could I talk to Jean, please?"

"Sure, whatever you say."

I catch a feeling of hurt in his voice. We usually pass the time of day before he turns the phone over.

"Hi, big brother. What's up?"

"I think you ought to sit down, Jean. I have bad news. Tell Leo to come on the extension."

"You've got me scared stiff, you big jerk."

She holds the phone down from her mouth, shouts. "Leo, would you pick up the extension?

"OK, I'm sitting down. What's the big news? I hope nothing's happened. Are you all right?"

"Jean, we just had a call from Bert's mother in Oregon. Bert, Kate, Dayiel, and Mia were killed yesterday in an automobile crash. We don't know any of the details yet."

"Oh, my God! Are you sure? I don't believe it."

"Neither do we, but it's true. We leave tomorrow, early, for the funeral on Tuesday. We've told the other kids and begged them not to come. There's nothing anybody can do. It's done. So don't you or Leo get any crazy ideas about coming up. There are going to be more than enough people out there, all upset, probably with not enough places to sleep. I don't think Bert's family has such a big house to put people up, and I'm sure there are no hotels in Falls City where they live. There are only 600 people. I guess that's 596 now."

"Honest, are you putting me on? If you are, I'll kill you!"

"I wish it weren't true as hard as I can wish, Jean. They're gone."

The sobs break out again. I'm crying hard.

"Jesus, Mary, and Joseph. How could a thing like this happen? Did you hear that, Leo?"

Leo comes on.

"Oh, my God! I saw it on TV yesterday! There were about thirty cars in a big crash on the I-5. Smoke blew over from burning fields or something. There was a huge fire with fire trucks, helicopters, everything. They still didn't know how many were killed. It must have happened about four or five o'clock yesterday. How is it they didn't get the news to you sooner?"

"Maybe it wasn't the same crash, Leo."

Rosemary gets up from the steps and comes over. She motions for the phone.

"I think it was, Leo. I didn't tell Will everything, but Claire Woodman, Bert's mother, told me it was a huge crash with a fire. Bert, Kate, and the babies were coming up from Eugene when it happened. Thank God, little Wills wasn't with them. It's something to be thankful for."

She hands me back the phone. Her face is pale green.

"Will, are you there?"

"Yes, I think I'm here, Jean."

She's crying but can talk.

"I know saying we're sorry is not much at such a time, but we are. We'll pray for all of them and you, Robert, Wills, and Rosemary as well. We're going over to Saint Joseph the Worker just as soon as I can get this food off the table."

She's crying and it's working up to sobs and long pauses. Hearing her cry sets me off again.

"Look, Will, after you've done everything that can be done there in Oregon, would you and Rosemary please come down here for a little rest? You're going to need it. Please?"

"All right. We'll see what we can work into our return flight. Robert's coming with us."

"You know we have plenty of space. Just come. We'll be ready. You two go to sleep now if you can. Take the phone off the hook and lock the door. If you have any sleeping pills take them. Sleep is what you need most now. I still can't believe it. It must be awful."

I hang up. I've no sooner hung up than the phone rings. It's Aunt Alice. I tell Rosemary who it is. She comes over to take the phone. I go to the front door and lock it. There are all kinds of other people we should call but I'm not up to it. Neither is Rosemary.

Rosemary is finished talking to Aunt Alice. She's smiling a flat smile.

"She called up not believing what she'd heard. You know how slow she is reacting. This was just too much for her. She thought maybe you were playing some kind of joke. Nobody wants to believe it." I also call Danny; he has to know.

She's moved into the kitchen and is unsetting the table she'd set for the pizza dinner. I go in and give her a hand. Twice, in passing, we stop, hug and hold onto each other. Neither of us can say a thing.

Robert comes in as we're finishing. He goes straight upstairs and into his bedroom. Rosemary sits in the reclining rocker. Now her face is swollen and red; her eyes are swollen, too.

"We should probably pack tonight, Will. There won't be much time in the morning."

"Right. I'll tell Robert."

"Give him a little more time, first, dear. I know he'll be up late: he usually is. Just before we go to bed, you can tell him about packing. Be sure to have him pack his suit, a shirt, and a tie, extra socks and underwear."

Going up the stairs behind Rosemary I'm reminded of the Myth of Sisyphus, a constant climbing and falling back. We each pull out a bag and start. It all seems so unnecessary. I bring a charcoal-gray suit, the only real suit I own. I also have a summer suit but it needs cleaning. I throw in socks, underwear, a few changes of shirts, an extra pair of shoes, more dressy than the ones I'll wear on the airplane. I peek over at Rosemary packing. She goes about it in her usual, methodical way, carefully folding each dress, skirt, blouse, putting rubber bands around her stockings, underwear.

I go into the bathroom. I look dreadful. I splash water onto my face. I take four Valium out of the medicine cabinet, two for me and two for Rosemary. They're the yellow kind, five milligrams. I've never taken two before. Once in a while I take one when I can't sleep. I hope two will be enough. I hope Rosemary will take hers. She doesn't like taking medicine of any kind, and has a terrible time swallowing pills.

We undress slowly, turn out the light, and climb into bed. The french doors onto the porch are open, letting in a fresh ocean breeze. Then I remember I haven't taken my medication. I slide out of bed and go back into the bathroom. I take my pills for blood pressure and blood sugar, plus some others. I also remember I haven't told Robert to pack.

On the way back to our bedroom, I knock at his door and open it. He's stretched out on his bed fully dressed. His eyes are red.

"Robert, we're leaving so early in the morning that you should pack before you go to sleep. Mom says be sure to pack your suit, a good white shirt, and tie. Take along your best shoes, too; a funeral is an awfully formal kind of thing."

"OK. But I'm not sure I'll sleep much."

"We're not sure we will either, but we're going to try. Tomorrow will be a long day, as will the next few days. So dress in your PJs and try to relax. If you want something to put you to sleep I have some pills."

"Oh, no, that won't be necessary."

I back out of the room, shut the door. Robert is the same as Rosemary when it comes to pills.

Our bed is basically two twin beds pushed together. We don't like to sleep apart but there's no double bed in this house, which we rent every summer. I usually start out in Rosemary's bed and then as she falls asleep, roll over into the other bed, the one by the french windows.

I close the bedroom door. Rosemary is stretched out on her back in her nightgown but not under the covers. In summer, I sleep without pajamas. I crawl across my bed to hers, snuggle in beside her, and put my arm across her breast. She has her arms up over her head against the bedstead and one leg cocked up. She often begins sleep this way. Her eyes are open, with tears rolling slowly down her cheeks, but there are no spasms of crying or sobbing. She's crying to herself. I put my face against hers; her tears are cold. I can't think of anything to say. I don't really want to say anything, but feel I should. Her voice seems so calm, so far away, so dry and emotionless, not like her at all. She turns to me.

"I never knew one's teeth could hurt so much from crying."

"For me it's the ears. I had no idea my ears could be so painful from trying not to cry. It's like the earache I used to have when I was a kid. Even swallowing hurts. Probably your teeth hurt from the same thing: trying to hold it in, you're biting down hard."

There's a long silence. We stay close. I snuggle closer but there's no response. We lie like this. It isn't very late. We're in bed mainly because it's the most private place we know.

We spend an hour this way, not moving; each, I think, pretending to sleep for the other. Finally, it's too much. I roll over to where I've put the pills and a glass of water. I turn back to Rosemary.

"I have some Valium here to help us. We really ought to sleep. Tomorrow's going to be tough, with the flight and then all the emotion in Oregon. I really think you ought to try swallowing these, Honey."

I hold out the pills. She doesn't move.

"I don't want to sleep, Will. I just want to lie here and think, remember. But you take something. One of us is going to need to be awake and going tomorrow. Have you set the alarm?"

"I've set the alarm on my wristwatch for six-thirty. That ought to give us enough time."

"Fine. Now listen, honestly, Will. Do you really think we should go all the way to Oregon? They're dead. There's nothing we can do. We'd only be going for the Woodmans. It doesn't seem like a good enough reason. Why don't we stay here where we were with them last and remember all the good times we had together? It was a miracle we had them that last week. Why ruin it by dashing off to the place where they were destroyed? I've never had any desire to visit Oregon. I know Kate was sure I wouldn't like it. Most of the people there are roughnecks, the country scraggly. We hardly know the Woodmans. Why don't we just keep it the way it is?"

I'm shocked. But I shouldn't be. It's the same thing we've been telling our kids. But it seems bizarre not going to the funeral of your own child, her husband, and two of your only three grandchildren. I begin to wonder if Rosemary is all right. She's so much for form, doing the proper thing. I keep quiet.

"Will, if there are any bodies to see, I don't want to see them. They're probably terribly crushed and burned. I don't need that, neither do you. Why are we doing this to ourselves?"

As usual, in her special way, she makes sense. I lie back, quietly, to see if she's going to go on. She knows I hate both weddings and funerals. I went to an aunt's wedding when I was eleven, then to my own, then to each of my daughters', but their weddings were so wonderfully relaxed they could hardly count.

I went to my grandmother's funeral when I was nine, then to my grandfather's when I was fifteen. I was a pallbearer. Then there were the funerals for my mother and father. That's a pretty good record for a man over sixty years old. I've been avoiding weddings and funerals all my life. In fact, I don't see much difference between the two. Rosemary knows this.

"All right, you're right, Rosemary. You know how I hate funerals. I'm sure if Kate and Bert can know what's going on, they'd agree with us. We haven't paid for any tickets so I'm sure we can cancel them. Tomorrow at six I'll call off the limousine. I'll tell Robert. I don't think that'll break his heart. I'll contact Camille and Matt, and tell them we're taking our own advice, staying home. If they want to go, that's their business. What else? Boy, I feel better already."

I roll out of bed to tell Robert.

"You're so sweet, darling. Don't. We must go. There's no way out of it. But as long as we both know this entire farce is for others, then I feel better about it. I'm sorry if I got your hopes up."

I roll back onto my bed, take the glass of water, and pop three of those Valium. Maybe we'll have a mass funeral. People who die together stay together.

The pills don't work at first and I can tell Rosemary is still awake when my watch "dedinks" midnight.

But the pills must work finally because when I drop back on the bed, I'm out like a light. It seems much later when I wake to the phone ringing. I stagger across the foot of the bed. Rosemary is rolling out her side.

"You go back to sleep, dear. I'll get it. It's probably one of the kids."

I dash past her and start down the steps. Rosemary is just behind me. I'm counting rings. It's the fifth ring I've heard when I pick up the phone. I sit down on a chair beside the table near to the desk. Rosemary hovers over me.

I've heard the little "dink" of a long-distance call but then that's all, except somebody breathing heavily into the phone. Nobody makes long-distance obscene phone calls, do they?

"Hello, who is this?"

Then I hear a thick rumbling, a clearing of a throat, the sound of a sob. Even from those, I recognize it's Jo Lancaster, my best friend.

"Jo, is that you?"

"I love you."

Then more hard sobbing. I can't respond; I'm sobbing so myself. I hand the phone to Rosemary.

"Jo, is that you?"

There's a long pause, then Rosemary walks over slowly to the table and puts the phone in its cradle.

"He just said he was sorry and hung up."

We look at each other and then break down again. I hold her in my arms. She buries her head into my chin. I can feel her silken skin under her light, white nightgown. Even now, her hair is tickling my nose. I rub my nose into her hair, knowing she'll know and not care. After almost forty years, she knows these things about me.

Finally, we push each other away.

"Rosemary, I think we ought to take a shower. Who knows when we'll have a shower available to us again?"

Without a word, she starts up the steps then turns back.

"Would you wake up Robert, please? You know how hard it is getting him going in the morning. Make sure he's out of bed. I know he slept because I could hear him snoring lightly last night."

She goes up the rest of the steps. I turn on the living-room light for the limo. Then I realize I'm stark naked and if any fool is up at this time, by Ocean Grove standards, I'm "exposing." I hurry up the stairs.

I wake Robert and wait until I'm sure he's awake and out of bed. I know better than to carry on a conversation with him. He's a slow starter but his heart's in the right place.

"I know, Dad. I'm up. Honest, I'm awake."

I go into the bedroom and dress myself in the clothes I laid out last night.

CHAPTER 7

WE'RE READY and on the porch when the limo arrives. It's a real limo with a dark blue, plush interior and strap-in seats, the kind that fold down from behind the front seat. Robert sits in front because he has such long legs. The driver is good, and we feel confident. I'm reminded of a funeral. I've rarely driven in a limo except for the few funerals I've been to.

The flight is long and boring. I'm torn between mourning and fatigue. Rosemary falls asleep until we get to Chicago where we change planes. Robert drops off to sleep immediately. I try not watching the film.

Chicago to Portland is even longer. Robert drops right off to sleep again, but Rosemary is just staring at the ceiling of the plane with tears running down her face. I don't feel I can interrupt her thinking. I know she's with Kate. I intrude only when the food arrives. I eat. I can always eat. Usually Rosemary can, too, but this time she only plays with the food, pushing most of it aside. She drinks a cup of tea.

At Portland, Steve and Wills are waiting for us. We give big hugs to Wills and try not to cry too much. Our Robert holds his ground. He never hugs anybody, hasn't since he was twelve years old.

Steve is tall and thin. It's hard to believe he's Bert's brother, but then I remember he has diabetes. He's been giving himself shots for over twenty years. His weight is an important part of his survival.

85

His eyes are red; we hug and shake hands. We're all trying hard to hold it in. He goes to pick up the car and brings it right to the curb. We throw the baggage in back and climb in. Robert is in front with Steve, and Wills is in back with us. Rosemary is hunting for a seat belt, but there isn't one.

Steve works his way out of the airport confusion and onto the highway. He tells us it's the same highway, I-5, on which Kate, Bert, Dayiel, and Mia were killed.

The traffic is horrendous. Steve drives carefully and stays to the right but it seems that just about every vehicle is towing something. I've never been on a highway like this, not even in Los Angeles, and they drive like kids playing bumper cars, constantly cutting in and out, ducking between the gigantic trucks and semi-trailers steaming along at over seventy miles an hour.

I thought, after what had happened to us in the past twenty-four hours, I'd never be scared to die again, but I am. I look over at Rosemary. She's white and white-knuckled. We turn our attention to Wills who's been rattling away about some horses they have at the Woodmans' and how this is "neat" or that is "neat." I begin to wonder if anyone's told him what's happened, or is he just so childish he can't comprehend? Then he puts his head on Rosemary's chest and in a choked voice says: "It was their nap time, Dayiel and Mia. They were probably asleep, weren't they? They just didn't wake up."

Rosemary looks over toward me and we both breathe deeply, trying to hold it down. She leans her head down so her face is in his hair.

"That's right, Wills. They just went to sleep and never knew what happened. It's terrible that they're gone, but I don't think they felt a thing."

He's quiet and so are the rest of us. Steve is trying to concentrate on his driving, but tears are rolling down his face. Wills looks over at me.

"Will anybody ever call me Wilzer again? I really like that name. Bert made it up you know."

"I'll call you Wilzer if you like, and I'm sure anybody you want to call you Wilzer, will."

He's quiet for several minutes. He looks back at me.

"I think I want only men to call me Wilzer. It's my man's name. I'd like you and Robert and Matt and Sam and Steve to call me Wilzer. Those are the only ones I can think of right now."

Soon after, Steve turns off the I-5 and we're on small roads. I lean back and try to let things flow by. Wills is asleep against Rosemary. He's got to be beat. He's been inside all the strain since the beginning.

I begin to dread arriving at this house where I've never been, meeting on such intimate and difficult terms people I hardly know. It's worse than any wedding.

We twist around a few dirt roads and then pull up in front of a rambling house newly painted, a sort of dark earth-pink. It looks good.

Claire Woodman is coming down from the front porch. Wills runs to meet her.

She pulls him to her as he's babbling away.

"See, they came. I told you they would. These are Mom's Mom and Dad. They'd be sure to come."

Just then, at this slightly embarrassing moment, I hear the sound of heavy, wide-track tires on the gravel driveway. It's a big, new, American car. Danny's driving it and he's alone.

He pulls up behind Steve's car and comes over. His eyes are red and his face puffed up. We give each other a big hug after a false start at a handshake. Danny and Rosemary kiss. He shakes hands with Steve and Claire. Wills can't wait any longer. He jumps into his dad's arms and breaks down. Danny nods to all of us and puts his arm around the almost hysterical, sobbing Wills, leads him off around the side of the house. I hate to admit it but I'm almost glad to see such an outburst. I didn't know how much he'd been holding in. Claire motions us inside.

During the course of the next hours, as people keep coming with more and more food, country style, we learn about what happened. They show us the newspapers. For the past two days it's been the headline event in the two Oregon newspapers. The faded, poor-quality color pictures are gruesome. I can't put it together with our family. It's like seeing the news about some drug-crazed nut in Dallas going up in a tower and shooting people, or the National Guard shooting students at Kent State.

It turns out a farmer named Paul Thompkins started the fire with what he thought was the approval of the Department of Environmental Quality. The DEQ, as it's called, keeps surveillance on the valley by air from light planes.

Mr. Thompkins won't speak to anyone and his son has told the reporters to go away.

Diane is Steve's fiancée. Diane's the one who first realized that Bert, Kate, and the little girls might be involved in the accident.

It was the next morning, after the accident, after watching the pictures on television all evening. She was listening to a portable radio in the shower when it was announced that two unidentified small children were found burned in a van with two adults. She came dashing out of the shower with a towel around her, and called Doug. Doug is Bert's best buddy, the friend from whom he'd borrowed the van. She told him what she'd heard and asked if he would be willing to go and try identifying the vehicle.

When he got there, he found his van, smashed halfway to the ground, with the license plate burned to a point where he could scarcely make out the registration number.

After that, the identification of Bert was made from dental X-rays. Kate's followed. There was no other way to identify the bodies.

I realize we should have stayed in Ocean Grove and spent the day at an isolated beach and talked to each other. We don't need this.

They've arranged for the mortician in the next town—which, oddly enough, is named Dallas—to have the bodies cremated. Claire is Catholic, but somewhere along the line, without my noticing, the Catholic church has let up on the temple of the Holy Ghost business.

For my own reasons, I'd rather they not be cremated but it's a bit late to stop this. I only insist that the members of the family not be cremated separately, as planned, but together. After a phone call to the mortuary in Dallas, this is confirmed. I find myself hoping the town was named before the TV show.

Jo Ellen and Diane come home from work. In America, it turns out you're only given one day off, the day of the funeral. Nothing more. We Americans are a hard-nosed bunch. There is pressure on me, as writer, to come up with something appropriate for the announcement (or whatever it is) that will be distributed at the funeral ceremony. This gets worse every moment.

But I have no trouble. They find me a pencil and paper. I don't even have to think about it. The thought just flows out the end of this dull pencil. It isn't even the kind of thing I'd usually write. I'm more of a mystical poet. I write:

> THEY CAME TOGETHER
> BECAME TOGETHER
> LIVED TOGETHER
> LEFT TOGETHER.

Everybody seems satisfied with this. Then they want me to design a monument for them. Again I know in my mind, as if I'm being prompted, exactly what it should be. It's like magic writing.

I take another piece of paper and design a slant-topped sundial with each of their names at the cardinal points. Around the sides I write the above poem. At least I have something to do. I want to carve a model of it in wax for the monument-maker. We melt all the sealing-wax they use for preserves and I put it in a number ten can. When it's hard, I pound it on the bottom and knock it out. I figure I'll work some more on it in the morning.

We start receiving telegrams and telephone calls from our friends all over the world. Several friends of ours and several of Kate's from Paris and in Munich are actually flying here for the funeral. Camille, Sam, and Matt phone from Boston to say they're on their way. So much for the fourth commandment.

Claire's in a dither. As I suspected, there's no hotel within twenty miles. We start pulling out quilts, blankets, sheets, sleeping-bags, blow-up mats, everything we can find. It's going to be a camping funeral. Some people will have to sleep on the lawn. There's no space at Steve's apartment. Jim, Bert's youngest brother, has space for horses but not people.

It turns out, as guests of honor, we're going to sleep in Bert's room. It's the room he had when he lived at home and where he and Kate spent their last night. The cribs are still up in there. Claire volunteers to take them down but we say it'll be OK. We're so frazzled, not tired, just frazzled, nerves on edge: we can sleep anywhere; that is, if we can sleep at all.

We go to bed early. Each of us, I know, is trying not to think about or mention the fact that the sheets we're sleeping on, the blankets we're under, were last slept on and under by Bert and Kate. I can even smell Kate's perfume, *Magie Noire*, chosen for her by Bert. I know Rosemary can, too.

We grab hold of each other and can't stop crying. It's the whole compilation of things, the actual knowing of how they died, how gruesome it was, the discussion of the cremation, the formalities. And we're absolutely dead tired. Rosemary's little snooze on the plane and mine in our bed in Ocean Grove last night weren't enough to support us.

For hours we cry intermittently, with long silences, and very little talk. There isn't much to talk about. How does one discuss such a thing?

Finally, sometime after midnight, Rosemary drops off. I can tell by her regular breathing, sometimes interrupted by a pitiful mewing sound or a sob, but, thank God, she's asleep. I carefully untangle myself and stretch out on the bed beside her, on top of the covers.

I must have gone to sleep rather quickly because I have no memory of a long wait for sleep. This would be real sleep without chemical assistance. I'm gone.

Sometime before morning, I wake. I don't need to use the toilet down by the front door. I wake naturally. I'm surprised at my inner calm. I know what has happened but it's somehow all inside me, integrated, accepted, in some astonishing way. I lie awake in the dark, in this strange, yet not-quite-strange bed, smelling the slight fragrance of Kate's perfume. I feel enormously comforted and comfortable. I begin to think I might be having some kind of psychic or psychotic experience. It isn't natural to feel so absolutely absolved, or separate, in such a circumstance. I fall back to sleep with this thought.

The event I'm going to tell next is out of most people's experience. It can be regarded as true by none of the criteria listed in the foreword. If you have not read the foreword, or have forgotten it, please go back and reread it.

This whole tale would be easier to write and more "true"—in the sense of "believable"—without this next part. However, if I am trying to represent truth, it is necessary to recount this experience as well.

I wake in the morning still in this state of unbelievable calm. I even entertain the idea I might have died in the night and this could be what death is, a totally involving peace.

I turn my head slowly, just enough to see that Rosemary is still asleep. I have no desire whatsoever to move. I stay like that, in some form of suspended animation, for an undefined length of time, watching the sun pass across the low window beside the bed.

Then, the concerns of what must be done this day invade my inner quiet. I carefully slide to the side of the bed, rise to a sitting position. I stay there several minutes looking out the window into the yard.

Then I stand up. Immediately, it's if I am struck hard in the back from behind. I fall to my knees. As I land, my hands are in fists on the worn, shag rug. It's as if I've been knocked down in a football game, clipped. I can't catch my breath for several seconds. Then I can, and begin to sob with such violence I almost throw up. I fight for breath between sobs, but that is only the outside.

Inside I'm knowing things I have no way of knowing. My head is spinning. I'm on the verge of fainting. I feel Rosemary behind me, hovering over me, her hands on my shaking shoulders. I feel her tears rolling on my bare back.

"What is it, dear? Are you all right? Should I go get someone?"

I have just enough contact, strength, to shake my head no. I stay like that on my knees, not able to stand. Rosemary eases herself onto the rug beside me, her arm over my shoulder, her hand on my quivering wrist. It's as if we're in the starting position of the second period in a college wrestling match. That image, that memory passes through my head, but they are then smothered by other images, strong images, images more powerfully imprinted than anything I've ever experienced.

I try taking deep breaths. Slowly, the shaking comes under control. Rosemary asks if I think I'm having a stroke or a heart attack: should she call a doctor? I must tell her something. My first impulse is to try passing off the entire experience as nothing, blame it on my hysterical state, keep it to myself. But I know I can't do this; it's not what I'm supposed to do. What I know, or think I know, must be shared, especially with Rosemary. In a certain peculiar way, I'm a messenger, a messenger to myself, if no one else.

"Dearest, I've had something happen to me and I don't know how to tell you and still maintain your respect. But I know I must tell you. It is meant that I tell you, even if you can't accept it."

I settle back to a sitting position on the floor, squatting between my legs. I'm suddenly aware of my nakedness. I'm in the sunlight coming through the window and I'm naked.

"Rosemary, would you lock the bedroom door? I didn't lock it last night in case we might be needed."

She pushes herself up, crosses the room, turns the old-fashioned key in the lock. She comes back, folds her legs under her and sits facing me in a modified yoga position. She looks in my eyes, waiting.

"It started, or happened, in the middle of the night. I'm not exactly sure.

"We'd both, happily, finally, gone to sleep. I woke with a sense of calm or clarity that's impossible to describe. It was something like the feeling you have after you've had a long fever and suddenly it's gone. The world seems new and you're part of it. It was something like that. I remember being frightened for my sanity. How could I feel like this when we've just lost Kate, Bert, Dayiel, and Mia? It didn't make sense. And yet it also didn't matter to me that I'd arrived at this strange psychic distance."

"Then, Rosemary, I woke this morning, refreshed. I didn't want to move, do anything but stay in this nirvana of peace. I still didn't know why I was so content, soothed; there are a hundred different things to do today and they'll all be waiting for us downstairs. I eased myself out of bed and stood up. This is where it starts being hard to believe. Don't interrupt, just listen, please. I want to get it all straight and right."

I'm trying to sound calm, but inside I'm shaking.

"When I stood, it was as if had been knocked down by some powerful force from behind. I found myself scarcely able to breathe, as I was when you found me when you woke up. But, more than that, I knew, all in a flash, what had happened to me in the night, what had calmed me, made me feel deeply comforted despite everything."

I take another deep breath, trying to convert something in my mind that wasn't words, into something Rosemary can understand as words, even though I know she'll never know or believe this. Still, I must tell her. It is part of the experience, telling her.

❆ ❆ ❆

"I'm sitting in one of our low beach chairs in Ocean Grove with my back to the land, the sun setting over the town behind me. You know how much I like that, the purple shadows, the shadows from the ridges in the sand, the changing color of the water, of the sky, matching the colors of the sunset. There are the sounds of water, at its calmest, rising and falling back on the pebbles of the beach. It is the most relaxing thing I know of, a natural meditation without effort. It has always been magic to me.

"Then I see the long shadows of people coming up behind me. I'm disappointed. This is, for me, a quiet time, not a social event. But it's Kate and Dayiel going past me to the edge of the water.

"Kate doesn't look back at me, neither does Dayiel. I'm surprised, because she's supposed to be helping you make dinner, but I'm even more surprised to see her on the beach. You know how she is about sand. She never could bear having sand between her toes. So, what's she doing at the beach, walking barefoot? At first, I think it's because she's mad at Bert, and it turns out this is part of it.

"Next, Bert comes up on my left side. Kate and Dayiel have passed on my right. Bert's wearing bathing trunks and one of his loud Hawaiian shirts. He's carrying Mia, the way he does, as if she's a football, in the crook of his huge arm, her little arms hanging over his forearm. He settles in the sand beside me, putting one leg out, his football knee, and he drapes Mia over it.

"She's wearing a diaper, also some kind of lightweight, white shirt and a sunbonnet with ruffles around her face. She's watching my eyes in a way she never has, not as if she's just curious about my eyes, but about me. Bert has started making marks in the sand in front of her, the sand collapsing completely, totally, without trace, each time. He looks up at me to see if I'm noticing. He has a quizzical smile on his face. He, too, stares into my eyes a long time, in a way he never has. I'm beginning to have an uncanny feeling in the pit of my stomach that something horrible, frightening, has happened. It has, but I have no idea, then. Bert starts that slow shaking of his head which is a sign with him, as it is with me, he can't comprehend or believe something.

" 'You know, Will, you're not going to believe this, but you're not here and I'm not either. You're in my bed in Falls City, Oregon, in my bedroom, the bedroom I grew up in, and I'm still not sure just where we are. We're not scared or anything, we just don't know. It seems right now we can be almost anywhere we want, just by wishing it. We're hoping to find out more fairly soon. It's only a feeling. I'll tell you, it's weird.'

"He stops. I don't know what he's talking about. It's so far from what I'm seeing, or think I'm seeing, feeling, or think I'm feeling, know, or think I'm knowing, that it's total nonsense, like some kind of crazy party game and I'm 'it.' I stare at him, waiting.

" 'Will, being dead is a hell of a lot different from what you might think. I'm still not sure what's going on, and I know I'm not supposed to be talking with you; nobody's actually said I shouldn't, but we just know. I only want you to know before it's too late. You deserve it.

" 'Kate's mad at me for telling you things like this, in what may seem like your dream, but everything was perfect: the place, the time, the way it happened to us. It all came together and I couldn't resist. We don't have much of what we've always called time, so I'll hurry.

" 'You see, the best way to explain it is this: we didn't leave you, you left us. It's as if we were all on a giant train or something like that and we just stepped off while you and everybody else kept going. That's not quite right either, but it's close as I can come. I've always been better at numbers than words.

" 'But I want you to know that we're fine, that we're still together. There's no way to know what's next, but we're not worried about it. That's the important thing. So don't you worry either.'

"He looks over, taking his eyes from mine. Kate's coming up the beach with Dayiel dancing around her. She's not coming toward us. She's going to pass right by us again without looking.

" 'Kate says I don't know how to let go. But would you do

me this one favor? Would you get hold of those bodies that used to be us, and take some good pictures of them? It's important. It might help stop this damned field burning. It's the field burning more than anything else that killed us. You'll learn more about it in the next months. Talk to Steve, tell him about this, he'll help you, I know.'

"He pushes himself up. Mia is still watching my eyes. He then joins Kate. I can watch their shadows, long and violet-colored in the sand. I don't turn around. Just as the last shadow is gone, I hear Kate's voice.

" 'Goodbye, Dad. We're sorry, but we're happy.'

"Then I turn around and they're gone. The beach is empty. I turn and watch the sea some more.

"At this point, I must have wakened. That would have been the first time, when I was so calm. I didn't know it then. Now I know it and I'll know it the rest of my life."

I stop. Rosemary is crying. She looks me deeply in the eyes.

"That's the most beautiful dream I've ever heard, Will. Even I, who didn't dream it, feel much more calmly accepting. I know I can live with it, now, too. I won't say I believe this really happened because I'm not that way. But I believe you believe it happened, and that's what's important. I think that's why Bert could come to you, because you'd believe. You know I never believe this kind of thing. What are you going to do now?"

"I think that's why I've been crying so hard. A dream like that should never make anyone cry. But I dread taking those photographs. I can't bear the idea of seeing them torn apart, burned. I want to remember them the way they were with us that week, or the way they all were in the 'dream.' I don't think I can hire anyone to take those pictures, even if I could find somebody who would. It might even be illegal, I don't know. I'll need to find someone to give me a hand. Bert suggested Steve. I think I'll try him first. Bert ought to know if anyone would."

I help Rosemary up off the floor and we make the bed together. I feel so close to her. I wonder what people are going to think when I go downstairs and seem so happy, so full of life instead of death.

CHAPTER 8

A FTER ROSEMARY washes up, I go in and shower. When I come downstairs, there's all sorts of breakfast fixings and it's serve-yourself. I have my blood-sugar automatic test-kit with me and I need to take a test before I eat. I go out on the front porch. Steve comes out behind me. He has his kit, too. It's a remarkable coincidence. We're pricking, making the blood blob, counting, wiping, waiting, while we talk.

"Steve, I don't know how to bring this up, but last night I had an amazing experience."

Then I tell it all as I told it to Rosemary. Steve looks at me in the strong, morning light.

"That's Bert, all right. He fought field burning tooth and nail. He could never let go, even if he was dead. You should have seen him play football or basketball. Never-say-die Woodman we called him."

"The main thing is, can you help me, Steve? Bert said you would. I need to see those bodies and take pictures of them. I dread the whole business, but I feel it's some kind of a mandate from Bert."

"Well, I can call John the mortician in Dallas and take you there. I have a camera, too. But let's eat first."

"I'd like to try keeping this to ourselves, Steve. It sounds so crazy, I don't want to try explaining to anybody else."

"I'll call from the upstairs phone."

We have a great breakfast, with pan after pan of good scrambled eggs. Rosemary tells me that Danny has decided to

97

take Wills directly back down to LA with him. They left about an hour ago. I'm sorry. I wanted to talk with Wills, let him know how I feel. But, we agree it's best. He doesn't need all this funeral business any more than we do.

About then, people start arriving from everywhere. These are Kate's friends from the American School in Paris, teachers and students, friends from Germany, people I don't know. There are telephone calls keeping the line busy. Friends of Bert and Kate are coming from different parts of America—Minneapolis, Connecticut, Florida, New York. Each time the phone rings, I listen to hear who it is. It's never the people I hope it will be.

Then, there are telegrams. I go through all of them. Most are addressed to us, all shocked, beautifully sympathetic and compassionate. But again, the ones I'm looking for aren't there.

The Woodman friends are generally within a few miles and are still hauling over cooked chickens, hams, cakes—the whole thing. It all has the quality of a giant picnic, except that everyone is talking in hushed tones. Everybody seems to be hitting it off as if they've known each other all their lives. I guess a real tragedy like this can do that, like after tough combat in a war. Death is on everybody's shoulder.

Each of us washes out his or her dishes in a huge kitchen sink. I've just finished mine when I catch Steve at the front door signaling me. I go over.

"John says the bodies are at the coroner's but he'll get them to the mortuary if we want. He says they're really awful and he doesn't recommend our looking at them."

"What'd you tell him?"

"I didn't tell him anything, but I made arrangements for us to be there at one o'clock. Is that OK?"

"Thanks, Steve. I'll work on the model for the monument while we're waiting."

"Dad had all the tools you'll ever need. They're out in the back shed. But you don't need to do this right now. It can wait."

"I want to. I'll be better off out there working with your dad's tools than inside with everybody talking about the accident. I need time to be alone. This will be my excuse."

Steve takes me out to a great workshop, all in wood, with nails driven into the walls for hanging tools and each tool marked in outline against the wall so anybody can see where each tool goes and his dad could see when a tool was missing. With three boys, I'm sure he had to keep track.

Steve brings out the wax mold from the number ten can and some knives. He clears the work table, putting tools back in place.

"This should be just the kind of place for you. I can't tell you how much we all appreciate your doing this."

He goes right out. I wonder if he believes I'd be doing this if we hadn't lost so many members of our family. I'm sure he's as upset as I am. A trauma like this can be very hard on a diabetic. I hope Bert knew what he was doing when he asked me to contact Steve for help.

I spend the morning carving away until the monument in my mind begins to appear. Around the sides I carve in the words of the poem. I find an old fourpenny nail and use it for the gnomon. I set it at an angle equal to the angle of the sundial face. For the cardinal points, I carve in Bert at north or twelve o'clock; Kate at south or six o'clock; Mia on one side, at nine o'clock, that is, west; and Dayiel at three o'clock, or east. I find some gold paint in the closet, and with a small brush fill in the indentations of the carving. I design it more as a yearly calendar than as a sundial for telling time.

It doesn't look funereal at all but it certainly makes me feel much better—as if, at least, I've done something. It helps me express, even if approximately, what Bert must have been suggesting when he talked about time. It's something we humans just thought up.

Throughout the whole job, I can feel Bert hovering nearby but I hear and see nothing. It's just my imagination. Sometimes one person or another drifts in but I don't look up. It doesn't happen too often, so I imagine Steve has given the word.

Rosemary comes briefly to sit by and watch quietly. I look up at her and we smile, but we don't say anything. I think it's as hard for her to speak as it is for me. She puts her hand on my shoulder as she leaves. I continue working, turning the model in different directions to see how it reacts to various lighting until it feels right. Just then, Steve comes in.

"We should eat first, then take off for Dallas. John phoned and said he managed to shift the bodies from the coroner's office but they aren't happy about it."

"Well, I assure you, Steve, it's something that must be done. I don't think any of us are exactly happy about it. It won't be much of a pleasure, but sometimes things just need to be. We don't have a choice. I have my camera with me, but I don't have much film. Is there a place in Dallas where we can buy film?"

"Sure, and I'll bring my camera too. We can buy any film we'll need. The same place does really good work on developing and printing. They're fast if we make it a rush order. We can take it right there after we have the pictures."

"Good, I'll clean this up and come in soon. What's the chance we can go to some place in Dallas where they cut marble and granite?"

"There's a place called Capitol Monuments. They cut the little plaque for Dad's grave. We can stop in there after we go to John's. In fact, we can do that while we're waiting for the film to be developed. Everything will be closed tomorrow, Sunday."

"That's what we'll do then. I'll be inside in a minute or two. Don't have anybody hold up anything for me."

Inside there's a mob scene. Everyone is so nervous and so glad to see each other it's more like a wedding than a funeral. I say hello to everybody, trying not to act too much the hypocrite, but not wanting to offend their sensibilities. I'm not as broken up as I was. Rosemary's in better form, too. These people must think we're the most cold-hearted parents and grandparents in the world. Camille is making up for us. She and Sam arrived this morning; she's crying up a storm. Those babies were practically like her own, so often did she come down from Stuttgart to take care of them. She and Kate were beginning to become close, too, even though they have entirely different personalities. Her face is swollen and wet all over as if she's been running.

It's good to see our eldest son, Matt, and his wife, Juliette. Matt is red-eyed and not talking too much. Juliette is doing her best to buck him up. So our entire family is there, except for Kate, Bert, Mia, and Dayiel. I begin to feel, for the first time, the quantitative as well as the qualitative loss. It's practically half our genetic future that's been destroyed—that is Rosemary's and mine. I hadn't thought about that part. There's now a vast, empty space.

I had no idea there would be such a crowd. It turns out there's a constant shuttle going between Portland Airport and Falls City. Bert's sister, his other brother Jim, and several friends and neighbors are ferrying the new arrivals. Falls City is a hard place to find unless you know where it is.

It's quarter-past twelve and I eat hurriedly. I'm not really hungry but I don't want to feel sick or weak, especially right now. Steve gives me the eye and goes out the front door. I wait about two minutes, then follow him out. He has his car parked outside the gate and the motor's running. I dash into the workshop and get my model; I've stashed my camera there, too, because I've been taking photos of the model as it's come along. I have the model mounted on a small piece of plywood. I climb into the front seat beside Steve.

The trip to Dallas is quick and we don't talk much. We stop first at the photo shop and buy three rolls of film, thirty-five millimeter, color, print, twenty-four exposures. We figure that should do it. Then we drive over to the mortuary. It isn't as ugly as I thought it would be; in fact it's quite handsome,

natural woods and tinted glass. It's also bigger than I'd
expected. I guess people die a lot around here.

But when we go in, it's a mortuary all right. There are the
smells and the quiet non-sounds. A sandy-haired, slightly
balding man comes out from a small office to greet us. Steve
shakes hands with him and introduces us. This is John. He
looks at me quizzically.

"Are you sure you want to do this? I don't recommend it
at all."

I nod. I don't want to talk much. I'm on the edge of what I
can handle. Actually being in the mortuary where my family
is being stored is getting to me.

"Have you ever seen badly burned human bodies before?"

I nod again, not trusting myself to speak. I must look white
or green. He suggests we sit down in some comfortable chairs
grouped in a semicircle in a small antechamber. We sit. I feel I
should say something but I don't want to tell him about Bert's
visit to me. I'm sure morticians hear more such crazy stories
than they really want to. I try answering his questions.

"I was in World War II and helped pull bodies out of tanks
after they'd burned, both American and German. I have a
good idea of what it's like. Mostly I remember the smell."

"Well, this will be different. This is your family, not complete strangers or enemies. I've sprinkled formaldehyde over
the bodies to keep down the smell and to slow down the
natural processes. Because we've had to hold the bodies for so
long, we've also kept them in a cold locker. That's one of the
reasons they were at the coroner's, because I don't have
enough cold storage space for them here."

"I understand."

I understand, but I'm beginning to want to back out of the
whole business. I can see by Steve's color he's having the
same feelings. I check my camera and stand up. Steve stands,
too. John, the mortician, stands with us. He leads the way
down a narrow corridor to the back of the building. There's a
door at the end of the corridor. I guess that's the entrance

through which they bring the bodies to cause a minimum of disturbance for the neighbors.

We walk in the last door on the right. There's the smell all right but it's covered partly by a chemical smell. It reminds me of my anatomy class at UCLA. There are four tables, a small one just where we came in, then another small one, then two larger tables deeper in the room. There are high windows over the tables. The ceilings are high, too. Each table is covered with a waterproof cover, black on one side and yellow on the other. John steps ahead of us. He takes hold of the cover on the first small table and turns to us.

"This is going to be difficult for you. If you feel it's too much, just give me a signal. I'll cover the body and we'll get out of here."

He pauses, watching us.

"This first one is the one who burned the least, the little baby, Mia."

Steve and I back off a little, and John slowly, gently removes the cover. My first reaction is that she looks exactly like the bodies which were dug up at Pompeii and Herculaneum. She's all white and her features are obliterated but it is definitely the form of a little girl. Her left foot has been broken off just above the ankle but is still hanging by a piece of what was once flesh. In places, we can see the charred sections of her body which were not covered by the formaldehyde powder.

Steve and I look at each other. We're both sighing and taking deep breaths. John is watching us carefully.

"Do you want me to cover her again?"

I figure I can make it. I look at Steve. He nods. I think he nods that we should go on, but I'm not sure. My hands are shaking so, I can hardly make the settings for my camera, then focus on the baby. I know I'm crying. This is so different from every memory I have of Mia. The last time I saw her she was smiling at me while Kate was holding her in the car. It's hard to keep it together. I take shots from the side; then from on top, leaning over; smelling this cloying yet sharp odor, the combination of the chemical and decomposition. Steve is doing the same thing. John covers Mia and leads us out into the corridor.

"Look, I don't know why you two are doing this but I don't want to have any more dead bodies around here. I think you're pushing yourself beyond what you can handle. I'm a professional, but I don't think I could take pictures like that of my family if something terrible like this happened."

Steve and I are leaning back against the wall of the corridor, breathing deeply, trying to recover. I have a feeling I could easily up-chuck if I let myself go.

"We're OK. It's just hard. We really want to have these pictures, the last part of what was once, for us, some of the most lovely people in the world. OK, Steve? Shall we go back?"

He nods his head. John opens the door again. The smell this time isn't so bad. It's in our clothes now, so the shock isn't so great. John goes to the other small table. He pulls off the cloth. This time it's much harder. Somehow, in the accident, Dayiel lost the top of her head. I think of JFK, of his wife stretching across the back of the limo in Dallas trying to retrieve his skull.

The striations of her brain are visible. She's also lost her arms from just above the elbows, and her legs from just above the knees. If she were alive, she'd be a "basket-case baby," like some of those Thalidomide cases in Germany. I can't believe this is the beautiful Dayiel, a child who never stopped, with deep blue eyes, a lively expression, and golden hair. There is a clump of darkened hair at her neck that I think could be her hair but there's no color, no life in it.

I start photographing and feel the room beginning to turn around me. I try to grab hold. I actually do grab hold of the edge of the table that Dayiel's on. John moves toward me, but then I'm better. I lean over to take a photo from on top. It's then that I hear Steve. He's leaned against the wall behind us and is slowly sliding down. John grabs him by the arm and takes him out. I stay on and take two more photos of Dayiel, knowing it isn't really her, impressed by how we are all fooled by the physical, thinking that's what we are. It might be the biggest farce of all. What must it be for her, having to change everything, be in another world when she's so young? But then the whole idea of age is only one of our limitations, our time-locked idea of reality. At best, it only deals with how long we've been in a particular body.

These thoughts comfort me, so I regain my equilibrium. I go out in the corridor. Steve and John have gone up to the antechamber and are sitting down. I join them. John turns toward me.

"Steve says he's ready to go back. He wants to see his brother for the last time. I'm not so sure it's a good idea."

I look at John and then at Steve.

"Don't come back, Steve, if it's too difficult. I know your family is Catholic. I don't know how much of it you believe, but if you accept the idea of the spirit, then you know that in there we're only looking at the empty body of what's been left behind. I know it's horrible, but it just isn't *them* any more. I know they're fine. Bert told me."

Steve has leaned over and is looking at his hands, fooling with his camera. His color is coming back. He looks up at me.

"OK, you're right. I'm ready. I have a feeling this is what Bert meant and this is a kind of test or something. Let's go."

We walk down the corridor again, John leading the way. I check to see how much film I have left on this roll, enough for two pictures, then I'll need to change rolls. I have a roll in my pocket.

We go into the room. I try not to breathe too deeply. John lifts the cover off one of the larger tables. It takes my breath away. It's Bert! He has his head arched back so I can see under his neck. This time it's like that wonderful statue in Rotterdam by Zadkine. The stumps of both his arms are thrown up over his head as if he's reaching for the sky. His mouth is full open as in a scream. It's a dreadful sight as a reality. Steve just stares. I look into his face. He's smiling a mirthless smile.

105

"It's the way I'd think he'd go, isn't it, screaming, reaching for a way out.

"I'm glad I've seen this. It helps me accept things. Bert was my big brother. He never gave up. Part of this whole horror for me has been that he didn't do anything. I see now he was trying the best he could, fighting to the end. He was good old Never-say-die Woodman, giving his all."

We start photographing. It's obvious that, even though burned to the bones, Bert was a big and powerful man. His legs are shattered into pieces, the largest one not more than three inches long. His arms are above his head, but his shoulders have been driven out of the sockets. In his open, screaming mouth, all his teeth are visible like a skull, the skin of the face burned away.

I'm noting all this as I take two photos, then change film. Mine is an old-fashioned camera with no automatic rewind and load. I hand rewind, then engage the spool with shaking hands, close the cover, cock it a few times, then start taking pictures. Steve is finished, and just stands there, looking at his brother. He's crying.

I ask if we can take a little break before I look at Kate. I know this is going to be the hardest part. All the games we've played together, the thousands of books I've read to her, the nights we've been up with her when she was sick, the fun of pushing her on a swing or on a playground carousel, or sometimes riding on a real carousel: trying to grab rings and never getting any. And she'd laugh. There's so much that binds people together, it makes it hard to let go.

We go back in. John pulls the cover back down toward her feet. The yellow and black plastic reminds me of so many auto accidents I've seen or helped with in my more than sixty years on the road. I never thought I'd see our first-born wrapped up in one.

She's the least recognizable. The lower part of her trunk is a mass of unburned but seared intestines, other organs. Here, she seems the least burned. But her legs, her wonderful, beautiful, long legs, are broken into pieces like a jigsaw puzzle or like the bones found in the ground and then pieced together to make a dinosaur. When I look at her face, calm, the mouth closed, her beautiful deep, green eyes, now only holes in blackened bone, I almost can't make it. I try to keep my eye to the viewfinder of my camera. It's as if I'm seeing it on TV, something artificial, not real.

Finally, I can't take any more. I go out the door into the hall. Steve follows me; John covers Kate, then comes out, too. Steve and I are both soaking wet from nervous sweat. My knees feel weak. The sweat on my forehead is cold. John leads us down to the couches and comes back in a few minutes with a shot of whiskey for each of us. I sip mine, Steve puts his down like a true Oregonian. John stands in front of us.

"Well, I didn't think you'd make it. That was bad. I want you both to know how sorry I am this had to happen. There's no excuse for a beautiful, civilized state like Oregon to have something like field burning still going on. These four young people aren't the first field-burning victims I've buried. It's a disgrace."

We take the film out of our cameras. John goes back into his office. By the time I've finished rolling the film out of my camera, I feel somewhat better. At least I'm not sweating. I head for the restroom. It's such a hot, sweaty day I want to freshen up some. I find the restroom in a corridor that leads away from the one where we saw the bodies.

I take off my shirt and undershirt. They're soaking wet. I'm a big sweater. I fill the little basin with water and dunk both shirt and undershirt into it. I push down and slosh it around to soak the nervous smell out. I can't get any wetter. Then I wring them out as best I can and slide them back on. It's refreshing. I'm just finished when Steve comes into the restroom. I tell him what I've done. He's only wearing a T-shirt. He pulls it over his head and does the same thing. He's thin but with strong arms and more hair than I thought he'd have, although still not as much as Bert or me.

"Lord, I smell like a stallion with the scurvy."

He uses his wet T-shirt to wipe under his arms and down his stomach, then rinses it before he wrings it out again and slides it back on. We go out of the restroom refreshed, wet, and ready for the Oregon heat.

The film place is nearby. We ask to have the negatives made first, then we'll choose which ones to print. They can do this all in one day.

We go out and head for Capitol Monuments. They're open. I lift the model out of the car. Steve is already talking to a round-faced man. They're surrounded by a stone forest of varying monuments, with slabs of marble against the wall. It's like an indoor cemetery. Steve is telling how he's the brother of Bert Woodman who was killed in the I-5 crash. He introduces me and the man is very sympathetic. Probably tombstone-builders need to learn sympathy almost as much as morticians.

I show him the model and explain what I want. He has trouble catching on that I'm not concerned about its being a functioning sundial or a religious symbol. I want it to be a symbol of the everlasting life, like the constant revolving of the sun, or at least its seeming revolution: another one of the delusions of time which has fooled men for thousands of years.

Then we start talking about what kind of stone. There must be fifty different sorts of stone to choose from. I like one which is a rich, warm gray but he tells me it wouldn't hold up against the weather the way another granite called "sierra" would.

There's not that much difference so I say OK to the "sierra." It turns out he doesn't have any in stock but he can order it. That's OK with me. There's no way I can stay around to see it anyhow. I'll most likely never see this monument.

Steve looks at his watch. We leave the graveyard of polished stones and enter into the heat again. We drive back to the film place. Steve has air-conditioning, but even so, it's hot.

❊ ❊ ❊

We're disappointed when we look at the negatives. Practically none of them is usable. We were so nervous and shaken up we seem to have made every mistake possible. It's three o'clock. The next day is Sunday and Tuesday's the funeral. We ask how soon they'd need to have new film in order to have them ready by Monday. They close at six. Steve uses their phone to call the mortuary. John says he hasn't sent the bodies back yet but can't hold them past four because the coroner's office closes at five on Saturdays.

We buy more film. We drive like madmen to the mortuary. We're out there and in the back room in five minutes. John shows us some Polaroid shots his son has taken. They'll probably be good enough if we don't do it right this time.

We're much more calm and collected as we work. I check every move, every setting on my camera to get it right. It's astonishing how the human mind can adjust to almost anything. We have the photos shot in half an hour. We're both crying as we go along but we're functioning. We thank John profusely. Nobody could be nicer under such conditions.

We take the film out of the camera and deliver it to the photo shop with time to spare, if there is such a thing as time to spare. Steve takes his camera from me. I was unloading as he was driving. They tell us we can see the negatives and maybe positive prints before they close, if we want to wait. I think they've looked at the work we did before and know what we're doing. Two young women run the place and they're very considerate. We say we'll be back at ten minutes to six and walk out into the heat again. Nobody should have to die in weather like this. Steve turns away from his car.

"I need a beer. I know a good, dark, air-conditioned place about half a block from here."

"Sounds good to me, Steve; I'll go any place that's cool."

We walk into the back of a wood-paneled inn with the bar up front. Steve orders two draft beers on the way past. I can feel myself fading. I lean back in my chair. Steve quaffs off his beer with only one stop. It's so cold it hurts my eyes.

"Steve, you know what I'd like to do while we're waiting for those photos to be done?"

It's obviously a rhetorical question, but I think Steve's expecting just about anything from me.

"How far is it from here to where the accident happened? Do you think we could make it from here to there and back before the photo shop closes?"

Steve stares at his watch, then sucks out the foamy dregs of his beer.

"We could do it, but it'd be close. I don't think we'd find anything there though. The road is all black and the grass is burned, and they've cleared everything away with big equipment. I watched some of it on TV."

"I'd really just like to see the last things they saw. I think it would bring me closer to them."

Steve stands up, pushes back his chair, leaves money on the table.

"OK, let's get going then. We'll have about two hours, that should do it."

He's already going out the door. I take one last slug of my beer and I catch up behind him. The heat hits us again.

Steve drives faster than before but still not so fast I'm uncomfortable. We don't talk much. Steve keeps looking at his watch.

"We'll make it and have ten minutes to look around if we want. I haven't been there myself, just didn't have the nerve. We'll need to drive about twelve miles past the place to find an on-ramp to the I-5. There's some kind of construction on the southbound lane. But I think we'll make it OK."

We drive onto the I-5 going north and I look out the windows, wondering what Kate or Bert, or either of the kids, might have seen. I'm also hoping for some contact from them. I'm now so close to where they last were in this world, although four days have passed. The newspapers said the accident seemed to have happened about four o'clock. We aren't far off that.

But all I experience is a weird frozen quality to the landscape, as if nobody has ever been here. To my right there's a lovely little hill in the generally flat country. Kate must have noticed that. As a geologist, this strange formation would have meant something to her.

Both north- and southbound traffic is on the north side with us. The trucks are enormous and, considering the density of traffic, they're going fast. There's no passing. These guys have got to make up time. About three miles after the highway opens up again, and the southbound traffic is back in its own lane, we see where the accident occurred. Steve pulls over. We get out in the pounding sun, and look. The roadbed is all cracked up from the intense heat of the crash. I looked only briefly at the newspapers everybody kept pushing into my face last night because I wasn't ready. But I remember the fire burned for hours. It seems diesel fuel leaked out of a truck and it, combined with a truck filled with wood chips, made quite a blaze. I find a piece of metal on the road. I shine it up: it's the name-plate of a Corvette. Steve and I need to be careful: the cars and trucks are tearing by us, nobody going under seventy. People don't seem to learn.

"Steve, we'd better get going. I don't know if I can take this any longer. It's hard to predict traffic at this time of night. Also that photo shop might close on us."

So, we hop back in the car and head north, continuing the trip Kate, Bert, Dayiel, and Mia never got to finish.

We arrive at the photo shop at ten till six. The girls pull out both the negatives and contact prints. They have a light-box and magnifying glasses. It's almost worse than the reality. This time we did it right. Steve wants me to make the choices. I'm not sure just what Bert really wanted, except that, somehow, these photos were supposed to help fight field burning. I try selecting the photos which best show the terrible damage done to their bodies. I know that, after the funeral, only these photos can ever prove that damage. Two days from now, the cremation will be completed and, as far as we mere mortals are concerned, the bodies won't exist any more.

For full-scale enlargement, I select twenty photos. The rest of the negatives and proofs I put in a separate packet.

"Are these photos of the victims of the I-5 crash Wednesday?"

"That's right."

Steve looks at me to see if it's OK to tell them.

"Are you from the police? How did you get these pictures? I couldn't help looking at them. They're horrible!"

We're both quiet for a moment. She has a right to know now.

"No, not the police. I'm the father of the woman and grandfather to the two babies. My friend here is the brother of the man and uncle to the two babies. We took these pictures so we'd have something to remember them by."

She looks to see if I'm kidding, sees I'm not, puts her hand to her mouth.

"But what a terrible way to remember them. I don't know how you could have taken these pictures. Didn't I just say that to you, Diana?"

"Well, it wasn't easy, but we did it. In a certain way, we had to. How much will I owe you for all this work? It's very well done. Could you write out the bill for the enlargements, also the development and proofs? I'll pay now. My friend will come pick them up when they're ready."

She takes out a form and checks the negatives that are to be enlarged, peering at the numbers in the margin. The cost comes to just under $200. I take two hundred-dollar bills out of my pocket. She peers at them just to check if they're real, I think. Then she gives me the change.

"We're terribly sorry about what happened. Isn't that field burning just awful?"

"I don't know, except it killed my family. We don't allow dumb things like this where I live."

We turn and leave. It's hot in the car. Even at six o'clock in the evening it's hot. But then, this is August. Steve turns up the air- conditioner. I lay my head back on the headrest. My eyes feel bare. But we did get it done, everything, the monument, the pictures. I need to give my address in Paris to Steve and some money to mail the pictures. This should finish up that part of things. Maybe I can relax.

I hope I sleep tonight. I should. I'm dead tired. I dread the funeral. I own one suit, one white shirt, one tie, one decent pair of shoes. Getting dressed up for things is not my style.

CHAPTER 9

WHEN I WAKE Tuesday morning, it sounds as if there's a party going on downstairs. I feel rested. I look over at Rosemary. She's watching me.

"You were even smiling in your sleep. It's so good to see you back to normal again."

"How about you, did you sleep well?"

"Like a dead person, but I didn't dream, not of Kate, not of anybody. You seemed to have been dreaming and having a good time and I'm sure it was with them."

"I don't remember anything."

We slide out of the bed. Rosemary showers first. My watch says nine o'clock. It's been a long time since I've slept this late.

When I come downstairs, I see that the house has filled with flowers as fast as it did with food. The center of all the action is the kitchen. I haven't eaten since lunch yesterday so I'm hungry. I help myself to some scrambled eggs and a few pieces of bacon. I surprise the hell out of Claire by kissing her good morning. I'm not tuned into Oregonian ways. Out in the streets on my own, I'd probably be nabbed as a rapist or child-molester.

Over breakfast there's talk about the music to be played. Rosemary wants Ravel's "Pavane for a Dead Infanta"—Kate's favorite—but no one has heard of it. Matthew suggests "Send in the Clowns," a favorite of both Kate and Bert, somehow "their" song. We played it at their wedding.

There's a young guitarist who says she'll play it. She'll also play some music she's written especially for Bert and Kate. It seems, in high school, she and Bert had been special friends.

114

Claire and Jo Ellen would like some religious music since we're not having a funeral mass. I suggest a *Stabat Mater*, but *Ave Maria* wins out.

Steve and I will be the principal speakers after the representative from Munich International School has spoken. He's flown over for the funeral. The students, faculty, and administrators had gotten the money together for him to join us.

The funeral cortège isn't much for fancy automobiles, but the numbers are amazing in such a small town. The local policeman leads the way; we're going about forty miles an hour all the way to Dallas.

At the mortuary, John has fixed up everything beautifully. We bring in the flowers from Steve's station-wagon and add them to the flowers already there. We go in quietly, two by two, Rosemary on my arm.

We slide in and take our places. The place is filled, and people are standing along the walls and at the doors. Bert was popular in this world; we've brought along our own mourners as well, and because of the publicity, many have come from far away.

I keep looking for an official, someone representing the state, or a farmer, but I don't see anyone. John, the mortician, has promised to look out for anyone he might recognize.

At the appropriate moment, he goes up to the rostrum and speaks briefly. Steve follows and talks about his brother. Midway, he almost breaks down. Doug, Bert's best friend, all six-foot-seven of him, is in the front row, his head in his hands, crying and sobbing, racked with grief. After Steve, John nods to me and I go to the rostrum. I have no notes, nor did Steve.

I tell how I came to Oregon for the first time in my life with bitterness in my heart. We'd reared our children so carefully, hoping to avoid this kind of reckless horror. Then, in a matter of minutes, all is lost. I want to know why they let this field burning go on. Aren't they afraid it might one day be them or one of their loved ones burned to a crisp, curled up in one of those coffins?

I turn to look behind me, wonder if I can go on. How can I stifle my bitterness?

"I've been learning more about the seed-growing phenomenon in Oregon. I've been reading the newspapers and listening to conversations. It seems brutally crude to me. I ask if there is anyone here at this service who can tell me why it continues, anyone who can defend this vulgarity? If so, speak now or see me after the service."

I don't want to talk long. But I want them to know something of what's been lost to all of us. I concentrate on Kate and the children. I recount briefly her life with us, then the all-too-short lives of the children. I tell how Bert was like a member of our family, in his looks, in his mannerisms, and in other ways, without ever denying his Oregon beginnings. He's been a credit to all of us and look at how he's been rewarded, smashed, burned, melted in the asphalt with his family on that dreaded I-5 highway.

"Although we, ourselves, our family, except for Bert Woodman, are not Oregonian, about half our family are now permanent residents. It wasn't their choice." Again, I turn to look back at those over-decorated caskets, hiding everything.

"Our family will be in the soil of Oregon for the rest of their existence on this earth. I hope those responsible for the horror of our family's deaths, the seed-dealers, growers, the government officials, will look again at this practice and stop it. They must! This can't go on in a civilized society."

I know I've been somewhat hard but the anger is deep within me. I did not intend to be so intractable.

Each of our own kids, including Robert, stands up to say a few words. Some of the Woodman family also speak. Jo Ellen, the practicing Catholic in their family, lends a religious note. She reads from the New Testament. Claire is too embarrassed to speak herself. I lean over toward Rosemary to see if she has anything to say but her face is wet with tears, and she smiles, shakes her head no.

The caskets are at the front of the room behind the rostrum. They are wooden and ornate; and they're closed, naturally. I'm not sure if they're smaller than normal; they don't need to be full-length caskets to hold the pitiful remains until cremation.

We file out and over to a place where refreshments are available. It's about three streets away. There are even more people than I saw at the ceremony. Perhaps they were outside. John had mounted loudspeakers so anyone outside could hear what was being said. On the way out, I ask him if he saw anyone I could speak to about field burning. He shakes his head no.

When the formalities of the funeral are over, we gather at Claire Woodman's. The almost-hysterical quality of this morning has burned itself out. Everyone is involved in packing, calling air-lines on the sole phone, saying goodbye. There's much emotion in the air and, with each leaving, many tears. It's as if it's only now that we're realizing the finality of it all. Steve is doing most of the ferrying up and down to the Portland airport. Camille and Sam are going up into Washington, on an island near Seattle to visit with Sam's sister for a while. Matt and Juliette will be flying to Philadelphia to visit close friends. I imagine all of them are searching out people, close, non-family friends with whom they can share their grief.

Rosemary and I are the last to leave. We do our best to straighten up the mess made by so many people living together in a limited space. It isn't as bad as I thought it would be. Claire must have slept little, cleaning up after all of us last night.

I pack my bag and go out into the corral and pet the horses. I'm always shocked by their tremendous strength, vitality. I don't know what it is, but something in their passivity sets me off again. I find myself leaning against Ginger, the smaller of the two horses, crying to the ends of my being. I don't know how long it lasts; it probably isn't long, but it seems like forever.

After I've wiped myself off with my handkerchief, dried my eyes, brushed off the hay and horse dust, I'm ready. I feel anger surging in me—at the wastefulness, at the uselessness, of it all—replacing the numbing sense of loss.

When I return to the house, Rosemary, Robert, and Steve are waiting. They've put all the bags, including mine, into Steve's car. I had said I might stay on to fight field burning. I guess no one was fooled.

I say goodbye to Claire, Jo Ellen, and Diane. I hold up pretty well; so do they, although we're only going through the motions. Steve is in the driver's seat for the fourth time this morning. Our plane flies out to Los Angeles at one o'clock. Jean, my sister, and Leo, her husband, will meet us. I want to share my feelings with them, especially Jean. I think it will help. I suspect Rosemary has similar feelings. She and Jean were close friends from before we were married. I slump in the back seat. Rosemary is looking at the Oregon scenery as it passes by. Robert is already asleep.

PART THREE

Settlement

CHAPTER 10

*T*HE FLIGHT down seems long but it's only a few hours. Rosemary and I sit next to each other, she in the window seat. Robert sits in another row in another window seat. The plane's about three-quarters full.

I'm going over all the newspaper articles about the accident. Many are devoted to eyewitness reports. The first are from the *Statesman Journal* and the *Oregonian*. They give the totals: thirty-seven hurt, twenty-three vehicles involved, seven dead, twenty-eight taken to Albany General hospital, and an unspecified number to Good Samaritan Hospital in Corvalis. Not much is given about the condition of the injured. The dead had not all been identified when this edition came out.

The accident was said to have occurred at about four p.m. A hundred yards of the northbound I-5 highway was covered with debris and burning vehicles. It was not until midnight, eight hours later, that the highway could be opened again.

I'm shocked to read a statement by a man named Brian Calligan, manager of the Department of Environmental Quality, that field burning would continue today, as planned, in Linn County and elsewhere. Linn County is where the accident occurred. He also says that, "Overall burn conditions were quite good today. What happened was a very unfortunate thing, but this state allows farmers to burn their fields."

I lean back to absorb this. To Mr. Calligan, this is a "very unfortunate thing." And, he's doing nothing to prevent it from happening again. New burning has been scheduled.

Earl Thompkins, the son of Paul Thompkins, who set the fire, tells reporters that his father doesn't want to talk about it. "I don't think anyone has anything to say at this time."

So, I have the answer to one of my questions: why none of the people involved has contacted us to express their condolences. One felt that it had been an "unfortunate thing." The other, who lit the fire, just didn't want to talk about it. Why?

The stories of the witnesses.

Dale Cronin, working nearby at a small plant, said, "The fire had already started when I came out. There were probably twenty-five or thirty people screaming, saying . . . 'Get out of the way! Get back from the fire, get back!' "

Some of the seriously injured were moved into the shade; the temperature, without the fire, approached a hundred degrees. Plant employees brought first-aid supplies, water, and blankets. A few of the less seriously injured were helped into the company's air-conditioned building.

I find also that, on Wednesday, the day before, there were three Mid-Willamette Valley wildfires that got away from the farmers who had started them. A spokeswoman from the field-burning office for the Department of Environmental Quality said that ryegrass farmers burned 3,000 acres in Benton, Linn, Washington, and Yamhill counties—all this on Wednesday. So far this year 18,000 acres had been burned. Tuesday's burning of 5,000 acres in Linn County and the Salem area produced fifty-eight complaints of smoke.

"It really made a lot of people miserable," the spokeswoman said. She also said that wildfires, many resulting from field fires, contributed to the problem. There were more wildfires in Marion, Polk, and Yamhill counties. Lieutenant Dale McKinney of the McMinnville Fire Department said fifty firefighters controlled a 140-acre burn on Hill Road, west of McMinnville.

I put down my paper. It all seems so totally irresponsible, and these tragedies, this "wildfire" business, is talked about like a sporting contest or football game, for which somebody is keeping statistics.

I pick up the next day's paper. The first thing I see is a picture of our little family. Some reporter must have gotten it from the Woodmans. It shows Kate and Bert standing, with Bert holding Mia, in almost the way he held her when he came to see me on the beach that lovely afternoon. Dayiel, with her beautiful strawberry blonde hair curled on top of their head, is pressing against their legs. Wills is on the other side of Kate, her arm around him.

It's a photo I haven't seen. I drink it in. How can they not be? There's an interview with the Woodman family, which mentions that Kate, Bert, and the babies were trapped in their van and burned beyond recognition. This is verified by State Trooper Richard Smith of the Albany State Police.

The big headline is:

DEADLY CRASH STOPS FIELD BURNING!

But will it?

The governor has ordered an investigation and a moratorium is announced at a press conference. Moratorium is the proper word. The accident is the fifth worst in Oregon's history. More statistics. State police say it may take two weeks to sort out how it occurred.

Tom Sims, a physician, says, "It's a political issue. It's an economic issue. I feel now it's a moral issue. When I heard about it, I was thinking it's time we do something about this field-burning issue. But it's too late for seven people. It brings you to tears."

This man's sympathy brings me to tears and I have to put down the paper. I find it hard to continue. I'd begun to feel that no one in the state of Oregon gives a tinker's damn, but here's this man who seems to care.

An editorial goes more deeply into the problem. It suggests that, for the time being, until legislation can stop field burning, large flashing signs should be mandatory and placed along the highway wherever field burning could reduce visibility. It says, "These spectacular—and tremendously unpopular—fires have been considered a relatively inexpensive way for farmers to sanitize their fields against diseases and insects. It also boosts yields." It asks, however, what the total cost will be from this latest pile-up. The property damage and medical services could be tens of millions of dollars, not taking into account the loss of life and the suffering.

How can anybody else take that into account? It's a closed account for our family.

> Moreover, the suffering of people with respiratory ailments for decades has been exacerbated by routine field burning, even people with healthy lungs find the smoke-filled air exceedingly irritating. Also, this accident is but one of a series. Highways shrouded by smoke because of field burning are common in Oregon, and that condition has resulted in other accidents.

Then it gets to the nitty-gritty part.

> Grass seed is big business in Oregon. The crop value of grass and legume seed in 1987 was $250 million and the total is expected to top $300 million this year. Grass seed, Oregon's fifth largest commodity, is distributed over the country and to more than sixty foreign nations. According to grass industry officials, it brings back hundreds of millions of dollars to the state's economy. The grass crop represents about eight percent of the state's total agricultural commodity sales, according to statistics from Oregon State University's Extension Service. The 1988 crop is expected to bring in close to $1.7 million profit for grass farmers. There are more grass seed growers in Oregon this year because of the higher prices, higher profits.

This is a big business, one intent on making huge profits, at whatever the cost to the ordinary person.

Bill Johnson, for over ten years a dedicated opponent to grass-seed burning, is quoted: "This business of saying field burning is the only way to sanitize fields is absolutely false." He is president and founder of the anti-field-burning group End Noxious Unhealthful Fumes (ENUF).

"There are over one hundred alternatives to field burning. There are so many that it's shameful we haven't picked up on them. Accidents like this are bound to happen again, the only way you can stop them is stop the burning. Period!"

I close the newspapers. They don't do me any good. All this is almost as hard to believe as the reality. The reality that Kate, Bert, Mia, Dayiel are all dead, cremated, probably while alive, in that van. All these statistics, these accounts of hundreds of millions of dollars being made, growing grass for people's lawns, for football stadiums, baseball fields, are depressing. Was any of this worth the lives of our family? I decide to do something about it—I don't quite know what yet—but something.

We start our descent into Los Angeles. In the arrivals' room, my sister Jean and her husband, Leo, are waving to us frantically. We run to each other, me to Jean, Rosemary to Leo. We hold on tight, rocking back and forth. We"re all crying. Leo's the first to break it up. Robert is standing apart.

"Hey, you guys, I'm parked in a no-parking zone. Let's get over there before I have a fifty-dollar fine to pay on top of everything."

He jogs off with a sort of hobble because of his bad knees. Jean takes hold of Rosemary's hand on one side and mine on the other. Robert stands to one side. I know he's suffering deeply. We fight our way out of the terminal, past the unending vocal notification, in varying voices, not to park. Leo pulls up beside us.

We load the van with our three suitcases and pile ourselves in. Leo starts the long drive over the Santa Monica Mountains to the San Fernando Valley, to Canoga Park where they live. For a while, we don't talk much. There isn't much to say. Normally, we'd all be talking at once.

Leo turns back from his driving.

"What really happened up there in Oregon, Will? We saw the pictures on TV and all, and read the newspapers, but none of it seems to make much sense."

Rosemary looks at me again. She still doesn't want to talk about it. But I want to try.

"Leo, basically, as far as I can see, none of it makes sense from any angle except pure greed and profit, plus, probably, some political shenanigans. I'd almost rather they'd been killed in a war or something, anything that would have some kind of reason."

Jean turns hard and looks at me.

"You don't mean that. Who can profit from the death of a young couple and two babies?"

I open the papers I'm still carrying and pass them over to her.

"Read 'em and weep. I've wept enough; I can hardly stand it any more. You won't believe what you read but you'll find out I'm right."

I tell them about sanitizing fields and the enormous amounts of money that are being made. It sounds just as crazy when I tell it myself as when I read it.

As I talk Jean reads through the papers. Her face has turned white.

"He's right, Leo. I can't believe what I'm reading here."

Rosemary looks at Jean, at me.

"Let's not talk about all this now, please, for me. I can't stand it. Tell me about your family. I want to hear about families that are alive."

There's a pause, then Leo starts talking. Generally, if Leo starts talking, nobody can stop him.

He goes on and on about their family, five kids, all graduated from university, all with jobs, all married. He goes into great detail about each of their jobs, how they got them, what they're earning, what they're thinking of doing. It's wonderful. Rosemary was right. It's the kind of thing we should be listening to, talking about. It makes sense, in what, for the past few days, has been such an insane world.

We sit back and listen for a while. It's almost like meditation. I look out the van windows, watching cars go by at fifty-five, sixty miles an hour, reasonable speeds, reasonable driving. We've taken the freeway just about all the way from the airport to their house. Everything looks so pale, dry, tired. The sky, the vegetation, the houses, even the automobiles, all look washed out, like old women with tinted hair, mix-and-match pastel-colored costumes with Easter-colored running shoes held on by Velcro latching. It looks like that.

I notice that Jean and Rosemary behind me are having a quiet conversation. I don't listen. I don't listen to Leo either, just nod or go "hmm" or grunt when he pauses. I try to answer any questions he has. I'm still not with it.

We pull into their driveway. The neighborhood hasn't really changed in the forty years they've lived here. It has just grown up. There are big trees and well-kept lawns, hedges. The houses were built in a tract after World War II to take advantage of the GI bill. Jean and Leo bought theirs new for less than $13,000, which they paid back over thirty years with a GI four-percent loan.

During those years they had their children, made additions to the house, continually kept it up so that even now it looks new, better than when they bought it. Their neighbors, similar kinds of people, have done the same. It represents the best of California living.

We climb out of the van. The house is air-conditioned, the drapes pulled against the incessant glare. Calm reigns. I drop down into a chair by the fireplace.

They've added a dining-room in what used to be the patio. Jean's fixed a full lunch for us. We're up to our ears with eating in Oregon, but this is love food and soon we start eating. We're both hungry.

During lunch, Rosemary asks if it would be OK if we go see Wills. Neither of us feels we had enough time with him before Danny drove him off to his new home. We want to know how he's handling all this.

Rosemary calls Danny and we make arrangements for the next day, to visit at eleven. Danny and his wife, Sally, might be at work, but Wills will be home. We each enjoy talking to Wills on the phone. We both manage it without crying. He seems glad to hear from us. Rosemary tells me later that when he heard her, he shouted, "Mom!" Rosemary and Kate have very similar voices and ways of speaking. It is several minutes before Rosemary recovers. I take the phone.

"How're things going, Wills? We'd love to see you."

"Where are you, Grandpa? Are you in New Jersey or Oregon?"

"No, we're right near you here in California."

By this time Rosemary has pulled herself together enough to take over. I listen on the extension as she talks, telling him we'd like to come see him. He's surprised we know his address. Rosemary verifies all the arrangements. Wills is sure it will be OK with his dad and Sally.

Wills tells us how happy he is to be with his dog, Trooper. He goes on about the things Trooper can do, and about his new bedroom. Finally, we say goodbye and hang up. Rosemary still has tears in her eyes.

After lunch I phone the Woodmans and talk to Claire. She tells me the governor has just announced that he's going to call off the moratorium, and that farmers will be burning fields again in a few days. I can hardly believe it.

I want to speak to the governor personally. But it's not the kind of thing I can do on a phone yet. I know I'd just break down. I'm still too upset. Besides, writing is my way of communicating. I spend two days composing a letter. Just putting it all down, expressing my feelings, helps a lot. Then I tear it up. I don't know enough yet about what actually happened. Just to make me feel better isn't a good enough reason.

❉ ❉ ❉

The next day, Wills is waiting on the front steps for us. Rosemary jumps out of the van almost before it's stopped and runs up to him. They hug and hug. Then I have my turn. He's a very affectionate child. He's holding hard onto me by the waist, burying his face into my stomach. I loosen his grip and he leads us inside the house. Jean and Leo each give him a good hug on the way in. He keeps wiping his eyes with the back of his hand.

But he plays the part of host wonderfully, showing us the living- and dining-rooms, the kitchen and then, proudly, his bedroom, up one floor, the perfect boy's room. He leads us on to the upstairs patio, to meet Trooper, his dog, who's so excited he runs from one to the other of us. Wills shows us how Trooper can sit and shake hands and pretend to pray. He and his dad spent most of last summer teaching Trooper these tricks. Wills isn't crying now. We go back downstairs.

He tells us how both his dad and mom are coming home early to see us. For me, it's uncomfortable hearing him call another woman his mom. Even in death, it's hard not to be possessive. I know I should be glad he has this feeling of "motherness" for Sally but I can't help myself.

We talk about everything except Kate and the babies. He tells us about Johnny, his little brother, who's at the baby-sitter's. He shows me some of his drawings and paintings and how he can type on his computer. Rosemary watches, and every now and then Wills runs and cuddles up against her on the couch. I look around. The house is perfectly kept, mostly white or off-whites with both real and artificial flowers for color. I hope Wills will be happy here. It's so different from the kind of home Bert and Kate kept. Theirs was messier.

But Wills seems happy. After all, this has been his second home for a few years. If this horror had to happen, it couldn't be better for Wills. But I still find myself wishing Rosemary and I could whisk him off with us.

Just then, Danny and Sally come through the door. We all hug and cry. How long will it be before getting together isn't so traumatic? We talk about how Wills is adapting. They feel he's doing well, but still wakes crying at night.

Sally brings out a cake she's baked and some ice-cream. We ask about the possibility of Wills spending summers with us. Danny and Sally look at each other quickly. It turns out, they're still undecided as to what to do for summers—they both work full-time jobs—and have already looked into sending Wills to summer camp as early as next week.

We say we'd love to have him summers, either at Ocean Grove or at the Mill. Rosemary says we'll pay his fare both ways. They check with each other and seem to think something like that might work. They'll let us know.

Sally says there's something else she wants to talk with us about.

"You know I work in a legal firm as a paralegal secretary. I've been talking to the people there about what's happened. They're really sympathetic, but they're concerned about all the legal problems we're liable to have. People will be suing each other left and right."

It's quiet for a moment. Rosemary leans forward.

"Do you mean somebody might sue us because Kate, Bert, Dayiel, and Mia were killed? I don't understand."

"I know it sounds awful but nobody really knows who hit whom in that smoke and it's just automatic that everybody will be pointing at everybody else.

"Danny and I are going to be using a legal firm in Oregon called Steele, Cutler and Walsh. My company says it's the best firm out there for this kind of thing. They're willing to work on a contingency basis, a good arrangement, where they take only twenty-five percent of any settlement. If you want, I'll have them contact you."

I've been listening. It seems to be getting off the subject.

"But, Sally, we don't want to sue anybody so there shouldn't be any settlements. Isn't there some way we can just defend ourselves without trying to sue somebody else? I really don't want to become involved with a bunch of lawyers."

"Well, maybe you could do it that way, but it would cost you a lot of money in legal fees. No law firm is going to take your case on a contingency basis if there's no chance for them to make money from it. That's the way it is."

"God, that makes me sick."

I look over at Rosemary and she shrugs her shoulders. She turns to Sally.

"Would you ask these people to contact us, Sally? You have our address in New Jersey, don't you? Then we can think it over. Maybe we can work together on this."

"Yes, I have your address upstairs in my files. I think it's the smart thing to do. Ask any legal friends you might have. You have enough assets to be at risk. You don't have the deepest pockets, but deep enough, and that's what they go for."

I'm ready to leave; it's been more than I can take; dead people and deep pockets! Rosemary stands, too. We shake hands with Danny and Sally. We all give good hugs to Wills. I feel myself going into shock again.

We fly next day and arrive back at our little house in Ocean Grove. It's dinner time and although we've eaten on the plane, we want to sit on the porch, going through the routines we've loved so in the past. There's cheese in the refrigerator and a bottle of wine. We don't say much at first, but as we eat, we begin to talk. Rosemary pours some wine.

"Shall we just get out of here," I ask her, "should we go back home, or stay on the rest of the month? I don't know if I can stand it here."

"If you can, I think we should go through the rest of the month as if nothing has happened. It may seem impossible and I think we'll both cry a lot, but it's probably best."

She's quiet. I realize she's right. It'll be tough, but we've got to start somewhere and the best place is where we left off. She's leaning toward me.

"I think tomorrow, early, we should bike along the boardwalk, all the way to the end and back."

I nod. I can't talk right away, then I pull myself together.

"You're right. It's the best thing. What about Robert?"

"He'll work it out his own way. I think sooner or later he'll want to talk to one or both of us; it'll probably be you."

I nod again and nibble on some more cheese. The light is declining; the sun seems to be setting just at the end of the street. I know Rosemary's watching my eyes. I feel as if I ought to say, do, something.

"How does a walk sound?"

We clear off the remaining cheese, the half-empty bottle of wine, and go inside. I look at the place where I'd been stretched out with my head against the couch. I'll never watch a ball game from there again. Maybe I'll never watch a ball game. Kate always thought it was so silly to stay inside evenings, watching baseball, when everything outside was so beautiful.

I sit in the rocker until I hear Rosemary coming downstairs. She goes out the door first, the screen door slams behind me. Will everything always make me think of them, even a sound behind my back?

We don't say much. We walk away from Asbury Park so there'll be less chance of meeting people we know. Neither of us is ready for that yet. We stop and watch the ocean. It's calming. We're holding hands.

On the way back, we talk. Rosemary thinks we should take Sally's advice. I agree but only nod. Kate would be so upset to know we need a lawyer because of her. She's spent most of her life trying not to make any waves. I think Bert would feel the same way. But it has to be done, and the sooner the better.

"Don't make yourself so miserable, dear. It's all bad enough. We'll just do what we have to do, try to continue our lives and make the most of it. Would you like to play some tennis tomorrow morning at seven? It'll be the way it was when you were first teaching me the game."

I look at her, Rosemary, my wife. She's a marvel and a mystery at the same time. And now she's being so brave and taking me along with her. I know inside she's got to be hurting even worse than I am.

"How are you doing it, Rosie? How do you manage? What keeps you going?"

"I know it's probably silly, but what I keep thinking is that they'd have been in Oregon for at least two years when we wouldn't have seen them—some letters, maybe, and a few phone calls. Also, don't forget, they were both thinking of going to some place like Southeast Asia to teach. You know how Bert loved his time there. That could be another three years. So, for the first five years, anyway, I can pretend that's where they are. If I want, I can write letters to them, maybe even phone. I just wouldn't dial. I could send Valentine cards, Christmas cards, make Easter eggs for them. Don't look at me like that. I don't think I'm crazy. You asked. This is how I'm going to do it. Some of the best communications in history have been through letters, some not even answered. It's something I can live with. Look at Benjamin Franklin, your hero."

I'm crying. I hold her close to me. I should have known. It's the way she'd do it, not deny it, but turn the thing into a fantasy, a personal re-creation. I wish I could do something like it. I know writing about the whole thing, what happened, what I'm feeling, will be my way, but not yet: it will all have to be finished, over with. I'll need to feel that something solid, real, positive, has come from this before I'll be satisfied, able to live with it. I'm supposed to be the fantasy merchant in our family, the writer, the painter, but it's Rosemary who's found the way.

I have a hard time talking again. Will it always be like this? I feel like such a neurotic. I wait several minutes as we walk along, our arms around each other. I look at her.

"OK, you're on."

"What do you mean?"

"I mean you're on for tennis. You're on for the whole damned thing, continuing as if they're still with us, maybe waiting for a chance to visit with us here. We'll keep our cup out. That's something I can live with."

We hold hands again. We talk about everything under the sun, or moon, but not about what's happened. I know we've independently decided the same thing. The worst has happened. The only thing worse would be to let it ruin our lives, our children's, our friends'.

*

The next morning we play tennis at seven. Rosemary beats me six-four. She plays like a demon. Her usually weak service is a bullet, or at least it seems like one to me. Then we take our bike ride, all the way to Spring Lake and back, then to the end of Asbury and back: that's better than ten miles. We don't talk much.

We're wearing our bathing-suits under our tennis outfits, so as soon as we return, we jump into the ocean. The lifeguards are just setting up the stands. Dave, Bobbie's husband, spots us and comes over. Bobbie was one of the ones who was with us that terrible evening.

We can tell this is going to be painful for him, too. He offers his condolences. There are tears in this big man's eyes. He's six-three and must weigh 220 pounds. We try to console him. We dry off, get onto our bicycles and return home. I go up to change. I peek into Robert's room. He's asleep. I'm not going to wake him. I wonder if he ever thinks about how much like death sleeping is. Maybe then he wouldn't sleep so much, or maybe that's why he does.

CHAPTER 11

W E GET through the day, then the next one, and the next one, until a week has gone by. I haven't heard from the governor—or from anyone else from the state of Oregon. I call the Woodmans to find out if they've been contacted, but they haven't heard anything either; I have the feeling they don't even expect to be.

Then I call the Oregon operator and ask for the phone number of the governor's office, his mansion. Am I doing the right thing? Have I been away from America so long I don't know how these things are handled any more?

I talk with a person at the State House who says the governor isn't there right now. She takes my name, address, and phone number, says the governor will call me back. I tell her I will only be at this address, and available at this phone, for one more week. I will then be in France. I give her my number in Paris. She assures me the governor will contact me. I hang up, then call his private phone at the governor's mansion. I don't get any answer, not even an answering machine. Rosemary watches and listens to me as if I'm crazy. I don't say anything; I know what she'll tell me if I do.

I go up to the attic where I write. I have my notes from the letter I'd written in California, plus some additional information I've gathered since. I write a new letter and mail it to the governor. I pedal on my bike to the post office and send it as a registered letter. I'm beginning to feel like a boy putting notes into bottles and throwing them into the sea.

❊ ❊ ❊

Two days before we're to leave, we receive a phone call from Steele, Cutler and Walsh, the legal firm in Portland recommended by Danny's wife, Sally. It's a woman named Mona Flores. We explain that we'll be leaving. She says if we like, she'll Federal Express a copy of the contract that was signed by Danny and Sally for Wills. It will reach us the next day.

I'm still not sure I want to get involved with lawyers. I don't want to sue anybody. "Do you want to sue anybody, Rosemary?"

She shakes her head no.

There is the slightest puddle of tears along the bottom of her eyes. Maybe we're running out of tears.

"Listen, Will. I've heard you calling. I know you're angry. In the end you're going to want to stop this field burning somehow. I understand. I know you. Forget about the suing part except for one thing. If they must pay a lot of money to us and everyone else, their insurance rates will go way up. Maybe they'll think twice before burning again, or at least be more careful."

"But what'll we do with the money? If it's a lot, it could ruin the lives of our kids. I like our life the way it is."

"How about Wills? They certainly owe him something. I know nothing can pay for what's happened, but they owe him. And I think with our own kids we don't need to worry. They're all quite sound that way. They can always say no."

The idea of doing something to make the field burners think twice before they burn is what convinces me.

The next day, the letter arrives. Steele, Cutler and Walsh will represent us for the "wrongful deaths" of Kate, Bert, Mia, and Dayiel. They will take twenty-five percent of any settlement and deduct their costs including filing fees, expert witness fees, travel expenses, and so forth. The whole document is one of suspicion and mistrust, calculating every possible advantage, any conceivable deception. But then, it is the law and these are lawyers.

Trouble is their business.

Rosemary and I sign the contract and date it August twenty-fourth, 1988, just three weeks after the deaths, and a day before we leave for France.

When we've settled into our home, the houseboat in France, I ask Steele, Cutler and Walsh to mail us a copy of the accident report. I receive it in early September. It was compiled on August eleventh by a Sergeant Richard Corrigan of the Oregon State Police. I read it carefully and find myself vacillating between grief and disbelief.

It seems that at three fifty-two p.m. on August third the Albany Patrol Office received numerous calls of a major motor vehicle accident and resulting fire. Sergeant Corrigan, Sergeant Steels, and Senior Trooper Tommy Nelson left for the scene at that time and arrived twenty-eight minutes later. The northbound lanes were ablaze. Six or seven cars and a large truck were in flames. Several other cars and trucks had stopped or had turned over on a shoulder north of where the wreck occurred. Approximately ten injured people were observed lying or sitting around these vehicles. They were being attended to by bystanders.

Sergeant Corrigan immediately requested all available fire and ambulance equipment to be dispatched. A request was made to notify the Linn County District Attorney and Medical Examiner.

The report goes on to list all the vehicles and people involved in the accident. Seventeen vehicles were damaged by the fire.

The van that Kate, Bert, and the babies were in is listed as Unit 19 in the report. It had been damaged in three different areas. According to the report, "The first very major contact damage area was from the front of the vehicle around the right front corner, straight back to the rear right wheel, near the passenger door." This is where Kate would have been sitting. Poor thing. "This damage," the report continues, "is from contact with Unit 5 while the van was being pushed into it by Unit 18." Unit 18 is the eighteen-wheeler trailer-truck that crashed into Kate and Bert from behind. Unit 5 is the vehicle in the next lane, the one the eighteen-wheeler pushed Kate and Bert's van into.

> Minor contact damage was also evidenced on the left front of Unit 19 from contact with another vehicle, Unit 20. Unit 19 also had very major contact damage distributed across the rear of the vehicle along with both rear wheels. This was from contact with Unit 18 as it rode up on top of the rear mounted engine of Unit 19.

This is where the two babies, Mia and Dayiel, would have been strapped into their safety belt seats. No safety belt could protect them from the momentum and weight of an eighteen-wheeler trailer truck coming through the roof of the van onto them.

The report continues: "All four (4) occupants of Unit 19 were found deceased in their respective positions, the vehicle having been involved extensively in the accident fire and ALL OCCUPANTS EVIDENCING DEATH FROM THAT CAUSE." The caps are mine—this is the information I most dreaded finding. Ideally, we like to say that someone was killed instantly. In this case, apparently, they were horribly maimed, crushed by the impact, but were still alive, perhaps conscious, and then burned alive.

"Having struck the van, Unit 18 then rode up on top of the rear."

Bert must have been scared out of his mind, in the right lane, trying to get to the verge, not able to see anything except the yellow, smoky headlights of the huge trailer-truck directly behind him.

> This impact caused an immediate ignition of both vehicles. Unit 18 pushed Unit 19 into Unit 5 . . . The vehicle, having much weight from Unit 18 pushing it down as well as forward, went under the left rear of Unit 5, pushing Unit 5 forward and slightly counter clockwise . . .

This chain reaction of collisions was *all* [my italics] caused by Unit 18. The fire then began to spread rapidly, causing the other vehicles nearby to catch fire and burn. Heat from these vehicle fires was intense enough to cause large chunks of concrete to break from the roadway surface.

The accident report goes on to describe the sequence of compounded crashes that followed in the total darkness of the smoke. It's more than I can bear. I close the report and sit numbed.

Maybe Rosemary's right: I should just let it be; there's nothing I can do now. But I can't quit; I owe it to Bert. Whatever it takes, I must do what I can to keep something like this from happening to some other family.

I review the medical reports attached to the accident report. Blood Alcohol Tests were made by the State Medical Examiner. Kate (then known only as "unidentified female passenger VW Bus"): no alcohol in blood, eighteen percent carbon-monoxide saturation. Bert, "unidentified male driver VW Bus": zero alcohol detected, carbon-monoxide saturation thirteen percent. Neither Dayiel nor Mia was tested. *Nor were any of the other drivers!* I can't believe it.

I look through the report to find the name of the driver of the eighteen-wheeler, "Unit 18." It's Bob Stone. He was not tested for alcohol, or if he was, it is not listed in the report.

According to the "in substance" statement he gave to Sergeant Corrigan, Stone was traveling northbound on I-5 in the right lane. He was, he said, going about forty miles per hour when he entered the smoke. He could see a hundred to 150 yards. He had seen the field burning and *knew* that he would pass through it in a short time. But then the smoke got so bad that he couldn't see his hood and he slowed to twenty miles per hour. He put on his headlights and his four-way flashers. He hit something but couldn't see what, when the flames started. Then he bailed out. He was not injured. *He ran away, with our family trapped under his truck!* According to witnesses, he went back to the truck to take something from it. He admitted this later. He claimed it was to remove a radar-detection scanner.

I take the report apart, it's held together with staples, and spread it along the walls of my writing room. I spend days going over it, reading all the eyewitness accounts, the field-burning rules and regulations, the statements by Mr. Thompkins and his son concerning this particular fire which got away from them. It all seems so senseless, so careless, so unnecessary.

I decide it's time to write another letter to the governor.

Dear Governor,

Today, it is exactly two months since we buried our daughter, Kathleen, her husband, Bert, and their two daughters, Dayiel and Mia, our only granddaughters.

One week from today we would have been celebrating our daughter Kathleen's thirty-sixth birthday. We'd hoped to fly out as a surprise for that celebration. Instead, we flew to Oregon, two months earlier, to bury her.

I've waited before writing you again until I could gather as much information as possible about the horrendous catastrophe which stilled our loved ones.

Our law firm in Oregon has warned us against writing to you, or anyone else, concerning the accident, but some-times personal concerns can outweigh the exigencies of legal procedures.

I'm still waiting for someone responsible to explain what has happened and why. I expected a call or a note from a public official, any public official: from the Department of Environmental Quality, the highway department, the police, or even the governor himself, expressing sympathy for our loss. I had hoped to hear from Mr. Thompkins who set the fire, or perhaps from someone representing the seed-growers' association. But there has been nothing. I mentioned that at the funeral, well publicized in Dallas, the funeral director had been asked by me to watch for representatives from any of the above categories. No one showed up.

I've been told since that it was probably on the advice of lawyers that they were not there.

"But Governor," I write, "an expression of sympathy is not an admission of guilt." The obvious culprit in all this is field burning itself. The fact that the field-burning farmer, Paul Thompkins, has complied with all the rules and regulations for a "controlled burn" while causing the deaths of seven people and injury to thirty-five others is, in itself, a condemnation of the practice. It doesn't matter what conditions the Department of Environmental Quality might impose; it's a hazardous activity. In fact, the Oregon Supreme Court has ruled that field burning is ultra-hazardous. Yet it goes on. This is, I write, a blight on the reputation of all Oregon, a state generally known for its ecological concern.

Governor, how do you defend the fact that this obviously deleterious activity continues? The land itself is being depleted, despite seed-growers' contentions to the contrary. Burning converts nitrogen to phosphates; the soil needs nitrates more than phosphates. The smoke is a summer-long pall over the length of the Willamette Valley. It is a menace to the health and well-being of those living there. The smoke is ugly and the burned fields are ugly. A beautiful part of the world is ravaged by a few, for the profit of a few, to the detriment of the many.

Governor, you can stop all this with a word. Why don't you? Would you defend marijuana growers or cocaine growers for the same economic reasons? They, too, would be profitable crops, only another kind of menace. Give the word, Governor!

It is only necessary to outlaw field burning, help the grass farmers find other alternatives to their current reckless system which despoils and desecrates your beau-

tiful state. Let us not have any other families go through
the grief, sorrow, sadness we have suffered.

I've enclosed photos of the bodies in the morgue in
Dallas along with other photos in better times, of our
children. I pray it gives you some idea of what we've lost.
I think, more than any statistic, it will help you understand what's involved.

Nearly two weeks later, October fifteenth, I receive a phone
call from Bill Buchs, Oregon Secretary of Agriculture. He is
phoning only to pass on his own and the governor's condolences for what happened. He's not going to defend or
explain it.

But I have many questions and we move into a discussion
which lasts almost two hours. Finally he says I must learn the
character of the Oregon grass-seed farmer, who does things
the way he's always done them and doesn't want to change
and doesn't want anybody else telling him what he ought to
do. I ask if it isn't his responsibility as Secretary of Agriculture
to make the farmer change his ways when what he's doing is
against the public welfare. He ducks that one. He says they're
just stubborn. Matt, who has picked up the listening device, a
second earphone on a French telephone, takes the phone from
me.

"Mr. Buchs, I am Matt Wharton, Kate's brother. I'm a biol-
ogist, a graduate of Trinity College in Dublin and I took my
advanced degrees in plant pathology at the Sorbonne here in
Paris. I have contacted friends in my field around the world at
various educational institutions—in New Zealand, Australia,
England, different parts of Europe, North Africa. I've studied
the problem of stubble disposal which killed our family and
here are some of the things I've found out.

"It seems that since Oregon planted its first grass seeds in
the forties, many new patents have been registered, mostly for
seeds resistant to the diseases and pests for which the growers
in Oregon claim it is necessary to 'sanitize' their fields. It

would cost little for Oregon farmers to pay these small patent costs and eliminate the problem which jeopardizes the lives of the people in the Willamette Valley.

"It is the Oregon Seed Growers' Council that still insists on its old grass seed patents, even though they have been superseded by superior versions.

"The solution recommended to me is to plant and then use the stubble as a field compost; that is, cut the grass and leave it there so that it can be plowed back into the land. This returns the nutrients to the soil and helps keep down weed growth. There will be no blind seed or molds or the other diseases which have plagued grass-seed farmers in Oregon. That makes more sense than burning."

Matt pauses and stares up at the ceiling. Then he continues. "You can't bring back my sister, my brother-in-law, or my two beautiful nieces, but it would help us to know that something is being done so no one else suffers as we have suffered."

Tears are running down his face as he hands me the phone.

Secretary of Agriculture Buchs insists that the governor is against field burning, that he'll do everything he can to stop it. That's what I've been wanting to hear. We finish the call in what seems to me to be agreement. Matt is listening in on the other earphone. We put down the phones and celebrate by opening up one of his prized bottles of Burgundy.

We celebrate too soon.

A few days later I receive a letter from the governor. It is written on October nineteenth.

Dear Dr. Wharton:

I apologize for not writing you sooner to express my personal sorrow and regret about the tragic death of your daughter and her family. Their deaths deeply grieve me and everyone else in Oregon. I can assure you that state officials responsible for administering the field burning program share this sorrow, even though they did not extend their sympathy to you directly.

Your letter reflects your serious efforts to understand field burning and grass seed growing in Oregon. The Oregon Legislature debated the practice extensively in the 1970s. The Legislature concluded then that banning field burning, given the lack of alternative practices, was not in the public interest. The Legislature directed the Environmental Quality Commission to regulate field burning to reduce air pollution and to seek alternatives to the practice. Millions of dollars have been spent by the state since then to develop alternative crops and ways to avoid burning. I am told that, so far, none of the alternatives found are complete solutions.

Field burning has now stopped for 1988. My staff is working with environmental organizations, seed growers and dealers, state agencies and members of the Legislature as legislation is developed for the 1989 Legislative Assembly to consider when it convenes in January. The tragic accident that killed your family has prompted review of the existing state laws.

I share your loss and anguish.

I'm happy to have the letter but concerned with what he means by "none of the alternatives found are complete solutions."

And then everything I fear seems to occur at once. It begins simply enough. I receive a copy of a letter from the law firm Steele, Cutler and Walsh. It has been retained, the letter says, to pursue the "wrongful death" claims for Kate, Bert, Dayiel, and Mia. The claims are filed against the state of Oregon and officials, agencies, departments or divisions, for negligence contributing to the deaths. The state of Oregon has filed claims as well. It is suing all those involved in the accident for carelessness and reckless driving. Mr. Thompkins, the farmer who started the fire, is also suing everybody— broadside. What could he be suing them for, blocking his smoke?

Pandora's box has definitely been opened. I find myself wishing to withdraw from the whole thing while recognizing that Sally was right: we need to protect ourselves. But no large law firm will protect us unless it can make money from the case. This means suing.

And so begin twelve months of voluminous correspondence with Steele, Cutler and Walsh, the first of which immediately makes us uncomfortable: we are asked for Kate's biography. We are asked: where she lived, what schools did she attend, what was her academic record, her work experience, as well as what kind of person, mother, and daughter she had been. We need to supply very specific details: how often did we visit her? How often did we communicate? How recently? What kinds of things did we do together?

We did not expect this. But we do it. We cry together but we do it, assuming it's to convince some jury of Kate's value so that her loss can be expressed in dollars and cents.

They also want the same information about Dayiel and Mia.

"Mia's academic record?" asks Rosemary. It's necessary to laugh a little; we're crying too much.

The correspondence continues, much of it devoted to two points of legal procedure. The points, according to Ms. Flores of Steele, Cutler and Walsh, are extremely important.

The first concerns where the case is to be heard. Ms. Flores wants it in a federal court instead of a state or a county one—especially Linn County, where the accident happened. This also ensures that our case will be heard on its own and not tied with the other cases. She has various arguments to back up her point—that the deaths were of people from a foreign country, that the deaths occurred on an interstate highway—and after much to-ing and fro-ing, a judge rules in our favor.

She also wants the state to treat each accident separately. In Oregon, as in most US states, there is a "cap," or maximum amount that the state can be sued for in a highway accident. In Oregon, the "cap" is only $300,000, even in this situation, in which the unlawful deaths, injuries, and property damage could mount into tens of millions of dollars in claims. The "cap" won't apply to the others we may also sue—the farmer who started the fire or the trucking company that owned the eighteen-wheeler that ran over the van—but the others can always go bankrupt, or die. The state of Oregon isn't going to go bankrupt, or die.

Eventually a federal judge, Judge Moody, finds in our favor and rules that the "cap" should apply to each case individually.

Ms. Flores is very enthusiastic; we are, too: by now we are determined to bring the state of Oregon before a jury and judge so it can be tried by due process in a court of law.

*

When the statement of complaint for the wrongful deaths of our family is finally filed in the United States District Court for the District of Oregon, it cites three defendants in addition to the state of Oregon itself: Paul Thompkins, the farmer; Sampson National Carriers, Inc., which owned the eighteen-wheeler truck; and Bob Stone, its driver.

The first claim for relief concerns Mr. Thompkins. This is what it says:

> On August third, 1988 at approximately 3 p.m., Thompkins began field-burning operations on his grass seed field within approximately one-eighth of a mile of the Interstate 5 freeway, just north of the Highway 34 overpass.
>
> Fire from Thompkins's field burn spread to adjacent fields and smoke from the burning fields was carried across Interstate 5 and enshrouded it with dense ground-level smoke, reducing the visibility of freeway travelers.
>
> At or about 3:50 p.m. on August third, 1988, the decedents were passengers in an automobile northbound on Interstate 5 that was struck from behind by a truck driven by Stone as the vehicle of the decedents slowed for traffic congestion caused by the smoke from Thompkins's field burn.

As a result of the collision described above, Kathleen Wharton Woodman and her infant daughters, Mia Woodman and Dayiel Woodman, were killed. [Bert Woodman is not mentioned because his family is involved in a separate suit in the state courts.]

The field-burning operation in which Thompkins was engaged was an abnormally dangerous and ultra-hazardous activity. It created a high degree of risk of harm of exceptional magnitude and probability to decedents and others traveling along Interstate 5, in that dense smoke inherent in field burning is substantially uncontrollable, despite the utmost care, once field burning begins.

The field burning in which Thompkins was engaged was a substantial factor in causing the deaths of Kathleen Wharton Woodman, Mia Woodman, and Dayiel Woodman.

As a result of the field-burning-related accident described above:

a. Kathleen Wharton Woodman, Mia Woodman, and Dayiel Woodman suffered pain and suffering between the time of the accident and the time of their deaths;

b. Funeral expenses, in an as yet undetermined amount, were incurred for Kathleen Wharton Woodman, Mia Woodman, and Dayiel Woodman;

c. Wills Billing, the surviving child of Kathleen Wharton Woodman and the half-brother of Mia Woodman and the half-brother of Dayiel Woodman, has been deprived of the decedents' society, companionship, and services; and

d. Decedents' estates have suffered pecuniary loss in an as yet undetermined amount, equivalent to the amount they would have saved during the remainder of their lives had they survived.

There is also an equally lengthy claim for negligence: that Thompkins should have known the field burning was likely to be carried across freeway traffic; that he should have surrounded the fire with noncombustible ground cover to prevent it from spreading; that, once it had, he should have alerted the emergency response agencies; that he had, thus, failed to control "the fire he started on his land"; and that "The injuries suffered by decedents and the damages incurred were the foreseeable result of his negligence."

The other claims are against the driver and his employer. Stone is said to have been negligent by driving at an excessive rate of speed, not keeping a proper lookout, and failing to maintain control over his truck. His employers, Sampson, which owned the trailer that Stone was pulling, were negligent because they knew that Stone's driving record included offences for exceeding the speed limit and driving under the influence of intoxicants.

Against Sampson, a million dollars in punitive damages is sought. Against the farmer and the driver the damages are described as a "yet undetermined amount."

The complaint is signed by Ted Mitchell and Mona Flores for the law firm of Steele, Cutler and Walsh.

CHAPTER 12

ROSEMARY AND I read the list of complaints. They seem to be legitimate from what I've learned but I'm uncomfortable with how the pending trial is out of our control.

In the meanwhile, the correspondence continues. How much did Bert and Kate save? How much did the funeral cost? How much did the monument I commissioned cost?

There are further arguments about court procedures. Paul Thompkins tries on two occasions to have the trial moved from a federal court to either a state or a county one, and both times loses. He then asks that all the cases be heard together, not one at a time. This, too, is rejected, but at the end of the judge's statement, I read the following: "While I am skeptical about this claim getting to a jury, or a motion to dismiss, I am bound to accept all allegations as true."

I read this statement several times. Our main reason for going through all this legal garbage is to bring this case before a jury: a public forum before the people of Oregon. Is this judge saying he doesn't think the case will go to a jury?

The hearings don't stop. There are questions and faxes and parcels arriving by Federal Express. And finally, worst of all, there is a demand for depositions—from Rosemary, Wills, and me. Why do we have to give depositions? Rosemary and I weren't even in the state at the time. I don't want to do it. I don't want to travel to Portland. I write to say I can't make it, that the trip will be expensive and difficult. We are assured it is absolutely necessary, that not going will seriously damage our case. We succumb. I'm not accustomed to spending this kind of money on plane fares, merely to give a deposition, a word I've never even seen or heard before.

Robert Wilson, our long-time friend, picks us up at the airport in Portland. Wills has travelled with us, having spent the summer in France. We'll be staying at the Wilsons' home. It's good to spend the first night in such family surroundings with old friends.

The next day we find the offices of Steele, Cutler and Walsh, a pink building in the center of town, and zip up the high-speed elevator to the wood-paneled offices of Ted Mitchell. He's a smooth-looking man in his middle fifties, well-dressed, his hair carefully cut. He'll be the one presenting our case in court.

His desk is located so that we have to look into the light, past him, to the view outside his huge plate window. We can't see his face clearly. But he can see us. I'm wearing a pair of stone-washed jeans, more or less clean. Rosemary is dressed in her usual ladylike way: low heels, her hair carefully combed. Wills is in typical pre-teen clothes.

We talk in generalities for several minutes, then two other people come into the office; the meeting seems to be well-orchestrated. There's an older man, introduced as Clint Williams, a former federal judge, and a younger woman, about forty, who is Mona Flores, with whom we've had so much correspondence. We all smile. They invite us to sit down.

Mr. Ted Mitchell describes what a deposition is, how it is an extension of the courtroom itself, how we are to answer the specific questions asked us and nothing more. He explains how the group asking the questions will consist mostly of insurance representatives and attorneys for other plaintiffs, as well as attorneys for the defendants. Rosemary is watching him as closely as he's watching us. I'm looking out the window. Wills is bored and restless. Clint Williams and Mona Flores contribute comments.

It is obvious who the boss is, and he doesn't want his steam stolen by subordinates. They, in turn, seem quite subordinate to him, or, at least, play the role well. I'm glad when we say goodbye and agree to meet the next day. I guess they were just looking us over. It seems such a waste of time and money. Thank God for Robert and Karen, the friends with whom we're staying.

The next day we dress up for the show. Even Wills, with Rosemary's help, spruces himself up. I wear a suit I bought at the Salvation Army for six dollars. It's a good suit, just a mite old-fashioned, vest and all.

We park and are met by Ms. Flores, who asks us to call her Mona. She cautions us.

"Don't answer quickly. If they say, 'Would you tell us your name?' you answer 'Yes.' Make them ask you for your name directly. That's a kind of general rule at depositions. Give nothing away."

We file into a long room with a gigantic table. Rosemary will be first. Wills and I are to wait in another room. This whole thing begins to take on some of the characteristics of an inquisition. I can't help wondering, who's working for whom here? It's our money which is being spent.

They close Rosemary in the room with what looks like fifteen or more people, mainly men. They're all dressed in lawyer-type clothes. Mona Flores and Clint Williams go in with her. I ask one of the secretaries for some paper and a pencil. Wills watches as I draw the scene out the window. I find some paper for him and he draws along with me. He's quite talented.

It seems forever before Rosemary comes out. Mona is with her. Rosemary is crying. I'm just old-fashioned enough that I don't like the idea of my wife crying. I jump up and take her hand. She's wiping her eyes with her handkerchief.

"What is it, Hon? What happened?" She's quiet for a minute, waves me off, trying to pull herself together.

"It was nothing they did. It was just talking about Kate and the questions they wanted answered, it upset me. I'll be all right in a minute."

Mona Flores has come forward.

"You don't need to go back if you don't want. Those damned lawyers: they just don't seem to know what's too much."

"No, I'm fine. It was my fault as much as it was his."

Rosemary leads the way back into the room where the deposition is being held. She's there another half-hour. Wills and I are beginning to tire of drawing. I start on a portrait of him. Just then, the door opens and they come out. They've been in there most of the morning. Rosemary seems to be all right. She's a little pale but she's not crying. Mona stays right beside her.

"She was great. She fended off those wolves like a queen. They're not used to dealing with a tough, classy lady like your wife."

Rosemary sits down, looks out at the view.

"I'm starving. Can we go look for something to eat?"

We find a good Mexican restaurant—not TexMex, but real Mexican food.

Mona is curious about our lives, why we're in France, about our living on a houseboat. I think she's genuinely interested. She's good-looking with dark hair and green-blue eyes. She has a nice figure but is wearing one of those weird suits that makes her look as if she's been pumping iron or is wearing football shoulder-pads, or both. She looks directly into your eyes—I can tell that Rosemary likes her, as does Wills—and is a good listener. I guess that's the way lawyers are supposed to be with their clients. She tells Rosemary she's not to talk with me about what happened in her deposition.

After lunch, it's Wills's turn. Mona is gentle with him, trying to prepare him. Mona has a five-year-old son of her own and is very sympathetic. But I still can't figure out what they expect to find out from him.

Rosemary has a book and starts reading while I go back to drawing. What would happen if she started telling me what occurred in there? Rosemary is not one to cry easily in public.

Ten minutes later Mona comes out with Wills. He's sobbing. This is even worse than it was with Rosemary. At least Rosemary is a grown woman, has a fair idea of what's going on. We both rush over to be with him. Mona waves us back to our seats and sits Wills in a chair between us. She's looking from Wills to us.

"He was very brave. But when they started asking about his mother, it just broke him down. I can't really say they were trying to do that, but there's a terrible lack of empathy and sympathy in lawyers as a group. When they want something badly enough, they can be incredibly cruel without even knowing it."

Wills looks at Rosemary.

"I'm OK now, Grandma. I just didn't expect so many people looking at me, and I have a hard time even thinking about Mom let alone talking about her to all those strange people."

Mona leans close, looks him in the eyes which are all reddened. His eyelids are swollen.

"You don't need to go back in if you don't want, Wills."

"No, we've come all this way, we should finish it anyway."

He stands up. Mona stands beside him, smoothing her black skirt over her hips. She looks at us. We both nod our heads, yes. Wills is right. After all this travel, we need to carry this thing through.

Mona turns to Rosemary.

"I think it would be better if you came in and sat beside him, Rosemary. That is, if you can bear it."

Rosemary stands and puts her arm around Wills.

"OK, Wills, sweetheart, let's go back. It can't last much longer."

They leave. This time I'm too upset to draw. I pace back and forth as if I'm an expectant father.

After about another hour, they come out. Wills's eyes are still red but not much worse than before. Rosemary and Mona are leaning over him. They look up at me and smile. Mona steps forward.

"You should really be proud of him. I am. He was wonderful. I don't think I've ever seen such a young person make monkeys of such a large group of lawyers in my life. It was well worth the price of admission."

Rosemary's smiling, too. She looks over at Mona.

"Is it all right if I tell Will about one incident that really established the mood of the entire deposition?"

"Let me. I don't think we'll be violating the deposition then. As your lawyer, we can have discourse regarding a thing like this. It's too good to keep to ourselves, anyway."

She looks at me.

"It was Harry Fox again. Out of the absolute blue, he asks Wills if his mom and dad ever had fights. Before I can catch Wills's eye, he's started answering. After he's started it would have been worse to try stopping him than just letting it go.

"Wills looked him in the eye and said, 'Sure they had fights sometimes, but not many.'

"Fox leaned in for the kill.

" 'What did they fight about?'

" 'Well, Mom is a very good cook and Bert was always putting pepper or catsup on his food. This would always make Mom mad.'

"Well, there was silence for a few seconds, then the laughing started. Even Fox had to smile. Rosemary's right, it sort of broke things up."

We talk some more. It's about quarter to four.

"Well, do I go in now?"

"No, they'll want to really lean on you. We'll start your deposition at nine o'clock tomorrow. Come on. I'll help you down to your car. The traffic will be picking up just about now. You can miss it if we hurry."

We get back to Karen and Robert's at about five. Neither one is home, but we have the key. We're tired. We flop out on the beds and before we know it, we're all asleep.

Next morning, Karen and Robert lend us their car. I know my way pretty well now. I head down Hawthorn and over the Hawthorn bridge. I can see the pink Steele, Cutler and Walsh office building as we go over the bridge. It seems ominous. I'm dreading the deposition. I swear it won't break me down.

When we come up, Mona and Clint Williams are waiting for us. The other lawyers are congregating, whispering softly to each other as if they're cardinals about to perform an exorcism, or maybe students going into a dreaded examination. I'm the subject. Mona and Clint pull me aside. Clint gives the instructions.

"Mr. Wharton, I have a feeling you're an impulsive person. This is not the time to be impulsive, just play it cool. Play it close to the vest. Most of all, don't start answering anything until you have paused to think it over."

They don't seem to have much confidence in me. I probably have too much confidence in myself and that's what scares them. It's as if we're playing a game like chess or contract bridge, one that's based on not showing what you think or feel. These are the games I don't like and am not good at. I should know better than to resist; they're probably right.

We enter the room and Mona leads me near the head of the table beside a window. There's a man at the end with an antiquated machine I recognize from movies as the stenographic machine of a court reporter. Mona sits beside me. Clint Williams sits on the other side of her. These are the only seats left in the room. One of the lawyers at the other end of the table stands up and closes the door.

The court reporter is about to have me swear in. I put up my hand to stop him.

"Before we start this deposition, I want to remind all you gentlemen and ladies that this is not an inquisition. I watched both my wife and grandson come out of this room crying. There could have been no need for that."

I pause.

"We are terribly upset by our loss. I hope all of you will keep this in mind. Sometimes, I shall probably not be able to speak. If this occurs, please have patience, just wait. I've found I cannot talk and cry at the same time. Do you understand?"

There are nods and smiles around the table. I lean forward to look at each of them in turn.

"If I feel that a question or implication is insulting or unfitting, I shall consult my attorneys here beside me and if they feel that something actionable has occurred, although I am not a suing man, I shall sue. Is that understood?"

I turn to look at Mona and Clint. I can tell they are not happy with this turn of events, but they dutifully nod.

"All right, now. Let's get on with it."

The man across from me looks like "the man in the butter-scotch ice-cream suit." He's to be my inquisitor, it seems. He can't be the dreadful Mr. Fox. He's slightly overweight, but perfectly tailored, with his hair combed neatly and flat against his head. He seems about fifty years old. He has a permanently unctuous smile, an almost Buddha-like calm.

The court reporter asks all at the table to identify themselves and he takes down the names with his rickety machine. We're ready. The Buddha, named Mr. Crosley, leans forward and pauses for about fifteen seconds.

"We don't want to antagonize you or cause you pain, Mr. Wharton. This is only an attempt to gather information which will help us in understanding this case and settling it amicably."

"I don't intend to settle, Mr. Crosley, let us get that straight first. I've told my lawyers this, so I guess they haven't passed on that information, but it is very important."

This slows things down again. Mr. Crosley consults the thin, wiry, bearded man beside him. I'm quite sure this is the notorious Mr. Fox.

Mr. Fox smiles and then asks a series of curt, almost insulting questions about my life. He's interested in how much money I make writing.

What's that have to do with Kate's death?

Mr. Crosley takes over. His concern is how much money I didn't earn during the greater part of my life.

I haven't worked for anyone but myself since I was thirty-five years old. I've been a painter, self-employed. This seems beyond his comprehension. He tries to portray me as a bum. In a way, I am, from his point of view. We're getting nowhere.

Mr. Crosley leans back, extending his thin-lipped smile.

"How about if you just tell us about yourself?"

I turn to Mona beside me. She shrugs.

"What do you want to know?"

"We just want to know about you."

"What's that have to do with the death of our daughter, her husband, our two granddaughters?"

"We'll decide that. Just start."

"Remember I'm a professional writer, a novelist by trade. I can give you the three-hour, the three-day, or the three-volume answer to an open question like this."

"Just begin. We'll tell you if it's not what we want. We'll interrupt if we have any questions."

I lean back and look at the ceiling. I keep my eyes on the ceiling, or on Mona, as I go on. I enjoy playing raconteur, and here I have a large, willing audience and a court reporter taking down everything I say. I didn't realize it then, but I was paying to play.

"Well, I was born in Philadelphia, Pennsylvania, in Saint Vincent's Hospital on November seventh, 1925, at five o'clock in the afternoon. I weighed over nine pounds. My mother was twenty years old when I was born, my father was twenty-three. I had colic for the first three months."

I stop and look over at Mona, then at Mr. Crosley and along the line at the others. There's no response. I thought they'd have stopped me by now.

I look up at the ceiling again and continue with all I can remember from those first few years, plus all the tales Mom told me: her pride at having toilet-trained me at thirteen months, or the time she prepared to take me, all dressed up, to her sister's in Kensington, on the other side of Philadelphia. She put me in a white suit into which, almost immediately, I proceeded to crap. She took off the diaper, wrapped it around my face and locked me in a closet.

Mr. Crosley leans forward with evident distaste. At least, it's a reaction.

"Did she really do that?"

"I don't know. It's what she told me. I was too young to remember. But I still don't like the insides of closets."

I get my first laughs and a giggle. They aren't dead.

I go on like this for three hours. Sometimes the court reporter stops me for a spelling, or one of the depositioners asks me a question, but generally I push forward with my life as I remember it. I begin to think this might make a great autobiography, under oath. I'll call it *Deposition*. I'll have to ask the court reporter for a copy. I should have a right to it.

At about twelve-fifteen, just when I'm up to my first year in high school, dropping a blivey from the third floor onto my algebra teacher, Mona puts her watch in front of my face. I get the message. Time to eat. Everyone shuffles out and leaves the room, without speaking or looking at me. The "blivey" bit might have been a little too much. Maybe they don't know what a "blivey" is.

Mona, Clint, and I stay in the room until they're gone. Clint is having a hard time keeping from laughing out loud.

"Jeez, you had me worried at first. I thought you were just shooting your mouth off, but you didn't tell them a damned thing, did you?"

Mona shuts the door. "I thought I'd pee my pants when you told them how you'd thrown the horse's leg under the porch of the man next door."

We come out. Rosemary and Wills are sitting in the waiting- room. They've gone to the science museum but not to the zoo. That will be for this afternoon.

After lunch, same place, we return for the second half of the deposition. It starts out fine. They've managed to pull themselves together and have some reasonable and demanding questions to ask. I check with Mona each time there's something awkward, and generally she gives me the nod, but sometimes objects and then they all argue. There are some fairly hot disputes.

By five o'clock, I'm up to 1963. Their questions have slowed me down. I'm never going to get my entire autobiography finished. At five, everybody starts shifting. It's that time again. One of them stands, looks at his watch, and speaks.

"I think we ought to stop now and continue the deposition tomorrow."

These guys are too much, after all the time they've wasted. I stand up myself.

"My wife and I have a very tight schedule. We can't stay here for another day of deposition. I was assured by our lawyers that two days would be enough and we have a plane leaving tomorrow at ten-thirty a.m."

He sits down. There's a mumbling and looking at watches. Mr. Crosley stands up.

"But we haven't finished the deposition."

Mona answers him.

"You've had more time than you needed. Mr. Wharton, are you willing to stay on until we finish the deposition today?"

"Sure, if you'll go down at six to the doorway where I'm supposed to meet my wife."

"I'll do that. Clint can take my place here. Gentlemen, the deposition is still on. If you have any more questions, ask them now. Mr. Wharton is willing to stay on until midnight if it proves necessary."

She sits down. There's some serious mumbling, one by one they start leaving.

Mona stands.

"All right. I warn you. By leaving, you are terminating the deposition. You've had your chance to continue it."

But the exodus goes on. I'm sorry. I'd like to have finished my autobiography. The court reporter is gathering up his tapes as if they're some kind of party streamers that have been sprinkled over the room. He, Mona, and I are the last to leave. Deposition over.

It's only five-fifteen. I walk with her to her office so she can pick up her bag and a few things. She says she'll show me the door where Rosemary will be for our rendezvous. We go down the elevator.

In the elevator she asks, "Have you ever tried some of the Northwest Macrobrewery beers? Do we have time while we wait for Rosemary? They sell them in a little cafeteria on the ground floor."

"Sounds great to me. My throat's sore from all that talking."

We settle into a booth and she orders. The beer comes fast. It's dark and tastes like a German beer, only sweeter and rawer. Mona's watching me.

"I shouldn't tell you this. Lawyers are supposed to stay out of the private lives of their clients, but . . . " She takes a long drink and then looks up over the glass. "Well, as I listened to Rosemary and then Wills, I had this incredible feeling that I actually know, or knew, Kate, maybe in some other life. It was so weird. It's not the kind of thing that happens to me. But I could hardly keep my concentration on that mob of lawyers during your deposition. Have you ever had that kind of feeling?"

"All the time. I haven't told you yet and I won't tell any of those people up there, but I had an absolutely incredible— right, incredible in the exact meaning of the word—experience just after the accident. Sometimes I have these unexpected openings, these loopholes, in the regular run of reality. I've had them since I was a kid. You should know that Kate had them, too. Tell me exactly what you felt, Mona."

"It was as if she were taking my place, or I was taking hers. I really don't understand and I know it sounds crazy to talk about it, especially with a client. Do you understand?"

"I not only understand, Mona, but I know what it was. It was Kate. Like Bert, she's having a hard time letting go. I'm beginning not to believe too much in coincidence. It's a word we use to explain too many things we just don't understand. Maybe they're God-incidences, events beyond normal reality.

"My conviction, that they're still here and caring in some way I don't understand, is important to me. It's my way of dealing with the events in this so-called real world, that are totally unacceptable, impossible. I'm here, fighting field burning because Bert asked me to, after he was burned to death, if you can believe that."

I finish the beer and look at my watch. It's five till six.

"I'd better look for Rosemary and Wills. Point me to the door. But let me get the bill here first."

Mona puts her hand over mine. "No, this was my idea."

Early in the next morning, Robert drives us to the airport. All goes well. The flights are on time—Wills's for Los Angeles, ours for New Jersey. We settle back and Rosemary goes to sleep almost immediately. But my mind is spinning. All this flying around, all that money down the drain, and for what?

CHAPTER 13

*I*N THREE WEEKS we're back home in France and just about settled into our old routine. But I'm about to leave again. I've agreed with my publisher to do a publicity tour for my new book, *Franky Furbo,* a book that Kate suggested I write and one which I've been working on between letters to governors and legislatures and all the other legal matters, as well as my painting.

I've always resisted requests for book tours or signings. I'm running out of time. I'm not thirty years old or hungering for fame. I want to preserve what's left of my private life. But I agree to go on this tour on the condition that both Portland and Eugene are included. I inform Mona. I also have my publisher send an extra 200 copies of my book to Portland and another hundred to Eugene. I then ask Bill Johnson of ENUF, who's running the Initiative, Petition, and Referendum movement, if he can have people with petitions at the doors of the places where I'll be speaking. Bill Johnson, who is about my age, is the most enthusiastic supporter for banning field burning that I've met in Oregon. It's his mission. My plan is to give a free copy of the book to anyone who can bring in a legitimate petition, twenty-five signatures, full.

In October, in New York, I start my tour. I work my way across the country, talking at universities, giving interviews for newspapers and radio, signing books in stores. I read the book's dedication to Kate, Bert, and the girls on each occasion. Once in Portland, I put into operation the STOP FIELD BURNING project. I speak wherever I can gather a group together, in libraries, schools, Powell's bookstore, any bookstore. I'm signing and selling books like mad, all the time letting people know how angry I am about the lethargy surrounding field burning. Bill Johnson's people are there too, and we're gathering thousands of signatures. But we need 65,000 if a referendum is to be held. It looks hopeless.

In the middle of all this, Mona asks if I can take time off to continue the deposition. The creeps from the first deposition are not satisfied.

I agree to give them three hours before the signing at the Powell bookstore that evening. This time, the lawyers are prepared and ask more specific questions—more and less pertinent at the same time. Among other things, they're concerned that I was trying to build a billboard along the highway where the accident occurred.

It seems that on the first anniversary of the deaths, a group of young people mounted white crosses along the road where the accident happened, without permission. I knew about this but had nothing to do with it. I tell how I'd tried to obtain permission to have some kind of memorial plaque set in the ground, but had been refused.

They want to know why I photographed the bodies and why I went out to the highway two days after the accident. I tell them the truth; after all, I'm under oath. It's simple enough; I only wanted to see what was left of my family before they were totally reduced to ashes, and I wanted to see the last things my family had seen before they were plunged into darkness, the seemingly final darkness. I also tell about my sense of obligation because of the "dream" I'd had. Anything other than "dream" would have been beyond them.

The next day, I rent a car and drive down to Eugene. The crowd is even more enthusiastic. The burning often blows smoke and grit over this lovely university town. I speak in

the public library and pass out petitions in all directions. I do
my best to impress on Oregonians how dangerous the field
burning is to all. The lecture and discussion are videoed for
local stations. Several other sessions are aired locally as well.
The next day I fly back to New York and from New York to
Paris. I'm acting like a jet-setter but I'm not feeling like one.
I'm dead tired. I'm losing steam and confidence: we have
fewer than 20,000 signatures for the referendum.

Forty-five percent of Oregonians do not live in cities, and
it's hard to reach them with our petitions. Also, the greater
part of Oregon doesn't suffer from the field burning: it's only
those in the Willamette Valley. Meanwhile the growers are
making more and more noise about how much revenue will
be lost to the state if grass growing is stopped. It lists all
kinds of public services which would, possibly, not be
available. People are dumb enough to believe it.

When I come home, I tell Rosemary that's the last time I go
to Oregon. Those people are just too damned ornery, thick-
headed, and I don't have the energy, time, or ability to
change them. I'm also beginning to feel I'm interfering with
the basic ecology of the area by asking them to think.

We continue to receive considerable mail from Mona Flores
who tries to keep us abreast with what's going on. They seem
to be taking depositions from anyone who had anything to
do with the accident or even knew it happened. And these
are all costing us money. Our own depositions cost us
$232.80, not counting plane fare. Even the one I did when I
interrupted my publicity tour at their request cost me more
than fifty dollars.

The reality seems to be that the firm covers the costs of the
suit only when it uses its own lawyers, but it can always hire
other lawyers when the firm deems it necessary—or investigators or so-called "expert witnesses": but all of them, finally,
are my financial responsibility. Even the cost of the trans-
portation, food, phone bills, accommodation for the experts
are paid for by Rosemary and me. I can see why everybody's

so anxious for us to settle. The money has to come from somewhere. We're locked in.

A little later, Mona writes again: Rosemary, as family representative, is required in Portland for a settlement conference. I write Mona to remind her that, as we have no intention of settling, we have no need to attend a settlement conference. She must know our whole reason for going through with this is to have a public trial and bring this horrendously irresponsible scandal out into the open as much as possible.

Besides, the conference is to be held in Portland at a time when Rosemary cannot leave her kindergarteners and when I'm in the middle of writing a new book. I tell Mona that we aren't coming. She says she'll check with Judge Joseph Murphy, who will be running the conference.

The next day she calls. It seems Judge Murphy has insisted that one of us come. If we don't appear, he will cite us for contempt of court. I hang up.

I go see a French lawyer friend who has some experience with American law. I explain the situation. I want to know what they can do if I don't go.

"He'll cite you and perhaps ask to have you extradited from France."

"And how would the French react if I'm extradited?"

"They'd be very wary about allowing you back. After all, you'd probably be a convicted criminal, depending on how harsh the judge might be."

"I don't believe it!"

"You'd better believe it."

He likes to use American phrases.

I return and tell Rosemary. She says I should probably go. She's concerned that I might hurt Wills's case, his chance to be compensated for the loss of his mother, stepfather, and two half-sisters.

I pack the only dark suit I have, the one I wore for the funeral, as well as my usual beat-up jeans, T-shirts, and underwear. I also pack three more-or-less dress shirts and a necktie. My life doesn't usually include this kind of dressing up. At the last moment, I throw in my old briefcase.

The flight's not bad, only boring, with a long layover in Minneapolis. Mona Flores is at the airport in Portland to meet me. This is a surprise. I'd told her my flight number, but didn't expect her to pick me up. I wave. She's wearing a dark pants suit with the shoulder-pads again.

"Are you surprised?"

"It's a wonderful surprise. What brings you all the way out here?"

"I could say I wanted to surprise you, but there's a reason."

"If you're going to tell me they've postponed the settlement conference, I'm jumping onto the next flight back and you'll never see me again until the trial."

"Not quite as bad as that, but bad enough."

She does the usual lawyer's trick of hanging fire, waiting for the other person to ask. I'm learning, slowly.

"OK, what's happened now?"

"Judge Murphy's moved the settlement conference down to Eugene."

"Why'd he do that?"

"I think it's his way of getting us all into the same courtroom: state cases and federal cases. Judge Murphy prides himself on the percentage of settlements he has presided over without having to go to court. He claims a ninety-five percent success rate, and that's probably about right. I suspect we're going to see him at his worst."

"Are you sure about that? Well, it doesn't mean anything to me, because I'm not settling, you know that. Doesn't this make a lot of trouble for everybody, the lawyers, the plaintiffs, the defendants, all for nothing?"

"A federal judge can do no wrong. There's no sense in trying to make him change his mind. He can't be removed from office, he has the job for life, and he can't even be sued."

166

Mona drives a new-looking, metallic brown Honda. I throw my bags in back.

"What else?"

"Ted Mitchell thinks Murphy's going to try for a mass execution, get everyone to settle at once. This is the biggest settlement conference in Oregon history. He's going to put tremendous pressure on everybody. If he settles all this mess in one conference, he'll have made a killing. His batting average will go up at least three points."

She looks over at me as she pays to get the car out of the garage.

"He has a reputation as a defendant's judge in these settlements."

"Well, that's nice, but, as I say, it doesn't matter to me. He can't make me settle, can he?"

"He'll try."

"Well, lots of luck, Judge Murphy. Even God has his limits."

"Well, where will you be staying?"

"The same as last time, with my friends Karen and Robert Wilson. I've phoned them I was coming but I didn't give them the flight number because I didn't want them coming all the way out here to pick me up. By the way, thank you again."

When we get to Karen and Robert's, it looks as if no one's home; both cars are gone. But I know where the key is. Mona leans out her car.

"You can always stay at my house if you want. Tom and I have just bought a big monster of an ugly old house built in the twenties. We have plenty of room."

I thank her but say I know where the key is.

"Don't get nabbed for breaking and entering."

"Would you turn me in?"

"Of course not."

"Never know with you lawyer folks. You're training me just fine. Soon, I'll be the perfect client."

"You'll never make a good client."

"Why not?"

"You always want to know too much for one thing, and you think you know too much for the other."

I leave my bags by the curb and go around to the back porch where I find the key just where Karen said it would be. Mona stays in the car with the motor running. I go to pick up my bags and say goodbye.

"I'll come by tomorrow and drive you down to Eugene. It's about a two-hour drive from here. The judge wants us all in the court-house by one o'clock. On the way down, I can explain what a settlement conference is."

The next morning Mona and I don't talk much until we're out of the Portland traffic and on that I-5 south. We'll go past the place where the accident occurred, but in the opposite direction. I stare out the windows. Several times, I catch Mona looking at me, as if she has something on her mind.

"Mona, you said we were going to talk about this settlement conference. Will you tell me or am I, lawyer style, going to have to pull it out of you with 10,000 bitty questions like a deposition?"

"You are definitely *not* a good client. You don't respect the law at all, do you?"

"I'm law-abiding, if that's what you mean. But from what I've seen so far of the way law is practiced in Oregon, no, I don't think much of it."

"Well, you're going to think even less of it before the next few days are finished. I have only hints as to what may happen and I'm not sure I should tell you. I know you're not going to like it."

"I don't get this, Mona. This is my suit. I'm paying you, Ted Mitchell, Clint Williams, and the whole company to represent me in this mess. How and why are you keeping secrets from me? I'll bet this 'settlement conference' is as stupid as those depositions."

"Worse."

"Oh, God! Don't make me drag it out of you, Mona."

"Well, I guess the first question you might ask is why we're going all the way to Eugene when the conference was scheduled in Portland."

"Right. Most of the people, defendants, lawyers, and all, must be closer to Portland."

"I don't know about that, but it's probably true."

"OK, I bite, then why?"

"You remember how hard we fought to have our cases separated from the cases that would be tried in the state courts?"

I nod.

"And according to what you wrote me, we won."

"Well, Judge Murphy's found a way to get around that. Judge Murphy is bringing all the cases to Eugene, to the courthouse there, for the settlement. It doesn't matter where the trials are scheduled to be, everybody, all cases, will be in Eugene today, like it or not."

"But this isn't the trial, is it?"

"As I've already told you, Judge Murphy is trying to settle all the cases at once. If that happens, there will be no trials anywhere. It won't make any difference whether it's a federal or a state trial. If Murphy has his way, he'll force everybody into settlements. He's surprised everyone, especially us. We're the only case scheduled for a federal court trial. Do you understand?"

"Sure, he outfoxed you. How'd you let him get away with it? Is it legal?"

"It's legal but it is unusual."

"Can't you do anything about it?"

"You are one damned curious client. This isn't easy on any of us, remember. I worked my ass off trying to move the venue of this case to a more neutral ground and it's all out the window like that."

"You didn't answer. Can we do anything about it?"

"No, I don't think so. Even if we could, we wouldn't."

I'm interested now.

"Tell me more."

"I've told you about federal judges. They're political appointees. Once they're appointed, it's for life, unless they do something incredibly stupid, or, are declared incapable of carrying out their duties. Even then, it's almost impossible to move them out, except to kick them upstairs. Not only that, as I said, one can't sue a federal judge. Now, you just think about that."

She gives me a hard look. I sit for a while staring out the window.

"Does a settlement judge like Murphy also sit on the bench and try civil or criminal cases, like an ordinary judge?"

"He's never an ordinary judge, he's a federal judge, don't you understand?"

"Yeah, I get it. And this judge might very well be sitting on the bench in the future for cases you or Mitchell or anybody else at Steele, Cutler and Walsh could be prosecuting or defending. Therefore, you all get down on your knees and do a 'yes, massah' scene to almost anything he wants."

She's quiet. She gives me a look that's supposed to drive me through the window.

She pulls over to the side of the road. The cars whizz past.

"So what do you want to do? Shall we just skip this settlement conference? The way you're acting, there's no sense going down there. Danny Billings can probably handle things for us. You wouldn't have a chance. Be reasonable."

"I don't want to settle, so why am I going to a settlement conference? That's reasonable, except, as far as I can see, if I don't go, it's jail for me and maybe being driven from the country where I want to live with my family. Imagine, me, the personal representative for my daughter, son-in-law, granddaughters, winding up in jail, exiled, because they were killed. Honestly, does that make sense to you, Mona? That's victimizing the victim."

"You're exaggerating and you know it. I'm only trying to explain the law to you as your lawyer. I didn't make up the law. I'm only your counselor. I'm trying my best to counsel you and you keep making it difficult."

"So, we're basically only trying to ferret out something reasonable from a system which is deeply flawed. Is that it?"

"Maybe. I'm not trying to defend the entire American judicial system."

"OK, I give up. As little Wills said at the deposition, we've come this far, it doesn't make sense going back now. Drive on, counselor."

"You're sure that's what you want?"

"No, it's not what I want, but I'm caught up in a skein of sticky threads and I don't see any way out. I only want a trial where we can present the case once more against field burning, and perhaps receive an award from the jury which will discourage field burners in the future. That's my whole point."

She puts the car in gear and looks for a break in the traffic. We're quiet for a while.

We drive along. I'm looking out the windows for the place where the family met death. As we approach it I recognize the little factory building on the other side of the road and see the mile marker. It's all so sad and it's led to this ridiculous business, driving down this road to Eugene.

"Could you tell me what to expect at this settlement conference? Tell me as much as you think I can understand, and I promise not to interrupt until you're finished."

She pauses, then begins.

"To start off with, there aren't enough courtrooms and judges for all the civil and criminal cases which need to be heard. The drug cases alone would keep most of the courts filled. A large portion of criminal cases are kept out of court by plea bargaining; that is, the accused agrees to a lesser sentence if he admits to being guilty, or volunteers testimony for the state."

She looks over at me; I nod, try to smile.

"With civil cases, most are 'settled'—that is, the defendant moves to settle the case by paying a certain amount of money to the plaintiff, and they negotiate. This saves the state and whichever side loses the case an enormous amount of money, because the court costs at a trial can be considerable. That's what this settlement conference is, basically, except that it's on a grand scale. In addition, we have the state claiming it will only pay $300,000 for the entire catastrophe—injuries, deaths, property loss, everything. This was the firm's first objective in this case, to have this 'cap' eliminated, because of the huge losses involved."

"Well, we won that one, didn't we? At least, that's what you wrote us. Don't tell me this 'win' is going to be like the 'win' concerning our right to a federal court trial."

She takes another deep breath, looks at me quickly. We're doing almost seventy. I hold onto the roof brace, tighter.

"We thought this had been decided, but apparently it hasn't. This makes a serious problem for all the plaintiffs. This override of the federal ruling is very recent, but Judge Murphy has accepted it, and there was scarcely time to inform those involved. Are you following me?"

"Can a federal judge's decision be put aside just like that?"

"We're not sure. Now it's a question of time, and we don't have enough of it to contest the ruling before Judge Murphy applies it to all the cases to be settled in this conference. I personally think we should apply for time to contest the ruling. Judge Murphy's acceptance of this definitely works against the plaintiffs."

"Why can't all the plaintiffs' lawyers just refuse to participate in the conference?"

"You heard what I just told you about the relationship between lawyers and judges. Nobody's willing to stick out his neck."

"OK, go on. I promised I wouldn't interrupt."

"Well, that's about all I can tell you now. We'll have to wait and see what Judge Murphy has in mind. There's nothing more we can think to do.

"By the way, something else you should know. Judge Murphy is a devout Christian. He's taken his vow to Christ.

There are other things, too, but you'll figure those out for yourself. Just remember that, for this day, we're in this man's hands whether we like it or not. He used to work for Steele, Cutler and Walsh, but they didn't ask him to stay. That doesn't really help our case, either."

I need time to think about all this. I can't believe it. None of this has much to do with the civics courses I had in element-ary school, or the "Problems of Democracy" classes in high school, or the one on United States government and political science at UCLA. Nobody mentioned anything about "settle-ments" or "plea bargaining." Maybe they hadn't invented those things yet. It was all over forty years ago.

I've slouched down in my seat as the beautiful scenery passes by the window. This is the same scenery which in a few months will again be shrouded with smoke. It's hard to believe.

We reach Eugene.

We shake hands all around and then go through huge doors, high enough for giants. The inside has the closed-in smell of all public buildings, of years of fear and conflict. There's a metal detector just inside the door, like the kind used in airports. I feel as if I'm being led into prison.

I'm carrying my briefcase. I have a peanut-butter sandwich packed in there and my tape recorder with a packet of ninety-minute tapes. When I go through, the detector buzzes, and I back out. The security guard goes through my briefcase and lifts out my small tape recorder. I have my earphones in there, too. He holds it up, glaring at me.

"What do you intend to do with this?"

"I'm the personal representative for my family as plaintiff in this case. I want to record what happens so they'll know."

"You can't bring this into a federal court-house. You aren't allowed to record any of the proceedings. It's against the law."

I turn to Mona.

"Is that so?"

"That's right. I didn't know you were bringing a tape recorder or I would have told you."

I look back at the cop.

"I don't intend to record any of the proceedings. I was only going to tape myself telling my reactions about what's been happening."

"Nope. Can't do that either."

"How about if I leave the tapes with you?"

I look over at Ted Mitchell. He's checking his watch. The cop opens the tape recorder and removes the tape. I watch him. He finds my peanut-butter sandwich, looks at it carefully, then takes out the pack of tapes.

"OK. I shouldn't do this, but you can keep the recorder in the briefcase and not use it. You can pick up these tapes when you leave."

He smiles. I smile back at him. I don't know if he senses how funny this all is. I smile at Mona, Clint, and Mitchell. They don't think it's funny at all. On the way up the steps from the entrance, Mona turns to me.

"If you use that tape machine and get caught, I promise I won't defend you."

We go up to a large room. It's apparently where the settlement conference is to be held. I spot Claire Woodman in the hall outside. She's knitting. She looks up as if she doesn't know me, but then grudgingly shakes hands.

"What's the matter, Claire? How's the family?"

"They're all fine, considering."

"Considering what?"

She shrugs and goes back to her work. Maybe she's catching "law," a contagious and dangerous disease. Mona comes over and urges me to follow her into the big room. Everybody's beginning to settle down. It's quite a crowd.

There's the main seating area, where I imagine visitors will sit. Then, along the right side, some plush swivel chairs. I count. Thirteen. It must be for the jury. Up front are some tables and chairs, and on a platform behind them is a large desk. It looks like a courtroom from any movie, only huge.

It's three o'clock. I'm thinking about that peanut-butter sandwich. I can smell it through the Saran wrap and the leather of the briefcase. Just then, a door opens on the left, behind the big desk. This must be Murphy, although he's dressed in civilian clothes, more like golfing togs, with checkered trousers, a shirt open at the top and a long-sleeved, loose sweater.

He crosses his legs tightly, left over right, and puts his hands up behind his head, fingers interlaced. He starts to speak. He speaks in a very soft, lyrical, lilting voice so we all lean forward to hear.

"I'm Judge Murphy, and I'm in charge of this settlement conference. We are going to settle all suits arising from the I-5 tragedy. We are not going to leave this building until every suit has been settled. I hope all of you understand that."

There isn't a voice of dissent.

"I am going to stay here twenty-four hours a day, working this out. And all of you are, too. I know we can come to compromises and reach agreement. This will not be easy for any of us. But I warn you that whatever the hour of my summons, day or night, you're to be in my chambers within five minutes—or I shall hold you in contempt of court."

At this, he looks around the room, hoping to find someone he can hold in contempt, I suppose.

"This is going to be a long session, as long as it has to be, as long as you make it. We could easily be here several days.

"Now, would each of you please stand one at a time, give your name, the reason you are here, and if it is appropriate, whom you are representing."

Again silence. I'm already feeling slightly claustrophobic. We're actually prisoners of this man. How can all these trained, educated people just sit there?

"We'll start with you, Mr. Stears."

Mr. Stears is on the extreme left of the room, but not in the jury box. He's up in the last row. He stands, says his name and that he represents a particular insurance company. We have a "thank you" from Judge Murphy, and he points to the next person in line.

This is going to take forever; there must be at least fifty people in the room. I'm between Mona and Ted Mitchell. Clint is on the other side of Mitchell. Danny is beside Clint. I was watching Judge Murphy so closely I didn't see Danny come in.

The lawyers, meanwhile, are already sounding as if they're tired of the whole thing. The plaintiffs or defendants are generally nervous. When the judge finally gets to my row, I'm surprised to find myself anxious as well. At my turn, I stand up.

"My name is William Wharton, father of Kathleen Wharton Woodman, grandfather to Dayiel and Mia Wharton Woodman, father-in-law to Bert Woodman, all of whom were killed in the accident on highway I-5 in this state. I am standing in for my wife as family representative. I am here under threat of being charged with contempt of court if I did not make the long voyage from France to this place. I have no intention of making settlement outside of court and resent having been forced to come here against my will."

So now it's out in public. I sit down. Ted Mitchell rises and identifies himself as lawyer to the plaintiffs, the Billings and Wharton families. He doesn't look happy.

After everyone has said their piece, Judge Murphy calls on the Assistant District Attorney for the state of Oregon, a heavy-set man wearing glasses.

"I am instructed as Assistant District Attorney to the state of Oregon to inform you that Judge Murphy, as settlement judge for this conference, has suggested to me, representing the state, that the maximum amount of money available from the state in these settlements for all claims relating to this accident is $300,000 as per the law."

There are no objections. I can't believe it. I look over at Mona; she puts her fingers to her lips to shush me. The judge takes over again.

"Also available for this settlement will be various amounts of insurance monies from different defendants. All of these have been entered into a general fund from which settlements will be allocated at your suggestion and my discretion.

"I suggest you gentlemen representing plaintiffs and defendants sit down and work out settlement amounts, proportionate to the general fund, which you feel appropriate to your particular case. I shall be calling you and your clients into my chambers a few at a time to see how well you are progressing with this difficult task. No one is to reveal to any client the total money in the general fund, nor the amounts of the settlements when they are made. This is an official injunction and violation of it will be dealt with severely."

On that note, he stands, turns, and walks back through the door by which he entered.

At first, there's not much movement or comment. Then, gradually, like birds searching for nesting places, lawyers, plaintiffs, defendants, drift into various corners, angles, or groups of chairs and, honest to God, pull out those innocuous, yellow, lined, legal pads. Mitchell, Mona, and Clint drift off together. Mona motions me to stay where I am. This is where the professionals get separated from the clients. Danny stays a while, then sees a newspaper on a table down at the front of the room and goes for it.

I'm still numb. I can't believe this is happening. It's like a kangaroo court, or secret fraternity initiation meeting. I'm furious.

After about ten minutes sitting alone, I pick up my briefcase and head for the door on the other side of the main desk, a matching door to the one the judge went through. I want a private place for myself. I have two ninety-minute tapes which were "accidentally" in my inside jacket pocket. If Mona wants to make an arrest, here's her chance. I want to get down some of my thoughts, and feelings.

The door, I find, leads into a relatively large room. It has a long table and comfortable chairs. There's another door at the other end which looks as if it might lead toward the judge's chambers. I settle myself with my back to the window. I put my briefcase on the table, slip a cassette into my recorder, pull out some papers and a pencil to look as if I'm writing, prop the edge of the top of the briefcase open with a ball-point pen, push the proper buttons on the recorder and start recording. I get down most of what's happened so far and how I'm feeling about it. This takes maybe ten minutes.

I go out again. I need to find our lawyers. How can they make decisions without the client?

It takes me half an hour to find them; actually, they find me. That is, Ted Mitchell does. He motions me to a chair.

"We've been thinking it over and we feel we should present our case against the trucking company, Sampson, first."

"Why not the state of Oregon? They're most responsible."

"You heard what's happened. We can't get much from the state by suing them; probably Judge Murphy won't even allow us to file suit."

"How about Thompkins? He lit the fire."

"He's filed for bankruptcy and has only $100,000 insurance available; the rest is protected by his bankruptcy, a special form of Chapter Eleven, for farmers. Everybody's going to be suing him and we'd only manage a limited portion of the whole. It wouldn't be worth it. Sampson's definitely our first choice."

"I don't want to settle. You know that, don't you?"

He doesn't answer at first.

"Yes, I know. But when Judge Murphy calls us in, he's going to put heavy pressure on us to settle. I, personally, think the case is worth close to a million dollars."

"But we won't settle."

He doesn't respond.

The day drags on. The few toilets are always occupied. There's only one phone on the courtroom floor. People keep being called in by Judge Murphy and coming out, still arguing with each other.

Meanwhile, I, at the insistence of my lawyers, have become involved in a terrible legal maneuver.

The van Bert was driving had been borrowed from his best friend Doug; it was insured for half a million dollars. This is because Doug has a garage and apparently insures all the vehicles on one policy. Another attorney wants us—that is Danny and me—to sue Bert, our Bert, for his involvement in the accident, so that this half-million can go into the "pot," this general settlement fund. Mona says Danny won't resist the idea.

I should be suing *Bert*, who was killed trying to save our family? And I should also be suing Doug because he was kind enough to lend Bert his van?

My lawyers point out that it's only the insurance company that loses, not Bert, who is dead, and not Doug. I don't care. There must be some line between right and wrong. For an hour, these lawyers keep badgering me: to them it is incomprehensible that I would keep this money out of the "pot." They act as if I'm robbing them.

Now I understand why Claire Woodman was so incommunicative: she thought I was going to sue her son. It's what her lawyer probably told her.

I go out and hunt for Claire Woodman's lawyer. I explain what has happened and confirm that there will be no suit coming from me, even at the cost of everyone's potential profit. The lawyer doesn't believe me at first, but then smiles and leads me over to Claire. She explains. Claire reaches up over her knitting, and we hug. I feel much better. She's crying. She has been sitting here, thinking the worst of me and not saying a thing. Very Oregonian, very John Wayne-ish, very lawyerish.

I walk along, looking out the windows into the courtyard. It's starting to get dark and I'm starved. Ted Mitchell and Clint say they'll cover for us while Mona and I go eat. There's a restaurant in the Hilton Hotel just down the street. We don't talk much. I bitch; she explains. I still want a jury trial, a chance to make the issue public again.

The food is expensive and isn't much good. I can see we're not going to see the judge today. I don't intend to spend the night sleeping on that courtroom floor and so, before leaving, I go to the front desk and reserve a room. I'll stick around in the courtroom till ten or so, but after that, I'm taking off. I'm pooped. I'll ask one of the team to phone me if the judge calls us to his chambers.

Mona isn't too happy with this idea. I tell her I can make it back in under ten minutes. Murphy's not going to cite me on contempt for five minutes.

When we return, neither Ted Mitchell nor Clint is there. Mona drifts around, trying to find out the latest. I see Danny and tell him what I've done concerning the suit against Bert. He doesn't seem too happy, either. I tell him if he wants to eat, I'll stand guard. I have the phone number of the restaurant at the Hilton.

I feel gritty. I'm sensing more and more that our lawyers want to settle as quickly as possible. A trial means higher costs to them, and they don't want to risk a jury.

The one phone in the court-house has a long line in front of it, educated men and women with hourly rates of a hundred and $200. The guy on the phone is screaming into it, at, I presume, his wife.

"But I've got to have at least a clean shirt. I'm beginning to smell like a sick dog."

At ten I leave. I give Mona the room number and ask her to phone me if the judge calls for us. I'm dead tired. I don't know how these people do this for a living. I close the door to my room, take my shoes, shirt, and pants off, and go right out.

And then the phone rings. I don't know where I am. Then I realize, it's probably someone phoning to tell me the judge has called for us. It's Mona. She's in her room and wants to know if we can have a drink downstairs.

We meet in the lobby. She's in an alcove, drinking a beer, an ordinary one. I slide into the chair across from her. She's watching me, lawyer fashion. She's smoking. There's a glass on the table but she's drinking from the bottle.

"What'd you think of today?"

"You mean, really? Or is this some lawyer 'lead-up-to-something' talk?"

"Really. I'd like to know. I watched you. I know you're not happy."

"Mona, would you be happy if you'd been dragged away from your work at a critical section, forced to spend $800 to fly to a place you did not want to go to, sitting in an airplane for more than ten hours, plus two hours in an airport, all because you want to live where you want to live, do what you want to do, and not go to jail?

"Then I arrive and am told I'm in the wrong town and am about 200 miles from where I'm really supposed to be. Next, I learn that the judge has pulled an end run on our lawyers, that I can't do what I want to do, that is, bring to court the state of Oregon and anyone else who was responsible for killing our daughter and practically her whole family. Then these assholes want me to sue my son-in-law just to grab his best friend's insurance money."

I break down. I put my forehead on the table and my tears splash on it. Just then, the waiter comes with another bottle of beer for Mona. When he leaves, I lift my head. He probably thinks we're lovers having some kind of quarrel, the pretty young lady leaving the bald-headed old man. Being angry and crying at the same time reminds me of when I was a kid getting beaten up in a fight. Swinging, ducking, bleeding, fighting, and crying all at once.

"Then this Judge Murphy tells us we can't sue anybody, and I'm beginning to see that nobody, not even our own lawyers, wants to go to court. They're afraid of this judge and don't trust juries, the basis of our judicial system. Judge Murphy has our hands tied, and I don't understand how he's done it, and I'm not getting an explanation. He has locked us into a courtroom that we can't leave for any reason for more than five minutes. I can't even take a crap in five minutes. And there aren't enough crappers in the whole place, if I needed to. And you ask me why I'm looking unhappy. Think about it! Are you happy?"

I spread my hands flat on the glass table, then reach for one of the little napkins which had come with the beer. I start wiping up the tears and the ring of moisture from the beer bottles. Mona reaches out and takes hold of both my hands.

"No, I'm not happy. I think a good part of what you say is true and I'm sorry to admit I'm part of it. But I have my job to keep and I'm the low woman on this particular totem-pole. There were things I wanted to tell you, warn you about, but I couldn't. I work for a large firm; Ted Mitchell is a partner in that firm. I'd like to become a partner myself, I think. This is the year I could make partner if everything goes right."

She lets go of my hands. I look her in the eyes.

"If you think it's so bad, then why don't you quit? I sure as hell would."

She looks me right back in the eyes.

"So, I feel guilty about some of these things. I don't think any of the plaintiffs' lawyers expected this. You're right: we were outmaneuvered by Judge Murphy, the state of Oregon, Thompkins's attorney, Sampson's attorney, and who knows who else. I'm sorry. That memory of your daughter and her family is being dragged through a travesty of justice. It's a trite phrase, but it seems to be what's happening."

She lights another cigarette and takes a gulp from her beer. She's pinning me down with her green-blue eyes.

"The reason I asked you to come down is that Ted Mitchell is convinced we'll be called into Judge Murphy's chambers tomorrow and has a pretty good idea of what is going to be offered us. He thinks it's too low. He doesn't want you to accept it. He'll probably say the same thing to Danny Billings. You should get together with Danny before we go see the judge."

She stops again.

"Please don't tell anyone I talked to you about this. I wasn't supposed to. Go to bed. We've worked out a watch just in case Judge Murphy decides to check out his power in the middle of the night. Do you know Murphy's law?"

"Yes, if anything can go wrong, it will."

"Keep it in mind, please. Don't shoot off your mouth tomorrow, if you can help it."

"I can't promise anything. Let me get the bill for your beers."

"No, don't bother. It'll be on the bill."

I don't ask if it's her bill, or my bill. Is this considered a legal consultation and the two beers part of my expenses?

"You go to bed yourself, Mona. Thanks for giving me some of the scoop. You should be sharp tomorrow; that's what you're paid for. By the way, what's with Ted Mitchell? He acts like a man whose mind isn't on what he's doing here."

"That's something I can't talk about either. But I tell you Ted Mitchell has a reputation as one of the best trial lawyers in the state of Oregon."

With that, we shake hands across the table and I turn away. As I'm standing at the elevator I look back and she's still sitting and is lighting another cigarette. Maybe she has another appointment, maybe with Danny.

I get upstairs to my room, undress completely, put on my pajamas, and drop off into the red blur of sleep.

CHAPTER 14

I PULLED the drapes before I went to sleep, so it's eight-thirty when I wake. I shower, dress, and walk across to the court-house to see what's going on. It looks as if everybody's there, but I don't see Mona, Clint, or Ted Mitchell. I hang around a few minutes, then go back to the hotel for breakfast. I order the continental style and rush it a bit. There's no telling with a guy like this Judge Murphy. Mona spots me and rushes up. Ted Mitchell is behind her.

"Where were you? We've been looking everywhere."

"At the hotel having breakfast. Where else?"

"We called your room and had you paged."

She's nervous. Ted Mitchell is nervous, too. I smile at him, and he sits down. Danny is behind him.

"Judge Murphy wants a conference. I told him you weren't here, so he took in another group but wanted us to make sure we were all together when they came out."

There is excitement in Mitchell's voice.

"Judge Murphy then called me in alone about fifteen minutes ago and told me that Sampson has offered to settle for $650,000."

He looks at me. I try not to react. I wait.

"I told him, in my opinion, it wasn't enough but I needed to consult our clients."

He waits again. The lawyer's expectant pause, waiting for the other person to commit. I jump in.

"If he's talking about settlement out of court, it isn't enough. But you know I don't want to settle. I want a jury trial. Money is not the reason I'm here. You know how I feel about this."

I turn toward Mona. She nods, but her face is white.

"Aside from protecting my wife and me against any possible suits that could be brought against us, my reason for entering this whole legal mess is to bring the dangers of field burning once more before the public eye."

Mitchell turns to Danny.

"How do you feel about this offer, Danny?"

"That's a lot of money. What do you think the case is worth?"

"I feel it's worth at least $800,000. Will, in the little time we have, maybe you and Danny ought to talk this over. We'll stay out of it."

I start up the aisle. Danny follows.

"Let's go outside where there's some air and sunshine, Dan."

We sit on a granite post. The sun feels soothing and warm. He starts.

"What do you have against settling, Will?"

"I think we have a strong case, Dan, one that any jury will settle in our favor. But that isn't the only reason. I want a jury trial. It's why I'm here. I want to bring this whole scandal out in the open. If we make Sampson defend itself in court, it'll start blaming the state of Oregon or Thompkins or anyone it can. This will put us in a good position when we go after those two later."

"Yeah, but the judge has thrown all that money in the pot. We can't sue them."

"Have you agreed to putting that money in the pot, Danny—or taking any of it? Has anybody asked you about it? Has Ted or Clint or Mona asked you if you want that?"

"Well, no, but they're lawyers, and it seems like a good idea to get all this over with. You never know about juries. They can decide almost anything. We could wind up with nothing."

185

"So, you'd like to settle rather than go to court. Is that it?"

"I'd hate to lose all that money on a gamble. I wouldn't feel right about Wills."

"OK. I'll compromise. I hate to take a chance on not having a jury trial, but let's push Sampson and Judge Murphy somewhat. How about a million even? I've heard Mona and Clint talk about those kinds of numbers. That's the figure given in the original complaint, a million against Sampson, and a million against Thompkins, just as punitive damages for negligence, let alone personal and property loss. Those are the specific claims for relief presented by Ted Mitchell and Mona Flores. We'd be letting them off easy at a million."

"Is that right? A million each, just for punitive damages? I didn't know that."

"Well, what do you say? Here comes Mona to lasso us into the corral."

"OK. I'll go along with that, a million, nothing less."

I stick out my hand and we shake. Mona comes up smiling.

"So you two have worked it out between you?"

"That's right, Mona. Danny and I are in total agreement."

She looks surprised and expectant.

We walk back into the courtroom.

As we enter, Judge Murphy emerges from his warren, three other people with him. He looks around until he spots Mitchell, then motions us toward him.

As we come to the door, he shakes hands with all of us, first with Mitchell, then Mona, along with a slight bow, then Danny and, finally, me. There's a row of chairs along one wall. Judge Murphy closes the door behind us. He's smiling as he moves toward a leather swivel chair and sits down. He looks us over, making a washing movement with his hands.

"Well, we're all together at last."

He looks quickly at me.

"I hope the Good Lord will help us reach some kind of agreement in this complicated and many-faceted case.

186

"I'd like each of you to tell me your feelings, honestly, about what you would consider an adequate and fair compensation for your loss or that of your clients. As you probably know, I've already told Mr. Ted Mitchell the amount I think would be a proper settlement. Has he informed you all of this?"

We bob our heads in agreement.

"Well, who'd like to speak first? I want each of you to be honest now and state your opinion of a fair settlement."

He waits.

Nobody speaks. There's a long silence. I start looking around the room. It's a lot more comfortable than what we've got out there in the bull pit. There's another door that probably leads to a bathroom and a bed.

He continues scanning us. I've volunteered enough; I'm learning the legal game. Danny is looking at his thumbs.

Judge Murphy turns to me.

"Well, Mr. Wharton, we've already had your opinions regarding this settlement conference at the beginning of our session. Would you mind starting by telling us more about your feelings now?"

I shift in my chair, leaning forward.

"Well, first, Judge Murphy, I'd like to say that the circus out there doesn't look like any legal system I was taught in school. I see nothing resembling the normal processes of law. It's more like a three-dimensional poker game. Secondly, I have no intention of settling out of court. You know this. My lawyers know it. I feel I was shanghaied here under threat of being cited for contempt of court. I consider that a form of blackmail, coercion."

I watch him. He's nodding but the sides of his mouth are turned down. I wonder when he'll stop me. It's time to drop my bomb.

"Judge Murphy, I understand you're a Christian, a dedicated Christian. Is that true?"

"Yes, Mr. Wharton. I'm a Christian, a believer in Our Lord Jesus Christ. What has this to do with the situation today?"

"Do you read the Bible, Judge Murphy?"

He straightens up in his seat, practically sitting at attention, military style.

"Yes, daily."

"New and Old Testament, Judge Murphy?"

"That's right."

"Do you consider the administration of justice to be a function of God Almighty?"

I almost expect him to stand up and salute. I'm afraid to look over at Mitchell or Mona.

"I say this to my friends in the law all the time. As lawyers and judges, we are functionaries of God Almighty and should regard our responsibilities accordingly."

I pause, a respectable imitation of a genuine lawyer's expectant pause.

"Judge Murphy, do you remember what Christ said to the tax collectors in the temple? I believe it's in Matthew, twenty-first chapter."

I hurry on. I don't want to be interrupted.

"To refresh your memory, it was, 'Render unto Caesar the things that are Caesar's and to God the things that are God's.'

"Judge Murphy, I believe that out there"—I point over my shoulder—"we are not living by the words of Jesus. Mammon is running riot, Judge Murphy. There's the smell of brimstone. No one speaks of justice or injustice, right or wrong, good or bad. Everything has been reduced to money, written out on those little yellow legal pads. The entire room reeks of corruption. Again, Matthew, chapter six, verse twenty-four: 'You cannot serve God and Mammon.'

"I want nothing to do with this sacrilege, Judge Murphy. I consider it blasphemy."

I stop while I'm ahead. There's a long silence. I keep focused on Judge Murphy's pale eyes until he turns away.

"Well, I guess we know pretty well where you stand, Mr. Wharton. It's obvious you don't have much knowledge of the law, respect for it, or how it operates. Let's hear from Mr. Billings, now."

Danny lifts his head but doesn't really look at Judge Murphy.

"I don't exactly agree with Mr. Wharton, but I think the figure you mention for settlement of this case is too low."

"You mean, Mr. Billings, that you want this case to go to a jury?"

"Not exactly. But I think my son deserves more than a part of $600,000."

There's a long silence. I'm wondering when a lawyer thinks he ought to give counsel.

"Think about it, Mr. Billings. Think about the possibility of your boy, Wills, hearing total strangers in a courtroom, talking about his mother, saying things he might remember all his life. Maybe some things he won't want to remember?"

It's right there that Danny starts to break down. At first I think he's kidding, but I should have seen it coming. He puts his head in his hands and begins to sob. I look at Ted Mitchell, then at Mona. They are like the statues at Abu Simbel, expressionless, immobile. We all watch as Judge Murphy plays the soap opera judge, sketching out a scenario with Wills on the witness stand, witnesses testifying to what nefarious acts we don't know. He goes on and on in his soft, lyrical voice.

Finally Danny gets it out.

"I don't want Wills in any courtroom. I don't want him to suffer like that. I'm willing to settle right now, your Honor."

There it is. I look at Mitchell, at Mona. They still don't budge. The case is going down the drain, and they're not making a move. I can't take it.

"Mr. Mitchell, as our chief counsel, representing Steele, Cutler and Walsh, could you please tell Danny the realities of what can actually happen if we go to court?"

Mitchell clears his throat, looks at Mona, then at me. He aims his speech at Danny, avoiding the eyes of Judge Murphy.

"Danny, if we go to court, Wills doesn't even need to appear in the courtroom if you don't want him to. He was not a witness to the accident; he has testified already in the deposition concerning almost any question the defendants might have. I would not recommend that he appear.

"If for some reason, he does appear, I would be the one who would ask for his testimony. We would not allow cross-examination. He's below age for that."

It's what I thought, but I wasn't quite sure. I chime in.

"You see, Dan, there's nothing to worry about here. Mr. Mitchell is our counselor. He would never allow the kind of thing Judge Murphy is talking about to happen."

But I can see Dan isn't hearing. He's just holding his head in his hands, shaking it slowly and saying over and over how he'd never allow Wills to hear people talk against his mother in a court. I'm trying to think of alternatives. I'm hoping for some help from Ted Mitchell and Mona Flores. They don't look at me. I try once more.

"Danny, you're the daddy. You must decide this. There's nothing I can do. I think you're making a wrong decision, but it's your decision to make. If you think you're protecting Wills, despite what Mr. Mitchell has just said, that's your right."

Still no reaction. I look at Judge Murphy. He's got the worst shit-eating grin on his face I've seen in years.

"Mr. Wharton, I guess you're from the 'tough guy' school, aren't you? Let the young people find out about the realities of life so they can handle themselves. Is that it?"

"Judge Murphy, you couldn't be more wrong. I love my children dearly and I'm here because one of the 'tough guys' in your state ran a semi-trailer truck over our beloved daughter, her husband, and her two lovely children, our grandchildren. Be careful what you say, it's on the verge of slander."

I turn to Ted Mitchell.

"Mr. Mitchell, although you and Ms. Flores have been treating our cases as one, in reality, it's two cases, isn't it? I am your client only because Dan's wife, who is a legal secretary, found you as a reputable legal firm in the state of Oregon and recommended you to my wife and me. She was concerned we might be sued. We did not intend to sue. It turns out her concerns were valid. There are several parties who have instituted suits against us."

They look at each other. They whisper back and forth. Mitchell turns to me.

"Technically, probably that position has some validity."

He looks at Judge Murphy. The judge nods his head. I go on.

"Well, if Dan insists on settling Wills's case this way, at any settlement figure, regardless of its insufficiency, I, as representative for my wife, Rosemary, and myself, wish to dissociate our case from his."

There's a long silence. Judge Murphy stands.

"Mr. Wharton, I think you and Ms. Flores may leave now. I'll stay here and discuss the situation with Mr. Mitchell and Mr. Billings."

We stand and leave, Mona working her way past Mitchell's knees. I'm still half hoping Danny will change his mind. This money belongs to our grandson, his son.

Outside, Mona goes up the aisle ahead of me. I follow. I think she's mad at me, but mostly she's rushing into that corridor to light a cigarette. First things first.

We stand, not speaking, while she takes that important long drag.

"Jesus, Will! Why couldn't you have told us what you were going to do?"

"You were there, Mona. I had no idea what was going to happen. Danny succumbed to the overwhelming badgering by Murphy. You two didn't help at all. What should I have done? I'm not a lawyer and I needed help. Did you want the entire case settled at Murphy's price? 'Murphy's law,' Murphy's kind of law? That's what was going to happen and you know it. Tell me what else I could have done."

She takes another drag, looks at me through the smoke.

"We could have asked for a recess to talk it over."

"Could I have done that? It seems that's what lawyers are for, or at least you could have told me then and there that I could have done it, and I would have. Everybody was doing nothing."

"You're impossible."

"All right. You're the professional lawyer. Tell me what I should have done, what I can still do."

"Oh, shit! It's all such a mess now. I'm not even sure we can divide this case. I've never heard of it happening before. Sure, Judge Murphy nodded his head as if it were OK, but do you trust him?"

"Of course not. Why should I?"

"Let's go have a beer until Ted and Danny come out from this conference."

By the time we return to the courtroom, Ted Mitchell is already there, waiting. He waves us over. I don't see Danny.

"Well, Judge Murphy made an offer to settle the case with Danny."

He pauses, looks at Mona and then at me.

"He's offering $550,000 for a settlement on Wills. Danny's accepted."

I try to read his face. My sense is that he isn't put out. I do some calculations in my head. Steele, Cutler and Walsh comes in for $137,750, for their twenty-five percent. That leaves $372,000, less all the other expenses. I'm sure $200,000 or $300,000 less than Wills would have gotten with a jury trial.

I'm frustrated.

"Where did the money come from? How much of it was Sampson money and what part of it came from the pot?"

It's the first time I see Mitchell look confused.

"I mean, did Murphy include my part of the pot along with what he gave Wills? I'm not settling, you know. I'm not settling with Sampson nor with Oregon nor with Thompkins. I'm convinced there have been some questionable decisions made by Judge Murphy in this conference. Murphy can't include money from the pot which was meant for Rosemary and me since we've never said we'd settle. In fact, I've said publicly and privately that I have no interest in an out-of-court settlement."

He doesn't move. Mona has that "I need a cigarette" look. She leans forward.

"But you want Wills to have the best settlement he can get, don't you? Considering what happened in our conference with Judge Murphy, with Danny surrendering his right to a jury trial, it would be hard to get more. It is quite a bit of money, you know."

"Yep, about $350,000 after all the nibbles have been taken out of it. It could be half again more, you know that."

There's silence again.

It's clear Rosemary and I are going to court on our own, at great disadvantage. I don't really want to make a big deal out of the money Murphy awarded Wills from our share of the "pot." I don't even accept the "pot" as valid.

CHAPTER 15

*T*HE NEXT DAY, early, Judge Murphy tells all the plaintiffs and defendants they may leave. Only their legal representatives need stay for the final summary of the settlement conference. I check out of the hotel. I put my bags in Mona's car. She has volunteered to drive me back up to Portland.

For the final summary, I dress in my "lawyer costume," including briefcase, but without the tape recorder. I'm about out of tape anyway. When we take our places, I smuggle myself between Mitchell and Mona as we go down the aisle. Mitchell looks surprised and unhappy to see me. I don't see Danny or any of the other plaintiffs. I turn toward Mona.

"This isn't exclusively for legal representatives, is it? Judge Murphy said defendants and plaintiffs may go home, but he didn't say they *must* go home. If he doesn't want me in here for the summary, he can just tell me. I promise not to make a scene."

"Why do you do things like this, Will? It just makes things more difficult."

"I've come a long way for this conference, Mona, and I still don't understand what's been going on. I feel like the blind man in a game of blind man's buff. I just want to know. What's so bad about that?"

She shakes her head and I tag along. They take a place about halfway toward the front. I sit beside Mona. A few lawyers turn their heads but keep their expressionless lawyer masks in place.

Settlement

Judge Murphy strides into the room, still not wearing robes. Behind him is a court reporter.

Judge Murphy seems very nervous. He crosses and uncrosses his legs, sometimes tucking his hands between them at the knees. It's obvious he's been through some hard times, although I can't feel sorry for him. I hope he doesn't spot me.

He briefly summarizes what has happened over the past few days. He's tired and he doesn't elaborate much.

He congratulates all who have participated in the settlement conference and is pleased to announce that as he had hoped, every suit has been settled to everyone's satisfaction.

I look over at Mona and Mitchell. Mitchell has reluctantly put up his hand.

"Your Honor, Judge Murphy, there is one exception. The suit involving my clients, Mr. and Mrs. Wharton, and Sampson National Carriers, Inc. has not been settled."

There's a long silence. Judge Murphy puts his hands over his mouth, joined together like a sign of prayer.

"Thank you for correcting me, Mr. Mitchell. But I think we can go through the rest of the roll to put this conference on the court record." He signals to the court reporter and announces that from this point on, all will be on record.

He then starts with another count-off. He's asked for representatives of each of the clients to stand and tell what the situation is in relation to their suits. Each stands and says basically the same thing, their names, the organization for which they work, the names of their clients, and a brief statement that a settlement for their suit has been agreed upon, no numbers. I'm waiting to see what Mitchell is going to say. If he says that all suits have been settled in our case, I'm going to break cover and deny it. Only the Sampson suit has been settled for Danny; it hasn't been settled for me and Rosemary. And there are also the two other suits, against the state of Oregon and against Thompkins. I do not consider those settled; in fact those weren't even discussed.

Finally, the Judge reaches our group. It isn't Mitchell who stands, but Mona. I lean forward, listening carefully. She says that all the suits, with the exception of the cases of Mr. and Mrs. Wharton, have been satisfactorily resolved. It was that word "cases" I was listening for. It's in the court record now. It's more than one case, it's not just Sampson.

After this count-off is finished, Judge Murphy scrunches down in his chair, hands still in front of his face. He checks to confirm that the court reporter is still taking down what he says.

"I'm putting all of you under an injunction to say nothing about this settlement conference to anyone."

There's another silence. Then one of the senior lawyers speaks up from the back.

"Judge Murphy, that's going to be difficult. I already have a battery of reporters at my office and on the phone. There's no way to pretend this didn't happen."

Murphy scrunches lower.

"All right, you can say it happened, but no one is to give any details or disclose the amount of money in the general settlement fund or the amounts of money involved in any of the settlements."

Another lawyer speaks up. It's Mr. Crosley, lawyer for Mr. Thompkins.

"Judge Murphy, I don't see how we can keep the amounts of the settlements from the public. You dismissed virtually all of the plaintiffs and defendants, who know those figures, and I don't think you can put such an injunction on them. There's no way to stop this information from being known to the general public."

Judge Murphy sinks lower, if that's possible; he has almost slid off the front of the chair and onto the floor. He's keeping his hands in front of his mouth in this praying position.

"OK. There's nothing we can do about that. But here is the official announcement which we will make."

He slides back and sits up.

"A settlement conference for the suits brought forward relating to the massive I-5 automobile and truck crash on August third, involving twenty-four vehicles, many injuries and seven deaths, was held in the federal courtroom in Eugene, Oregon. The conference continued day and night for three days. Federal Judge Thomas Murphy presided.

"All suits were settled to the satisfaction of all concerned. This was one of the largest settlement conferences ever held in the state of Oregon."

I look over at Mitchell and Mona. Mitchell already has his arm up to get Murphy's attention.

"Judge Murphy, my clients Mr. and Mrs. Wharton have not settled."

There's another long silence as Murphy gradually starts sliding down in his chair again. He looks to the ceiling, maybe to God. Who knows?

"All right. We change it to: *virtually* all suits brought before this conference were satisfactorily settled."

Mitchell seems more satisfied with this. It's close enough to the truth, so I sit on my hands. Murphy sits up straight again and points his finger.

"Remember, all of you are under an injunction not to talk about any details of this conference."

There's not a murmur. Judge Murphy stands and returns to his little room. It's all so anticlimactic. We walk out to the hall. Mona lights a cigarette. She tells Mitchell that she and I are driving to Portland in her car. He nods. In his mind, he has already left.

CHAPTER 16

*M*ONA AND I go out to the car. She says there's still time to avoid some of the Eugene "coming home traffic."

"You see, Will, I grew up in Tacoma, but I worked for the appellate court here. I know this town well. I also went to the university in Corvalis. Now, that's a nice town, fewer than 40,000 people and beautiful country all around. I think you'll like Oregon better after you see the way we're going to go, not up the I-5."

And she's right. The country is different from what I've seen, more green, orchards of fruit-trees, some in bloom. The road isn't a big highway, just twisting, easy curves, rolling hills.

But I'm still carrying the load of the conference on my shoulders. I have so many questions. A magician has done all his tricks and I haven't figured out one of them. I feel miserably frustrated. Mona catches my mood and doesn't say much except to point out some of the more beautiful sights.

We stop at a bar in Corvalis, one of her favorites from the days when she was a student. It's more a coffee-house than a bar, filled with young people, loud chatter and loud music. We manage to find a table against a back wall, as far from the music as possible, and she goes up to the bar for some beer.

She returns with two steins as big as those the Germans drink in Munich, only made of faceted glass.

"Here, this might be good for what ails you."

She laughs.

"Mona, can you tell me now what was happening down there? I'm not stupid but I still don't understand. There seemed to be so much maneuvering behind the scenes."

"That's the way Judge Murphy set it up. Probably there was no other way it would work, a gigantic settlement like this. I didn't like it, but it worked for just about everybody. Danny seemed to get what he wanted, so did Claire Woodman."

"But did Wills? I feel awful that I couldn't protect him from something like this happening. I've known Danny since he was a sophomore in high school, dating Kate. He has trouble with this kind of thing. So I was worried, and it turned out I had every reason. But for the life of me, I can't think of what I could have done without some on-the-spot legal advice, and neither you nor Mitchell jumped in to help."

"You've got to understand. I do what Ted Mitchell tells me to do. I am only in charge of the little things that have to be done to advance the case. The big decisions were Mitchell's. Let's not talk about it, huh?"

She starts looking in her purse. I think it's for a cigarette, but it's for her wallet. I pull mine out.

"I'll get it. This doesn't have to go on the expense account, even though I've been pumping you as a lawyer."

"Oh, shit! Lawyers always talk about problem clients, and now I understand what they mean."

I pull out my money, check the bill, and leave enough. I stand up.

"As far as I can see, lawyers think they're gods and clients are supposed to behave like clouds, just going where they're blown."

I follow her out to the car. The sun is going down fast. It should be a beautiful sunset. I wish I could get the hostility out of my mind and enjoy myself, remember how lucky I am to be alive, not burned to a crisp like Kate and the rest of them, to be riding with a bright, good-looking woman through this lovely countryside. I should appreciate all that

199

Mona has been doing to make the entire thing less painful. As we slide into the car and she puts the key into the ignition, I turn so she has to look at me. Her face is in that frozen lawyer mode.

"Listen, Mona. I'm sorry for being such a creep, but I am deeply upset. I feel I've failed my dead daughter and I've failed Wills. Everything I've done seems to have backfired.

"I know you're doing your best to get me through this mess and I appreciate it. Just have a little more patience. You live with it. I don't. It's hard to change. I hate feeling I'm being pushed around, even when it's supposed to be for my own good; maybe especially. Do you understand?"

"Wow, you don't sound like a client after all. Maybe I'll be able to drive us up to Portland without running into a pole, if you can keep talking like that."

And we do. The drive is pleasant. I tell her about my books and my painting. She knows more about me as a person, not just as a client, than I thought. She has recently read *Birdy* and *Dad*, likes them both. She tries to explain why she has had so many husbands—she's in her third marriage—and how much she loves her little boy, Jonah, and how she is worried that her current husband feels guilty because she's the prime earner in the house. She admits to being the kind of person who doesn't save, just keeps ahead of her credit cards.

I tell her what a skinflint I am. How I hate to spend money for things that don't last. I try explaining why I live in France, didn't want our children to grow up in America. Some of this she knows, most of the real reasons she doesn't.

We eventually reach Portland, where Mona drops me off at my friends the Wilsons'. We shake hands goodbye. Because I refused to settle, my claims against Sampson, the truck firm, will go to trial. Maybe later we'll be able to take on Thompkins and the state of Oregon. It's my one consolation. Mona says that the trial will be in late September and that I should be there a week or two before then.

Settlement

Karen and Robert are on the porch. Robert turns on the light. He walks down the steps. I introduce them all around.

Karen comes up to give me a kiss and I shake hands with Rob. It's great to be with friendly people and not to be on my guard all the time.

I stagger into the bedroom and find the bed all made and ready for me. I drop my bag, hang my clothes over it, and fall into the bed. I'm getting to be a regular vagabond—or is that tramp? On that thought I drop off.

In the morning, I take a shower before going into the kitchen. I'm still feeling bleary-eyed. Rob is reading the newspaper at the breakfast table. He looks up at me. Karen is out, I guess.

"I see you settled after all."

He passes over the front page of the newspaper. There it is in big print. LEGAL FEUD IN FATAL I-5 PILE-UP ENDS. I start reading. I can't believe it.

The settlement of numerous lawsuits stemming from a fatal twenty-eight vehicle collision on I-5 in 1988 brought expressions of relief Saturday from persons involved in the mammoth legal battle.

"It's just a relief," said Claire Woodman of Falls City. "It's been a long time." Woodman's son, Bert, died in the crash along with his wife Kate and two young daughters.

"I'm certainly pleased that it's been disposed of to everyone's satisfaction," said Arthur Johnson, an assistant District Attorney General for the state of Oregon . . . [Lord, I can't believe it! They're denying it to the very end.] US magistrate Joseph Murphy and a battalion of lawyers negotiated the settlements in a series of meetings between Tuesday and Friday. All parties in the claims agreed not to make public the amounts of the monetary awards to eighteen plaintiffs involved. ["Agreed" isn't quite the word.]

The fiery, chain-reaction accident occurred August eighth, 1988, south of Albany, when an out-of-control field burn cloaked the freeway with smoke. Seven persons were killed and eighty-seven others were injured.

An eleven-day moratorium on field burning followed, and attempts to have the practice banned or curtailed, continue. Willamette Valley grass seed farmers use field burning to destroy excess straw, pests, and diseases. Most of the claims named the state of Oregon and Albany area farmer, Paul Thompkins.

Woodman said that she was "basically" satisfied with the settlement made to her son's estate.

"I think Judge Murphy bent over backwards to reach an agreement," she said . . . Woodman said that justice really would be served in the case when stricter controls are placed on field burning . . . [How is letting these people off the hook going to stop field burning?] "That's what we wanted all along," she said. "We're afraid it's going to happen again." Woodman said that she has been surprised by the increase in traffic along I-5 in recent years and fears that another such accident there could be even more catastrophic . . .

Woodman said that she has been energetically working in support of a ballot initiative being circulated by Oregonians Against Field Burning . . .

Arthur Johnson stressed that the federal magistrate did not settle the claims by decree. Instead, the settlement work came about through concerted legal work from many parties . . . [This is too much! There's no question that Judge Murphy announced at the beginning that we, all of us, were to be there twenty-four hours a day for as long as he wanted, and if anyone he called was not there within five minutes they would be charged with contempt of court. If that isn't being forced, what is?]

Johnson said that the case had been one of the most investigated and documented cases in the state. But although it was complex, because of the number of vehicles, injuries and lawsuits [not to mention deaths!] it did not pose unusually difficult legal issues. A ruling was made in April. A Linn County Circuit Judge said the state would pay no more than $300,000 for all claims from the incident. [When? In April, just days before the settlement conference: an appeal in a *lower* court concerning a *federal* court ruling which was then accepted by Judge Murphy! And the appeal was granted by a Linn County Circuit Judge, right in the middle of the seed-growing area where the accident happened!]

"Once the court ruled that the maximum liability of the state was going to be $300,000, then everything else fell into place," Johnson said. "Without that ruling, everyone was thinking, 'The state's going to pay me a million dollars.' "

Johnson said that although claims were settled with regard to the state, one case involving two of the parties in the collision has yet to be resolved. [I think: "Here it comes at last."]

Jimmy Phillips of Kaymond, Washington, said Saturday night he had not been informed of a settlement. Phillips was moving his family from Arizona to Washington when they were caught in the crash and lost their vehicle and most of their belongings.

"I'd like to see it come to an end," he said. "They keep saying it's going to soon, but we haven't had word yet of anything definite." Phillips's sister-in-law, Joy Phillips, who was also injured in the accident, would not comment on the matter.

Rob looks up at me as I put the paper down on the table. I have a hard time speaking at first.

"This entire report is untrue, Rob. No, I didn't settle, never had any intention to, as you know. I can't believe all those lawyers, even mine, were so thoroughly fooled."

"You sure, Will? The AP is usually pretty careful about those things. So is the *Oregonian*."

"May I use your phone, Rob?"

I'm so mad I'm beginning to shake. I want to do this right.

I pull down the phone directory and look up AP. I'm surprised it's there. I phone. A woman answers. I give my name and my relationship to the I-5 crash. I tell her that the AP report in the *Oregonian* is incorrect.

There's a pause.

"One minute, would you hold onto the line, please?"

Rob is watching me. I'm trying to keep it all together. I have the newspaper in my hand; my hand's trembling. After about five minutes, another voice comes over the phone. It sounds like a slightly older woman. I explain again. She apparently has the article in front of her.

"What, exactly, was reported incorrectly?"

"The fact that all claims were settled. I was a plaintiff of one of the most important cases at that conference. We lost our daughter, two granddaughters, and a son-in-law. My wife and I did not settle with anyone."

There's a pause again. I don't want to lose her.

"It's in the court record if you wish to verify my statement."

"Mr. Wharton, are you sure of this information?"

"Absolutely. I had no intention of settling. At the summary, the judge tried to make a statement that all claims had been settled, but our lawyers there corrected him. He reluctantly agreed to change the phrasing to 'virtually" all cases were settled. This was agreed to by the lawyers involved. As you can see, that word is not given in the headline nor the article. I should think AP would want to report the correct version of what happened at this important conference. I, and my wife, have no desire to settle this case out of court."

Again, there's a long pause.

"Would you give me your name once more and your relation to the settlement conference? Could you tell me again in detail what actually happened."

I do this. I wait.

"Mr. Wharton, we'll check this out with the reporter and with Judge Murphy and, if necessary, the court record. We certainly appreciate your having called our attention to this potential misinformation."

"You're very welcome."

I hang up. I look over at Robert.

"Well, I've done what I can. I don't really expect anything to come of it. I've lost most of any confidence in large organizations, and I guess AP has to qualify as one."

"You're positive about this, Will? I wonder why they'd do a thing like that? It could make a body lose confidence in just about everything."

"I know what you mean, Rob."

I spend most of that day taping all my remembrances and reactions. Probably none of the kids, nor Rosemary, will take the time to listen to this, but it will be a good record for me when it comes to writing my book. This book is beginning to look like my last-ditch effort to fulfill Bert's mandate about field burning. If the book is published, it might help Oregonians see how they've been, are being, ripped off by big business and big government.

It also helps get some of it out of my system. I'm burying it alive in that little black, battery-driven box. I sit down and fill seven ninety-minute tapes, and I'm hoarse when I'm finished.

The next morning Rob takes me to the airport. We're out of the house by six-thirty. It isn't too bad a drive at that time in the morning. Rob drops me off at the departure gate. I check in, carrying my bags straight through to avoid waiting for them in Paris. I sit in a lounge chair near a window. There aren't many people. I've never seen an airport so empty. I look up.

There's Mona running toward me. She's holding a newspaper. She has a big unlawyerlike smile on her face. She gives me a good kiss and then shows me the newspaper. She holds it out flat in both hands, facing me. I would never have believed it. The headline is:

I-5 CLAIM REMAINS UNSETTLED
The Associated Press
Contrary to earlier reports, not all legal claims stemming from the deadly 1988 chain reaction crash on I-5 have been settled.

US Magistrate Joseph Murphy said Monday that he was quoted incorrectly and did not say last week that all claims had been resolved.

One claim, by William Wharton, has not been settled. Trial is set for September twenty-fifth.

Four members of the Wharton family were killed in the crash.

"I have no desire to settle . . . I was blackmailed into coming here," Wharton said.

Murphy said he was aware that Wharton was not satisfied with the legal processes that resulted in the settlement in Eugene last week of all other claims in the crash.

"He has strong feelings about his idea of the judicial process," Murphy said.

Wharton, who lives in France, said Murphy required all eighteen plaintiffs and their lawyers involved in the court case to be no more than five minutes away from the courthouse for three days.

"We were virtually locked in. He just wore everybody down," Wharton said. "I'm very unhappy about it all."

Murphy said no one was forced to settle. "All I will say is the settlement conference process is a mediation process," Murphy said. "The court does not require anyone to settle. They settle of their own free will if they choose to, and that prerogative is strongly protected by the court . . . " [Yes, but all the lawyers did not want to antagonize Judge Murphy. They did not want to put their law or insurance firms at a disadvantage some other time. So, they held their tongues, afraid of the judge's power.]

Except for Wharton, all eighteen parties who made claims agreed to out-of-court settlements.

The lead defense counsel Henry Crosley called it "One of the most complex pieces of litigation in Oregon history."

Nearly all of the lawsuits were against the state of Oregon and Paul Thompkins, the Albany area farmer whose field burning investigators blamed for the collision.

I can't believe it. I can hardly talk to Mona. I thank her for bringing me the newspaper. She has an extra copy for me. I don't want to look at it again. My sense of correct behavior has been vindicated, and I'm not capable of making any logical comment. We hold onto each other for a minute, kiss, slowly, once on each cheek, French style. I pick up my bag; my flight is boarding. I look back. Mona yells, "I'll see you in September."

I nod, smile, and turn.

CHAPTER 17

W E S P E N D the summer in New Jersey, as usual. It's difficult, being in the place where we last saw Kate and her family, but while there, on the beach, I prepare for the upcoming trial, listening to all the tapes I made just after the conference. I take notes on my own yellow legal pad. I have so many questions. I still can't put it together.

After a few weeks, Ted Mitchell phones personally. He says, without prologue, that he is dissociating himself from the case. He will not elaborate. He suggests that I find another lawyer. Steele, Cutler and Walsh will then give the new lawyer what it has already discovered.

I'm stunned. The trial is only two months away. I ask if he could recommend a lawyer. He says that Ms. Flores may have some ideas. I ask if this means that Steele, Cutler and Walsh is abandoning the case. How does this relate to our contract for contingency? There's a pause.

"You can work that out with Ms. Flores. I'm only telling you I am no longer associated with your case."

With that, he hangs up. For a few minutes I sit by the phone. Then I tell Rosemary. She knows how unhappy I've been. She suggests that I phone Bud for advice. Bud is our family lawyer.

"He'll know somebody in Portland he can recommend. At least he can tell us what to do."

I phone and go through all the secretaries until I reach Bud. I explain the situation. He asks if I could fax him my correspondence with Steele, Cutler and Walsh as well as my notes.

I go up to the local drugstore and fax what he's asked for. I set a time for him to fax me back. I bike home. But instead of faxing, he phones. "Look, Will. It seems as if your lawyers aren't exactly doing you any favors. I think you're right: they just want to settle."

"But what do we do, Bud? We don't know any lawyers in Portland."

"Well, I don't either. The first thing is to do nothing. There's no hurry. With this situation, any judge, despite your opinion of judges, is going to delay your trial.

"You've made the big mistake of asking questions of your lawyers which are not easy to answer. They may be thinking that you might want to sue them. From so little information, I don't know if you have grounds, but I can tell you one thing: never sue your lawyer. Especially if it's an outfit as big as this one seems. They have salaried people walking the corridors all day, looking for something to do. It won't cost the partnership anything to keep them busy fighting you. The legal and court costs would wipe you out before you could blink. So, just sit tight. Let them contact you."

I'm pleased to have Bud on our side. It's nerve-racking, but we follow his advice: we do nothing.

Three days later there's a phone call. It's Mona and Clint. They have a speaker phone, and when I get Rosemary on the extension, we have a four-way conversation. Mona is the first to speak.

"Ted says we can talk to you. But he's definitely off the case."

"I got that message. What is it you want, Mona?"

"He says, if it's OK with you, Clint and I can take over the case without Ted. I'd be your trial lawyer."

"You mean you'd actually go all the way to trial?"

"Of course. That's what you want, isn't it?"

"I wasn't sure anybody at Steele, Cutler and Walsh wanted it, not even you. Judge Murphy in Eugene didn't want it, and I didn't see anybody else rushing around encouraging me to go on with it."

"Well, do you want to go with us?"

"Sure. It's what I want. To be honest, I'd rather go with you two than with Mitchell."

"OK, then, we're on. I'll write you, explaining what's happened and what I hope will happen next. For the trial, we'll need expert witnesses and they will cost money. That cost has to come out of your pocket: that is, from what is awarded you by the jury. I'll explain it all in the letter."

In fact, she feels there's so much to prepare for the trial that she suggests I consider coming to Portland early. She has, she says, a very large house and I can stay with her. And so, on September tenth, I return, once again, to Oregon.

Mona's house is huge. It's brick and frame construction, very turn-of-the-century in feeling, a huge porch across the front. It has three floors, plus a large basement.

She takes me up to the top floor and shows me an unfinished room with a comfortable bed. At some time in the past, someone tried to redecorate the room but used a flame-jet to burn off the old paint and melted most of it into clumps, then gave up. There are beautiful windows looking out onto a small grove of trees.

The trial is set for the end of the month, when Rosemary will join me. Although I am here early to help, most of the pre-trial work is done by Mona in the office. While Mona is there, I figure I'll use my time getting this room into shape. I tell Mona of my plan. She's enthusiastic. She says if I drive her to work and pick her up, I can have the car to buy the things I need. She'll pay for paint or anything else I'll use. So, that's the deal.

The windows, I soon discover, must have been painted by a blind man. There's more paint on the panes than on the wood. I spend hours with a razor-blade, scraping.

Tom, Mona's husband, is a huge man, at least six-four and more than 200 pounds. He's on the phone a good part of the day, arranging listings on houses for sale. He doesn't seem to mind my being there. He's up by four or five in the morning, reading the newspaper at the breakfast table. He sits alone, drinking his coffee. Mona comes down by seven or eight, dressed in jogging clothes. I develop the habit of following her along on a bicycle while she runs. She moves at a fairly stiff pace. I could never keep up with her on foot. She usually does about two miles, mostly in a local park. I like to think of what she could do if she didn't smoke.

Throughout, she briefs me for the trial. She asks me hard questions. What if Harry Fox starts blaming you for writing a book about the death of your family? Doesn't the book invade their privacy?

I say, "I don't think so. I know they would like to stop field burning as much as I would and would be very happy with what I'm doing."

Fox, again: "But you're going to make money from this book. Doesn't that make you feel like some kind of vampire?"

"No. Most likely the book won't make any money. It's written for us, for the family."

I still can't stop from asking questions.

"I know you're trying to prepare me for what might happen at the trial, Mona, but what does all this have to do with Sampson's responsibility for the deaths?"

"You still don't understand, do you?"

"I guess not."

"Why, at the deposition, do you think Fox wanted to know exactly how much money you made?"

"Just a nosey bastard, I guess."

"I'll tell you something. Harry Fox never does anything for no reason, or just to be nosey. Remember that. When it comes to the settlement, your assets will be a factor in what an ordinary jury awards you."

The next morning, when I'm driving Mona to work, she says she wants me to go with her to see the people we hope to use as our main expert witnesses. It's an outfit called Lee's

Forensic and Metallurgical Engineers Inc. It's located in a small, one-story building near the outer limits of Portland.

There's no question as to which Mr. Lee is. His number one and number two sons stand at attention on either side of him. They have a huge drawing-board before them with complicated drawings in blue and black ink. Mr. Lee bows toward Mona and they shake hands. Mona turns to me.

"Mr. Lee has some experiments he wants to carry out to establish whether the impact which killed your family was from the front or from the back."

"What's the difference? The accident report says both impacts were a direct result of the momentum from Sampson's truck."

"But you can be sure Harry Fox is going to make a big issue of this with the jury. He'll try to claim Bert drove into the car in front of him *before* the Sampson truck hit him. It could affect the case."

I say nothing. Mr. Lee begins his presentation. He wants to make a video using small models to demonstrate the sequence of the vehicles slamming into each other.

I don't understand. "You mean you're going to make little models and push them around a few frames at a time—filming them like kids playing with toys?"

He doesn't blink an eye. He illustrates how it will work, using the little wooden trucks and cars on his drawing-board. I look at Mona.

"Honestly, Will. We need to do this. Harry Fox will have his own film showing just the opposite sequence, with Bert slamming into the vehicle in front of him before being hit by Sampson's truck. A video re-enactment is standard in auto accident trials. It's something that interests juries, that they can understand, not all that different from what they see on TV or films."

"So, at great expense, we're going to sponsor a motion picture Academy Award contest for miniature automobile crashes, with the jury as judges. You've got to be kidding. No jury is going to believe this. The judges must be filled up to the gullet with these kinds of make-believe dramas. They must know it's all phoney."

The technocrats for Forensic and Metallurgical Engineers Inc. stand there, not smiling, not arguing. Mona's lips are tightly pursed.

"Mr. Lee also has a wonderful way with juries. He has the right blend of seriousness, so they believe him, and humor, so they can enjoy him."

"So, we're also paying for Mr. Lee's thespian skills. I'm sorry, Mona, I don't see it. All I want is for us to gather the information concerning the accident, put this in a reasonable form, then present it to the judge and jury so they can make a decision. Does that make sense to you?"

"All right, we'll talk about this later. Mr. Lee has another idea. He's convinced from the positions of the bodies and the damage to the vehicles that he can prove our version is the correct one. He would like to purchase a VW van exactly like the one Bert was driving, same model, same year, and put it through some metallurgical tests. As I understand it, there's a metal connection of the front seat to the floor which he's convinced gave way so that the seats went over backward as a result of the Sampson impact from behind."

"Lord, Mona, you only have to look at the pictures taken when they were still in the van. They're stretched out on their backs. What else do we need? If he really wants to do some kind of metallurgical monkey-business test, I'm sure he can buy a van for five bucks from any junkyard. There's no reason to buy a whole Volkswagen."

I turn to Mr. Lee and his helpers.

"I'm sorry, gentlemen. But I'm the one who will pay for all this nonsense in the end, and I don't think it's necessary. Thank you for your help."

I go toward the door. Mona continues to talk to them, shaking hands all around. I realize I forgot to shake hands goodbye, but I'm not going back in. The place feels like a coroner's lab.

We walk out to the car, not talking. Mona gets her key out of her bag. I stand waiting by the passenger side door. Her face is white. She can scarcely talk. And then she starts shouting over the top of the Honda.

"Why are you like this? You can be so nice, and then at the critical moment you become vicious."

"Mona, I hate to think this case could be decided by such a childish technique."

"Don't you trust my professional judgment?"

"I think, Mona, you're out of touch with reality. I think you don't believe we can win this case. You're afraid of Harry Fox, and you don't trust juries. I imagine that not trusting juries is an occupational hazard. If anything, you're being *too* professional."

"So you don't trust my professional judgment."

"If I didn't, I'd have another lawyer. I think you're a good lawyer and we have a good relationship. We're friends and, as friends, we should say what we think and feel. It's our responsibility to each other."

"Don't talk to me about responsibility."

Suddenly, I feel terrible. Maybe she's right. Maybe my natural resistance to all authority, all experts, is the problem.

"I'm sorry, Mona. I know how much you want to win this case. But I'm being honest: I think your desire to prove yourself professionally is getting in the way. Maybe I should have an 'amateur' lawyer. Perhaps this whole business of being 'professional' rings a wrong bell with me. Professional, to me, means doing something for money. I think of professional baseball players, professional artists, the entire bag of professionals. Amateur in French means lover. It means someone who loves what they do for the work itself. They can be active or passive amateurs, it doesn't matter. These people are real lovers."

I sneak a look over at the speedometer. We're doing seventy. I'm holding onto the handle built into the roof over the window and the other hand is locked onto the holder on the armrest.

"Mona, you're a good driver, maybe a lover of driving, but you're not a professional. Please, for me, would you slow down, I'm a real wimp about fast driving."

"Boy, you really are a wussy, aren't you?"

"You bet, a professional wussy, wimp, or whatever you want to call me. I love life and I'm not ready to leave it yet, especially not broken into pieces and scraped all over a macadam road."

She slows down. She looks at me again. I look back at her. I wish she'd keep her eyes on the road, but I'm enjoying looking at her, too. Cross purposes.

"Mona, is there time for us to stop and have a beer?"

As quickly as I can think, she's swung the car across the entire road, both lanes, and pulled into a little parking-lot in front of a bar. Either she was considering the same thing, or she knows every bar within twenty miles of Portland's city center. Or maybe she is a professional driver. The way she made that turn, she could have been screeching around the curves at Le Mans.

Inside is dark and cool. We take tables in the back.

We sit, not saying anything. The drinks arrive. I hope a cop doesn't stop us on the way home.

Then, I can feel myself about ready to cry, but if it comes, it comes. I'm getting better at crying. I even cry when I don't know what I'm crying about. I can cry over a picture in a newspaper or when I hear about a kind, loving act that somebody's done, or a piece of music, or, as I said, over nothing at all. I imagine this is the sign of some neurosis with a complicated name.

I put five dollars down on the table, hoping it will cover the beers. Mona and I walk out the door, slowly, so they can stop us if it isn't enough.

The next day, Mona tells me we're going to a pre-trial conference. It's been called by Judge Higgins, the trial judge.

I dress in my lawyer clothes. We park in a parking-lot near the courtroom. Clint is already there waiting for us on the steps. I'm reminded of the settlement conference, with Ted Mitchell and Clint waiting for us. But no Mitchell this time, no security check either.

We go to a small room. Harry Fox is there with another guy, a big heavy fellow, and we shake hands all around. About five minutes later a middle-aged woman peeks in the door, and nods for Fox and Mona to come with her. We sit in silence waiting.

They come back quickly. Mona walks in her high-heeled-booted walk over to me.

"Judge Higgins doesn't want either plaintiffs or defendants at the pre-trial conference, only the attorneys. I'm really sorry to drag you all the way over here."

"It fits."

"Whatever you do, don't talk to the defendant. You'll probably be told to stay in the same room. Don't trust this guy, he's standing in for Sampson. He'll try his damnedest to wangle something, anything, out of you."

The middle-aged woman returns. She motions Mona, Clint, Harry Fox, and his fat lawyer helper into the room with the judge. She takes the Sampson man and me through the door. It opens into a medium-sized courtroom, the kind I'm accustomed to in films.

At first I wander around the room, trying some of the chairs, first the jury's, then the judge's. It's comfortable and swivels. I wish I had something to read; the other guy has a couple magazines.

"Like to borrow one of these? They're the latest *Newsweek* and *Time*."

He holds them out like the witch in *Snow White* with her poisoned apple. I take *Newsweek*. Maybe it's a test to see which one I'd choose, get some information as to my political preferences. But no, he keeps on reading.

Five minutes later he begins talking about one of the articles he's reading. I figure, the hell with it. I'll just be careful about what I say, nothing about the accident, my lawyers, the case in general, my personal opinions.

We have a great time chatting. As far as I can tell, he asks no leading questions. We talk about skiing, the baseball season, the pennant races, our children, neutral stuff. It's a good thing we have something to talk about, because the pre-trial conference goes on for over two hours. I feel guilty when Mona comes out. Should I tell her I've been friendly with the enemy?

She and Clint are all smiles. But then, so are Harry Fox and his blimp. We again shake hands, just as if we're in a boxing match before the starting bell. I don't like the feeling.

We stop at a bar around the corner from the courtroom. They're jabbering away as we go along. They seem to think they've won every point that was raised. I wonder what Harry Fox was smiling about. Maybe this is the way lawyers hide their real feelings, smiling and jabbering. I try to stop my mind from thinking that way. I'll listen.

It turns out that in most points of procedure and of admissible evidence, "we've" won. Then, Mona speaks to me directly.

"Judge Higgins wants to close the courtroom to TV. He says this issue is too controversial in Oregon, and could possibly generate a media-inspired mass hysteria. He pounded his fist and said his courtroom would not be a circus."

I look at her, then at Clint. It's so diabolical, and it isn't even their fault. They still don't understand what I want, why I want it. The only person who seems to have been listening was Harry Fox. Now I know why he was smiling.

"I give up! There's no use having a trial if nobody's going to be there to see it, to hear it. If no media can be used to put it before the people, the whole farce is an exercise in futility. How hard did you fight Judge Higgins when he tried to put this one over?"

Clint speaks.

"But we got everything we wanted, Will. We're going to win this trial and win it big. There's only a question of how much Judge Higgins will limit any award the jury makes. You have nothing to worry about."

I turn to Mona.

"And what did you say?"

"Clint's right. We've practically won the case already. Most of our time was spent arguing whether he would or would not deduct the money awarded to Wills by Judge Murphy from your jury award, and what he would do if Sampson appeals."

"And that's all?"

"Well, what else?"

"You won the battle and lost the war, that's all! Don't you see it? I know Harry Fox does. I'm sure all the seed growers and farmers will see it when they get to know about this fiasco.

"As far as I'm concerned, this trial might as well not take place. It's going to be a non-event, a total waste of two years' work on your part and mine, an insane parody of a real trial!

"I've said it all along, over and over. WE WANT AN UP FRONT JURY TRIAL! We've wanted it because we want to rub the filth and the stubble and the ashes into the faces of everyone who has anything to do with field burning, want them to experience, in total, complete detail, the destruction of my family. You had to know that. I've said it often enough.

"I don't think I'm a vindictive person, but as some compensation to my daughter, her husband, her lovely children, I want these Oregon grass-growing hicks to know what they've been a part of, what they'll be a part of again, when the next fire burns, when more autos and trucks tangle and are crushed, and their drivers along with them, into oblivion.

"Now, it will be just another private black mass in the back chapel, dry tears, echoes of muffled snickers by the people responsible; from your wonderful governor, to the last person who would not sign the petition for the referendum. How could the two of you have missed it. Didn't you listen? Or were you so caught up in the ultimate trivia game, called law, that you forgot to look at or listen to what was happening?

"It's easy to see why plaintiffs and defendants were excluded from that pre-trial conference. I'll bet our Mr. Fox was somehow behind it as I'm sure Mr. Crosley, the lawyer for the man who lit the fire, in his ice-cream suit and Buddha smile, was behind the settlement conference."

I stand up, drop some money on the table, and walk out. I don't know how to get around by public transport in Portland but I have Robert and Karen's phone number.

I find a phone booth around the corner. I'm in it when I see Mona running along the street. I don't duck, but I don't signal where I am, either. Let chance be a factor. In her high-heeled boots, she isn't quite running, but she's moving fast enough. She passes my booth, then, apparently having seen me in the corner of her eye, comes back. As I slip coins into the phone, she's outside watching me. I look back at her while the phone rings. After nine rings I put the receiver down. Chance! I go out. I don't see Clint.

"Hi there, good, old, bloodbuddy chum. What do you think of yourself as a friend now?"

I start to walk away, not knowing where I'm going. She follows, stride for stride, even in those dumb boots.

"Please, Will. Stop! Listen to me! You tried to explain but I didn't really hear you. I thought I did, but I didn't. I should have known, just by watching Harry Fox. Jesus, law can be such a fucking stupid business."

"Yes. Law sure is, at least as it's practiced in Oregon, and probably over all America, and perhaps the entire world, but it's lawyers who make it stupid. The kinds of people it attracts, the way they're trained, separated from real life, made to believe they're somehow superior to others. It makes any possibility for real justice almost negligible. Our negligent law and its indigent practitioners. It makes me sick.

"Mona, let's stop running and sit down somewhere, please."

I flop on the green bench in a small park. I spread my arms across the back. Mona sits on the edge of the bench beside me. I'm soaking wet from nervous perspiration; I must stink like a raunchy old boar.

We're both breathing heavily—me from frustration and pent-up emotion, she from trying to run in those crazy boots, and probably something else.

"Are you going through with the trial or shall I phone Judge Higgins and everybody else to call it off? If we don't notify them and then you don't show, the judge will have a good reason to call us in contempt, all of us."

"Well, as you know, Mona, I'm definitely in contempt, more so now than ever. I don't know yet what I'm going to do. But whatever I do, don't feel you have to go through with this farce because of me. I'll work it out somehow."

"Will. Are we still friends?"

I don't know how to answer. I feel so betrayed, but I know I was betrayed by a situation beyond my control and hers, or Clint's. Only another trapdoor mind like Fox's, or perhaps Judge Higgins's, with some nudging from Fox, could understand and know what was going to happen.

"I'm still your friend, Mona, and I'd like you still to be mine. It's just we don't always dance to the same music."

I can feel myself filling up, choking, on the brink of breaking down. I don't want that, not now. Mona looks away across this little park, this green oasis between high buildings. We're quiet again. She knows I'm trying to pull myself together.

"Will, I'd like you to come home with me. You can pull me off the case, never speak to me, but come home with me."

She stops, bites her lips. I see she's having a hard time, too.

I can't speak. I can't look at her either. The whole shitty thing seems such a mess. I stand up. I barely get it out.

"OK, Mona, let's go. Lawyer and client, riding off into the sunset."

CHAPTER 18

A FTER A quiet dinner, where Mona's son, Jonah, does most of the talking and Mona makes noncommittal sounds at appropriate places and Tom grunts approval in the same way, I get up and clear the table.

Over Mona's objections, I fill the sink and prepare to wash things up. This is the kind of work I always do when I'm upset at home. It smooths things out, makes them better, organizes disorganization.

Twice Mona comes in, and twice I shoo her out of her own kitchen. She knows. After the dishes, I clean everything within reach, starting with the stove, the microwave, all the counters. I'm about ready to start scrubbing floors when Mona comes in again.

"They've all gone up to bed, Will. I'd like to go sit on the porch. I can smoke there without blowing my diseased lungs all over you and maybe we can talk."

I follow her out the screen door. She reaches behind me and pulls the big door shut so it latches.

She sits on the wide railing, tests the wind with her forefinger, and lights up. I watch how, with only about four movements, she opens the pack, knocks one out, puts it in her mouth, and lights it. The smoke, illuminated by the street lamp in the dark, is like a fog. I pull a chair over from the other side of the porch and tuck it in the corner. She looks through the smoke at me.

"So where do we start?"

"I thought the question was how do we end it?"

She blows smoke slowly out her lips in what seems an unending stream. I could contemplate the twistings of that smoke in the back lighting of the street light for a long time.

"Well, Mona, I've been thinking while I was futzing around in your kitchen. I feel strongly that if I'd just stayed closer, pushed harder, paid more attention, I wouldn't be in the spot I'm in now. I succumbed to my own grief and anger. I didn't keep my eyes and ears open. I let experts do the things I should have been doing for myself. That was dumb. I trusted more than I should have. I was lazy.

"So now I don't have many alternatives. I will hate having to explain to Bert in my dreams what's happened. What I want to tell you now is strictly confidential between client and lawyer. Mona, I'm thinking of settling after all. I don't want any part of the animal act that's going to happen in that courtroom. This is between us, personally, professionally. Do you agree to that?"

"You mean I'm still part of the act?"

"Yes, you can play lion-tamer and double as the double-jointed lady."

"It can't be this simple. What are you planning?"

"A 180-degree turn, but at top speed. You can be the driver, if you want, or just step out now. I'll need a navigator."

"Come on, stop being such a wise-ass."

"What's the latest figure Sampson has come up with for a settlement? I haven't been paying much attention because it didn't mean anything to me."

"He's offered $60,000. It's Morgan who's in charge of these negotiations."

"It's all so disgusting. Imagine, one can kill four people at only $15,000 a head. Bargain-basement murder."

"It's not as simple as that, and you know it."

"Yes, I know it, but I don't like it.

"There's obviously no sum of money which can compensate for what's happened. But, I won't accept anything less than twice that on any condition. Yes, it's blood-money, black, burned, blood-money, but that's where I am now."

"So what are you going to do?"

"I hope it's 'we.'"

"I do, too."

"Thanks. We'll go the way we've been going, refusing any offer. But no more expert witness crap. Let's see if we can cut our losses a bit.

"We give off vibes to Sampson, Fox, everybody, as if we're dead sure we have the trial in our pocket and don't intend anything except a jury decision. We make out as if we intend the trial to go on as long as we can keep it going. Steele, Cutler and Walsh isn't going to like that, neither is Judge Higgins. This might make Mr. Fox think a second time, too. They don't want a trial any more than anyone else."

She starts to light another cigarette, then stops.

"So, what happens? Don't we do anything? What do I do with all the trial preparations I've made?"

"Save them, you might need them yet, Mona. I'm sorry. This is one aspect of this entire ploy that bothers me. You've worked hard and you'd have won, I know it.

"But you know that I've been aced out of what I needed to win—a big, live court-case with heavy coverage: we're not going to get that. And after the expenses and the pot money, legal and illegal, there wouldn't be much real money left at the end.

"Anyway, if we win we'd be forced into probate, then to an appeals court, waiting a year or more while the pittance that's left is reduced even more. You see, I've been reading some of your law books, and I have been listening to you.

"Then, by contract, I need to pay lawyer's fees to Steele, Cutler and Walsh for the appeals out of my pocket. I'd be lucky to pay off the debts I've already run up. Do you get the picture, Mona? Tell me where I'm wrong."

Now she lights that cigarette. She puts her feet up onto the porch railing. She's staring up the street to the next street-lamp.

"I can't tell you where you're wrong. I'm not sure you're right all the way, but it could go that way. Don't worry about me and the case. I've been on salary. I'm not a partner, only an associate. I have a regular monthly salary just like any high-class secretary. But I still don't understand what you intend to do. Are you going to skip the trial or settle? And when?"

"Wait and see, Mona. They'll come after us soon enough. They think I'm a nutcase. They haven't yet made anything resembling a serious offer. So, for now, we're just not listening. As far as they know, we're only preparing to put them through the hoops in a courtroom."

"Mitchell will be all over us to settle."

"Yeah, he and just about everybody involved."

She puts out her cigarette and stands up. I hope I've convinced her. I stand and open the door. She looks at me as she passes.

"I hope you know what you're doing."

"You, as a lawyer, have only one thing to lose, and it isn't the case; it's the chance to win the case. In their eyes, and on their terms, I have everything to lose, but I've already lost it, so I have nothing more to lose. I don't think they've figured that one out.

"Think about it. In the morning, after you've slept on it, and you decide you want out, just tell me. I'll understand, I really will, and respect you for it."

She goes up the stairs and I stay out on the porch a little longer. I'm wishing I could have the family with me.

CHAPTER 19

*T*HE NEXT MORNING, while I'm driving Mona to her office, she keeps looking at me, not smoking, not saying anything until we're on the Hawthorne Bridge.

"OK, I've decided. I thought I'd never fall asleep last night. You deserve a chance to play it your way, crazy as it seems to me. But first I need to find out how late one can call off a civil trial without being cited for contempt. And I must do this without alerting anyone. I think I can trust Paula. She's an expert on these kinds of things. She's my best friend at the office."

She looks at her watch and runs for the door.

"Boy, are there going to be a bunch of scared, shocked people in that office. It's almost worth getting fired just to see this. Stay at the house. I'll call probably in about an hour. I think Paula will have what I need by then and I'll have started pushing the buttons to abort lift-off."

I return, and some time after breakfast the phone rings. I let it ring seven times for luck.

"Paula says we have until midnight tonight to cancel the trial. The bees are buzzing here. Mitchell took it out on me, then on Clint. But he really took it out on you. I told him you weren't going to abandon the trial, just push for a maximum settlement and what's wrong with that? According to him, everything. He says you're playing with the law and so forth. It was great.

"Now the bad news. Everybody insists that you come in and talk with Judge Steiner, another federal judge, who specializes in mediations. They've asked Fox to be there, too."

"OK. When should I be there?"

"The first conference is scheduled for ten. I'll come get you. Put on your 'lawyer's outfit.' You're really going to have to play lawyer, defendant, and plaintiff today."

An hour later we're at the court-house. Clint, Mona, and I sit on one side of a little room; Fox, with Morgan, on the other. We don't even go through the handshaking ceremony, just short nods. There's an aura of hurry. I like that; it's a good sign. A secretary comes out and asks Mr. Fox and Mr. Morgan to follow her. Mona leans close to me.

"I think we're about to have a mediation toward settlement, or Morgan wouldn't be here. Everyone's turning desperate."

Clint leans in close from the other side.

"I think you're right, Mona. They sure waited long enough."

"I think they're beginning to suspect our client's really going for a trial, even if it's closed to the media."

We sit there for the greater part of an hour. Then Fox and Morgan come out. They don't look at us. A few minutes later we're called into the room.

This mediation judge is tall with a pallid complexion. He doesn't look well. He asks us to sit down. He speaks briefly about the case, offers his condolences to me. He speaks slowly with his hands flat on the large table. He turns to me.

"You've indicated you do not wish to settle. Is that correct, Mr. Wharton?"

I nod, then remember the protocol and speak.

"That's right, your Honor."

"Then why are you here in Portland?"

"For the trial, your Honor."

"Well, I've just spoken to Mr. Fox and Mr. Morgan who represent Sampson National Carriers, Inc. in this matter and they've made what I consider a generous offer for settlement."

I sit. It's starting. He looks me in the eyes. He's been in the game a long time. It's like staring into the eyes of Steve Carlton with a bat on your shoulder. He leans forward.

"They've offered $90,000 as a settlement. What do you feel about that?"

"I think I've made it clear enough that I do not intend to settle, your Honor. Even with the restrictions placed upon the trial by Judge Higgins, I'd prefer a jury trial to an out-of-court settlement. I believe strongly in the American system of law, your Honor, and out-of-court settlements are, to me, a denial of that system."

He lifts his eyebrows, leans back and then looks down at his hands on the table, first one hand then the other.

"This trial is going to cost everybody a great deal of money and time. Our courts are full, mostly with drug or drug-related cases. Civil cases such as this can't take precedence. You do understand that, don't you?"

"The case is scheduled in Judge Higgins's court for tomorrow, sir."

"Would you prefer a postponement?"

"No, your Honor. I've already been away from my family and work too long."

"I see. Is there some figure you have in mind that you would consider a proper settlement?"

"I'd prefer not to settle, your Honor. A settlement such as you've presented would be an insult to my daughter, her husband, and their two babies. It's not possible."

"That's how you feel?"

"Yes, your Honor."

He turns to Clint and Mona.

"Would all of you please go back to the waiting-room? Ask Miss Gaitskill if she'll send in Mr. Fox and Mr. Morgan again."

We stand up to leave. We pass Fox and Morgan on the way in. We keep straight faces, not really looking away, but not looking at them. It reminds me of bargaining for a rug in the Casbah in Algiers. We sit down. Mona nervously smiles at me.

We sit about fifteen minutes and are called in again. Judge Steiner is sitting in the same place. Fox and Morgan pass us on our way in. Something about it all seems so silly. Why, since we're obviously negotiating, not just all sit around this big table and talk it out?

We sit down again in the same places.

The judge is smiling—the first smile I've seen on a face that I don't think smiles very often.

"Mr. Fox, in an effort to avoid jamming the courts and to save his client and yours considerable sums of money"—a nod to Mona and Clint—"has offered $100,000 as a settlement. I'll be honest, this is beyond what I consider the case to be worth."

He stares at me again. Now he has his hands wrapped around each other in front of his mouth, in a sort of double-handed fist. A vision of Judge Murphy, with his prayer-pointed fingers in front of his mouth, rushes through my mind.

"I'm sorry, your Honor, but I submit that neither you, nor Mr. Fox, nor Mr. Morgan can have any idea of the worth, to my wife and me, of our daughter. I'm sure, if you have children of your own, you understand my feelings. I very much dislike hearing the 'case' discussed as to its worth. It is demeaning."

I can hear Clint shifting in his chair. Mona is absolutely still.

The judge takes his hands from his mouth, puts them back on the table, pushes his chair slightly back. He's pretty good. He turns to Mona and Clint.

"Would you two be so kind as to leave your client alone with me for a few minutes? I'd like to speak to him in private."

They leave. I sit as still as I can. We're both waiting for the other to open. Now, we've progressed to an all-night, high-stakes poker game, a small step up from the Casbah.

"Mr. Wharton, are you sincere in saying you consider set-tling out of court a violation of due process of law, the intent of law?"

"Yes, your Honor."

"This, despite the fact that there are enormous backlogs of cases pending in just about every state in the union?"

"That's right, your Honor. I consider this backlog of cases to be scandalous. One of the rights guaranteed in our Bill of Rights, and spelled out in the seventh amendment, is a right to a fair trial. If our society is not prepared to support this right, by expenditure of money, to expand the courts, the judgeships, all the ancillary necessities to ensure proper justice, adequate and timely jury trials, the system is at fault. The price of two aircraft carriers and their support backup could probably be enough to rectify a good part of the problem.

"However, I am not obligated to participate in this failure, by agreeing to circumvent the courtroom, the judges, and the jury. In fact, despite the difficulties to my family, I feel obligated to insist on my constitutional right."

He pushes his chair all the way back and stands up. I stand, too. He motions for me to sit down again.

"I'd like you to just ponder on what you've said and think of what would happen to our present judicial system, with all its strengths and faults, if everyone took your position. I'll be right back."

I sit for several minutes. This man is nicer than Judge Murphy and much more effective. I wonder what he'll come up with next. I'm sure he has Fox and Morgan in another room, trying to encourage them to up the ante. I stand and go over to the window. Lunch traffic is beginning. I'm just starting to think that the judge himself has gone out for lunch when he comes back. He has Mona and Clint with him. They all sit down. The judge is back to his double-handed, fist over his mouth, position. He stares at me. I stare back. He starts speaking from behind his hands.

"Obviously, I disagree with your analysis of the use of the settlement process as a legal procedure. To me it is the civilized way to settle these kinds of conflicts. A jury trial is a failure of our legal methods. It is a much more primitive way to resolve differences."

"If that is so, your Honor, why is the right to a jury so carefully defined in the Bill of Rights? The whole chicanery of settlements has come to dominate civil law, as plea bargaining dominates criminal law, but I don't remember ever reading about 'settlements,' or 'settlement conferences,' or 'plea bargaining' in those original documents of our forefathers.

"As I said to Judge Murphy, entrusting the resolution and declaration of justice to money only, in itself, is a terrible retreat to the most primitive methods, only one step away from direct violence, an eye for an eye, a tooth for a tooth. It is vulgar.

"Your Honor, I'm sorry we hold such divergent positions and I know your expressed opinion is the prevalent ethical code in the legal and business world. It's most usually expressed as 'money talks.' But I am not comfortable with it, and I don't think I should be."

I consider throwing in another "your Honor," but decide it isn't appropriate.

Judge Steiner leans back in his chair. He looks at Mona and Clint, his eyebrows up, his eyes finally wide open.

"I have sent away Mr. Fox and Mr. Morgan. I explained your position, Mr. Wharton, as best I could. I think they were convinced as to your sincerity, as I am."

OK, there's the piece of chocolate cake, the come-on. What comes next?

"They have decided, and, I assure you, against my advice, to make a 'once and for all' offer of $120,000. It is a significant increase over the last offer, by $20,000. It's a lot of money. It's tax free and could be set up as a very comfortable twenty-year trust for you and your wife. I'm sure you must agree they are being very generous."

"Yes, if I were interested in a settlement, I would consider it, as you do, most generous. However, I state once more that I do not want to settle. I shall take your kindly advice into consideration regarding the function of 'settlements' in today's law, the urgent need to clear the docks for criminal cases. I shall phone my wife this evening and ask for her opinion. I guess that's all I can say."

The judge stares at me uncomprehendingly. He looks at his watch.

"All right. I hear you. I think you are being stubborn and unreasonable, despite, or maybe because of, your sincerity. I'd like you to think this offer over. I can be reached at my home any time before eleven o'clock this evening. Miss Gaitskill will give you my card with my home telephone number. Thank you very much, all three of you."

He stands, gives a slight bow, and we leave. We note that Fox and Morgan are not in the waiting-room but they could be stashed away in some other room.

Clint suggests we have lunch together. We eat in an Italian place.

"My God, Will, $120,000! How could you refuse it? I told Mona the most we could expect was $100,000, and this with a favorable jury and judge."

I slice my lasagne.

"I think they'll push it up another $5,000. We go to trial tomorrow if they don't, so be prepared everybody."

Mona drops her salad fork into her lap. We all scramble to wipe it off her new $300 black suit. She bought it for the trial.

After dinner that night, Mona and I go out on the porch again. I try not to look at my watch. Mona is doing the same. It's past ten.

"Mona, first I want to thank you for sticking by us. I know you risked your job, but I think that if we arrange the kind of settlement we're heading toward, all will be forgiven. As I said, money talks, especially with Steele, Cutler and Walsh, which is, above all, a business. I've made them about $15,000 in the past day or two.

"What bothers me is the conscientiousness with which you've prepared our case. I can't think of anyone who could have done it better. We won't talk about the settlement conference, that was a mousetrap operation, and you weren't the only one caught in it.

"I've told you I'm not happy with the costs of the expert witness business, but that's my fault. I should have paid more attention. You were only carrying through as you've been trained to do."

She's keeping her eyes on me, smoking slowly, the way one smokes to keep calm.

"You know I've been writing a book about this entire ordeal up to right now, here, this moment on this porch. It's titled *Ever After* because sometimes when Kate would have had too many Franky Furbo stories or stories from my childhood, she'd like a fairy story. I've always enjoyed making up fantasy, fairytale-like stories. When she wanted one of those, she'd ask for an Ever After story, meaning one that ended with 'and they lived happily ever after.' It seems like the right title in many ways.

"Believe it or not, another title I considered, for a while, was *Expert Witness*. I wanted to be my own expert witness, tell my truth of what happened in my own way. But the more I learned about expert witnesses and how they are 'jury rigged' literally, the less interested I was in that title. *Ever After* also means they will live 'ever after,' despite all.

"Now, I've seen that the practice of field burning is horrible and yet no one can stop it. Even the people devoted to stopping it, obsessed by it, can't stop it. They've passed out petitions but couldn't manage enough signatures to hold a referendum.

"We've tried the legal solution. As you know, Mona, I never wanted to be involved in this suit. If, at any time, the field burning had been stopped, I would have called the whole thing off, settled at whatever Steele, Cutler and Walsh considered the case to be 'worth.' But it came to the point where nothing else seemed possible. We were cornered.

"Then, with the settlement conference, it became more and more apparent that the law wasn't going to work. There would be no way of bringing the subject of field burning into the public eye, no way of punishing those responsible for the horror. No way of encouraging them to admit responsibility. All I heard from the moment I arrived was 'settlement.' How much money? What's it worth? Well, you know how it went, you were in the middle of it all. I can't tell you how it disturbed me, but you know that, too."

I look at my watch. It's twenty to eleven. If I'm not careful, I'll be going to court tomorrow, whether I want to or not, all alone, without my witnesses, maybe without a lawyer.

I smile at Mona in the dark. She's not looking at me now, still staring down the length of that tree-lined Portland residential street. She's a handsome woman, feminine but very strong, determined yet sensitive. I hadn't noticed it much before. I must be getting old.

"Some last questions, Mona, then I promise I'll stop all this preaching, and I'll call Judge Steiner.

"If we settle, accept Sampson's money, is that an admission of guilt on their part? Are they agreeing they're responsible for what happened? Are they even saying they're sorry? Or does our taking this settlement money exonerate them, everybody in fact, for what's happened?

"Mona, I've read through all the documents and one phrase keeps coming up. It set my nerves on edge each time I see it.

"The term 'wrongful deaths' is used when referring to our family. Now, if no one is held responsible for these deaths, if no one is found guilty, are they now 'rightful deaths'? Is there such a thing?"

She shakes her head.

"I don't think so."

"Each of us has a right to death. But when is a death rightful? Is a suicide rightful, because it is a sought-for death, a desired death? The death of our family was the opposite of a suicide: there was no desperation, no despair, no desire to end it all.

"They were each of a wonderful age, from Mia, just discovering the physical world, to Dayiel, discovering herself, to Kate and Bert, deeply in love; a whole future with loved ones in front of them.

"Naturally, in time, this would have changed, as most things do. Call it inertia, entropy, senility. These are many names for the same thing: the tiring out, the wearing down, the gradual reduction to physical nothingness. They won't need to experience any of it. Perhaps that's a blessing.

"Perhaps they did have a 'rightful death,' such as most of us will never know. I can live with that. Can you?"

She turns to me and nods. There are tears in her eyes. She starts to speak, can't. She nods her head. We stare at each other a second, and then, simultaneously, we're in each other's arms. She's sobbing deeply, pulling in gasps of air into those nicotine-coated lungs. I'm shaking at first, then sobbing, hard sobs: I begin rocking my head back and forth the way I did when we first found out they were all dead. I can accept their deaths now, feel they were a preordained ending, for reasons I don't know, will never know. That's what Bert was trying to tell me and I misunderstood. It's the way it had to be.

Mona's speaking against my neck.

"I'm so sorry, Will. I tried. What should have been simple became so complex. The answer to your question is, no, by settling they do not admit to responsibility, to guilt: they do not need to be sorry."

"That's what I thought, Mona. Nobody came out ahead, did they? No winners. Kate, Bert, and the babies were already gone, beyond our struggles. I should have known better than to think I could stop a big operation such as field burning. The people I've been fighting helped design the system, they want to keep it running just the way it is.

"The people of Oregon, for reasons of their own, don't seem to mind field burning as much as I do; some do but, apparently, not enough. Probably TV has made them think it's

234

normal for people to be killed in big accidents, to die slowly of respiratory disease. I don't know; I'll never understand.

"Sampson's lost a wad of money, just because they hired an inept driver. Steele, Cutler and Walsh didn't make the kind of money they thought they could. Bob Stone will be driving trucks again, maybe even big eighteen-wheelers. Mr. Thompkins will go back to burning fields, growing grass, making tens or hundreds of thousands of dollars a year, protected by the state. And the state of Oregon will continue to protect itself against its own citizens at all costs.

"It will be the same as if we hadn't done one damned thing. The legislature has another chance next year to do as little as possible to curb the problem and they'll pocket seed grower and dealer money to help them be elected again. Nothing's changed.

"But the important thing is this: you, and I, and maybe Clint know we did our best. We tried. We lost the war, but we won a few battles. We can live with ourselves. At least I think I can, and I want you to, too.

"I'd better make that phone call, let's go inside.

"Mona, I'm going to ask Sampson for an additional $5,000 to compensate me for my expenses running back and forth from Paris to Oregon."

Mona leans back from me. She stares into my eyes.

"Will, you can't do that, it's not ethical, probably not even legal. Sure you have them over a barrel in a certain way, but Judge Steiner did everything he could to help you. It's not fair to him.

"I'm telling you now, Will, I won't go along with this. If you insist on this idiocy, I'm no longer your lawyer, I disassociate myself, you're on your own."

I look into her eyes. She's serious. She looks lovely in the reflected gleams from the streetlight, her face tight with concern and strain. I feel like a real shit.

"I'd better make the phone call now, Mona, or we're liable to wind up in that 'kangaroo court' they have planned."

We pull apart and go through the door into the living-room. Mona still won't look at me. My hands are shaking as I dial. Quietly, staring me in the eyes now, Mona picks up the other phone. The phone on the other end is answered after three rings.

"Your Honor, this is William Wharton. I'm sorry to keep you up so late. But, I've decided at your advice to settle with Sampson for $120,000."

Pause.

"Yes, I understand. My counsel, Ms. Flores, will contact everyone concerned."

Pause.

"Thank you, Your Honor, for presenting your opinion so well. I disagree, but I agree to the settlement. It's obvious I can never have the kind of public jury trial I want."

Pause.

"I understand your position, Your Honor, and I'm sure you understand mine. I'm not happy, but probably this is the best solution available. Good night, Your Honor. Thank you for all your help."

I hang up.

Mona is smiling with tears in her eyes. She puts down the phone. We stand looking at each other.

"I'm proud of you, Will. And I'm ashamed of myself for the pressure I put on you. But it had to be this way. It really is for the best."

"I don't think so, Mona. But I'm tired of fighting. It all gets to a point where the money, a trial, justice, right or wrong mean nothing. It's all a technical exercise of experts, witnesses, lawyers, judges all. A dumb individual citizen like me hasn't a chance. I'm not ready to spend the rest of my life trying to change the system. I give up.

"Despite the laws in our land, the inertia of the people of Oregon, the cowardice of its elected government, the evasions and deceits of political leaders and their minions, I still believe the obvious reality that our beloved family, Kate, Bert, Dayiel, and Mia, in their personal Ever After, have joined the vast legions of heroes; all those who have died rightfully, from firemen trying to save lives, to martyrs dying for their faith, to soldiers killed in wars for reasons they couldn't comprehend, to babies dying from crib death, to all those who die young because of diseases such as cancer, leukemia, cystic fibrosis, yes, even those new killers of many innocents, drugs and AIDS. Are they the rightful dead? Is there such a thing as a rightful death?".

Mona looks up at me, tears still in her eyes.

"No, Will, there are no rightful deaths."

"Right."

EPILOGUE

IT'S BEEN more than five years since the events described in this book. The pain fades with the overlay of our personal lives we must lead, but the memories, in some strange way, become stronger. All of our family, still living, are different than we would have been without that horror on 1-5 at four o'clock on a hot August afternoon in 1988.

Our only remaining daughter, Camille, is teaching UNESCO children in Hanoi, Vietnam. She has made four attempts to have a child by in vitro, without success. Now she is in the process of trying to adopt two little Vietnamese babies.

Our older son, Matt, is teaching in Ankara, Turkey. He and his wife, Juliette, have two daughters: Emilia, now five, and Clara, who is just short of two.

It's almost as if they're trying to fill the blank spot in our lives.

Our younger son, Will—Robert in the book—is taking a teaching credential and master's degree at a university in New Jersey. I changed his name for the book because there were so many people named Will or Wills that it was confusing.

Rosemary, my wife, pretended for a long time that what happened hadn't, and buried herself in reading. She's retired from teaching and seems happy. We can now talk about our lost loved ones with comfort, and often do.

The monument we ordered from Capitol Monuments still hadn't been completed and erected at last hearing. Perhaps they don't want to admit the inadmissible either.

But we have our own personal family monuments: two sundials, built from millstones we extracted from our water-mill in France. One is perched on the edge of the millpond. We hang our towels from the gnomon when we dive from the stone into the pond. It's as if Kate and her family are still there, playing with us, and it helps me feel they aren't gone.

Inside the millstone we've placed the ashes of our departed family. Over the top of them, we've built a small pyramid supporting the gnomon. Each of the quadrants has one of their names and a single letter spelling L-O-V-E. Around the outside of the stone is lettered the small poem we used at the funeral in Oregon.

The other monument is up on the land we gave Kate as a wedding present. It's a matching millstone and is mounted on a platform of native Morvan rock. We try to keep flowers at the base when we're there.

My experience with Bert (whose real name was Bill), the dream, visitation, whatever it was, has made me much more sensitive to my own spiritual identity and that of everyone else. I've become convinced the physical life we must live out is but ephemeral. It gives me much comfort and has allowed for new experiences of a spiritual nature I've never had before.

This is an example:

In the spring after the accident in Oregon, I returned alone to our mill in Burgundy to paint. It's a lovely time of year there, with lambs gamboling in the fields beside calves cavorting and feeding from their mothers. It's a time of duck-lings and chicks hatching in the midst of an increasing haze of greens and yellows over everything. The hills are punctuated by flowering trees and hawthorn. I had a devouring hunger to paint this proof of continuity.

The second evening I was there, after a day's painting, trying to capture the magic of wild flowers in the shade of overhanging trees, I went to bed while the sky was still light—the sun doesn't leave the sky until almost ten o"clock at that time of year. I was falling asleep, when I thought I heard knocking. At first I was convinced it was at the door. I rose to check who could be there at that time, but there was no one. I went back to bed, but the knocking began again. It seemed to be coming from above me, from directly over my head, but that was impossible because the stone wall is high and two feet thick, with only a small ventilation window set under the peak of the roof. Eventually the knocking stopped, and I fell asleep.

Three days later, as planned, my very good friend Jo Lancaster, another artist, arrived. He's the one who called us at six a.m. the day after the tragedy, the one we cried with long distance. I found out later, he was the first one Camille had called; he's been a friend of the family a long time, and has five children, several matching our own in age.

We share a studio in Paris. He had come down to paint with me and keep me company.

We had a wonderful day painting. We're both figurative artists and we discovered a barn of weathered wood with bundles of yellowing hay hanging through the cracks in the boards. It made a stimulating subject. Painting is a lonesome art, but it's great to share the experience, the process, with someone who has the same reasons for painting as you.

We ate a simple dinner early, and again were ready to sleep before the light had gone from the sky. We also wanted to make an early start the next day.

Jo was sleeping up in the loft, the place usually reserved for our son Will [Robert], who lives at the mill more than the rest of us. Early the next morning, Jo called down to me: "Hey, Will. There's some kind of crazy bird doing a dance outside this window up here. It's beautiful, yellow, with a long body and a long tail. It's acting as if it wants to come in."

I climbed out of bed and went part-way up the steps to the loft. Sure enough, just as Jo said, there was a bird jumping up and down on the outside ledge of the window. It was pounding its head against the glass, and looked as though it were dancing.

I didn't recognize the bird although I have a strong interest in ornithology. My first book, *Birdy*, was about an intimate relationship between a small boy and his canaries. I've kept birds most of my life, they mean much to me. Their ability to fly, to sing, to have a broad view of things, has always entranced me. Each bird is something of an angel to me.

"This is really weird, Jo. You're right, it does seem to want to come in. From its sharp, pointed beak, it looks like some sort of insect-eating bird; maybe it's picking bugs off the window."

We watched a while, fascinated. The bird kept on with its wild gyrations. I have a long pole with a hook on the end with which I can open that little window. I went into the granary and brought it back into the main mill room. The bird was still there. I reached up and pulled open the window. The bird flew straight in and landed on the railing to the open loft. It didn't seem frightened at all. It was giving me a typical bird checking-out look, tilting its head back and forth to see me with one eye, then the other. It was an exceptionally beautiful creature, its movement graceful and like a dance, with its long, dark tail dipping up and down on each change of direction.

When we were eating breakfast, the bird flew down and perched on one of the empty chairs at the table. Jo and I were having fried eggs and bacon. I tried feeding some bacon to the bird, but it backed off; it then returned, continuing its head-twisting movement as if to say "no."

The bird hopped onto the table. We stared. "It must be tame," Jo said in a low voice. "It's probably escaped from a cage somewhere. It's not afraid at all."

"I don't think so, Jo. A bird like this is impossible to cage. I don't know why she's acting so strangely, but she isn't tame. Maybe she's just curious, or maybe she likes us."

"What makes you think it's a 'she'? Is it some kind of marking?"

I was surprised myself. I had no reason for calling the bird a she. It just came out that way. I didn't answer.

We left it at that. The light was just right for painting. A low morning sun can create colors and shadows beyond human reckoning. As we left the mill, I pulled open the small, high window again. I also opened the door out onto the terrace. A bird can panic when it's trapped in a house; in fact, it usually does. I figured when we came back for lunch, she'd be gone. And she was. But at least I now knew who'd been knocking.

To make things even more peculiar, from then on the bird arrived knocking on a window—any window—at exactly seven o'clock every morning. It was like a wake-up call. We came to expect her.

Jo had his opinions.

"Couldn't she make it seven-thirty or eight o'clock? It's like having a baby crying and waking everybody up soon as the sun rises."

I was beginning to realize in a certain way that, for me, it was a baby waking me, our baby.

Jo and I painted for a week and finished three paintings apiece, some better than others, but all above our usual standards. The bird began swooping around us when we were out in the field painting, up and down, flying almost like a swift or a swallow catching insects. Once she landed on the edge of my canvas.

I began calling her "Katiebird." It was a good feeling. I convinced myself she was trying to comfort me in the bad times. All this started at about the same time as the depositions in Portland.

In June, when school was out, Rosemary, Will [Robert], and I went down to the mill. I had a full roll of canvas, a good supply of paints, turps, oil, and varnish. I also had my computer. Things had been heating up in Portland, but here all was calm.

The first night we were there, just going to sleep, I was waiting. She came. I heard the knocking at the original window high on the wall. Rosemary was about asleep beside me. I waited. She didn't seem to hear; could I be imagining the entire thing? No, Jo heard it. He saw it. I turned to Rosemary.

"Dear, can you hear that knocking?"

"What is it, rats or dormice doing some syncopated rustling in the hustings?"

"No, listen. It's like someone knocking."

She sprang up.

"Who could it be at this time of night? Do you think something could have happened to Camille or Matt?"

"No, it's all right. It's only a bird knocking at the window. It's my Katiebird."

"What Katiebird? What are you talking about?"

So I told her about the bird, about Jo hearing it and seeing it, and what happened.

She stared at me and listened. I knew she was worried about me now. Whenever you try to share an experience like this—such as when Bill [Bert] came to me in Oregon before the funeral—people think you're either going crazy, are crazy, or are lying to them. No matter what, you can't win. But I like to tell the truth, especially with an experience like this, and to the woman I love, the one I chose to live with. Rosemary settled back onto the bed.

"Go to sleep, dear. And if you have any control over this Katiebird, would you please tell her to stop knocking so I can go to sleep."

She kissed me, and we both lay back in bed. I listened until the knocking stopped. I shouldn't tell Rosemary these kinds of things. They don't seem to calm her at all, only scare her. Maybe we were told too many ghost stories when we were children.

After she fell asleep, I slipped out of bed, pulled out the pole from the corner and opened the window. I didn't want Rosemary to be shocked by the knocking in the morning.

Instead, I was the one who was shocked. I tend to sleep on my back with my hands folded across my chest. I also usually wake up before I open my eyes, enjoying the peace of non-vision before my mind starts racing.

That morning, I could feel something on my hand. I opened my eyes slowly, and saw Katiebird, less than a foot from my eyes. Rosemary was still asleep. I wanted her to see this. I knew she was supposed to. It was the way it was with Bill [Bert].

I nudged her gently; she moaned and slowly wakened.

"Don't move too quickly, dear. Just open your eyes, there's something you should see."

She turned her head slowly, opening her eyes. At first she said nothing, only stared. Katiebird looked at her.

"What is this, Will, some kind of trick? Is this a bird you've trained? Isn't she beautiful?"

"It's no trick, this is a wild bird and I didn't train her. Her name is Katiebird as I told you, and she really is beautiful, isn't she."

I slowly unfolded my hands and held out a finger for Katiebird to stand on. She hopped right onto it. It was a magic moment. Finally Rosemary spoke.

"It's a 'visitation,' Will. I don't want to believe it, I can't, but it's the only way I can explain this."

"It is the explanation. This is a visitation. I'm convinced Kate is worried about me with all this mess in Oregon, and wants to comfort me, and you, too. You don't need to believe, just enjoy, relax."

I climbed out of bed with Katiebird on my finger. I walked her over to her chair at the breakfast table. She sang for us— she had a lovely voice, but only for two melodious notes.

We washed up and she watched. We ate and she watched. I was worried that she felt trapped in the house with us, and approached her with my finger out. She hopped onto it as before. I walked her out the door, then cast her away to the sky. She sang her simple song, circled the mill twice, and then flew off over the pond.

❋ ❋ ❋

After that, every time we went to the mill, she was there. Maurice, our neighbor across the street, said he could always tell when we were coming because the yellow bird would come just before we arrived. The whole experience was so magical. And it lasted three years. Every morning as my wristwatch made its little ding at seven, Katiebird was there. She was there in spring, summer, autumn, and winter. The second spring, she nested on a small outcropping of rock just below the window over our bed. I discovered it quite by accident, while washing the window. There were five eggs in the clutch. Will [Robert] wondered why five when there were only four of them. On a hunch, I said that only four would hatch.

And that's the way it happened. Katiebird wasn't frightened at all as we watched the babies grow. One egg didn't hatch, so Will [Robert] was impressed, and he's hard to impress. One day, the babies flew away, and the nest was empty. I leaned out of the window to rescue it and put it on the mantel of the fireplace in case Katiebird should want it again. But she'd given us her message.

Once the case was settled, we never saw Katiebird again. She'd come back for only one purpose, to comfort us in our distress, and it was finished. I knew she had a life of her own to live, or whatever it is that spirits without bodies do, and was not even disappointed when the spring came and she wasn't there. I know there are many logical explanations for this experience, but for me, the only one that holds is spiritual. We've been blessed.

My editor at Granta, Bill Buford, is convinced I wrote this book as therapy, to help rid myself of the pain, the agony of the trauma. I don't think this is so, but I'd be the last to know. He says: "Is it possible—looking back on this now—to say that, on some level, you may actually have needed a legal struggle such as this, that it became a way of deflecting you from feeling too much? (One of the benefits of the court action was that your daughter was no longer your daughter, but a fact in the lawsuit; it allowed you—I'm speculating—not to have to feel the full intensity of the pain.)"

I don't think this was the case. My prime reason for the maneuvering in Oregon, and it is said often in the book, was to stop field burning. It's the reason I started writing this book. I felt I didn't want anyone else to suffer what we were forced to experience. I don't have that reason now. If Oregonians, for their own reasons, want to burn down the barn, that's their business. As I say at the end of the book, the deaths of loved ones are sometimes meant to be. Maybe it's some kind of lesson to all of us not to hold onto life so ferociously, bitterly. It's been so for me.

Next year, I will be seventy. Soon enough I'll find out if Bert, Kate, Mia, and Dayiel will be available to me. There's no way of knowing except to die.

As to the others in the book, Mona Flores earned her partnership in the firm, divorced her husband, sold her house, started a legal practice with a good friend, and found a new man. I'm happy for her.

We hope to visit with our friends the Wilsons this summer. They're still living in Portland.

So life goes on. It does for all of us, longer than most of us permit ourselves to believe.

WILLIAM WHARTON,
9 *May* 1994, *Port Marly*